IMAGES
of America

JEWS OF GREATER MIAMI

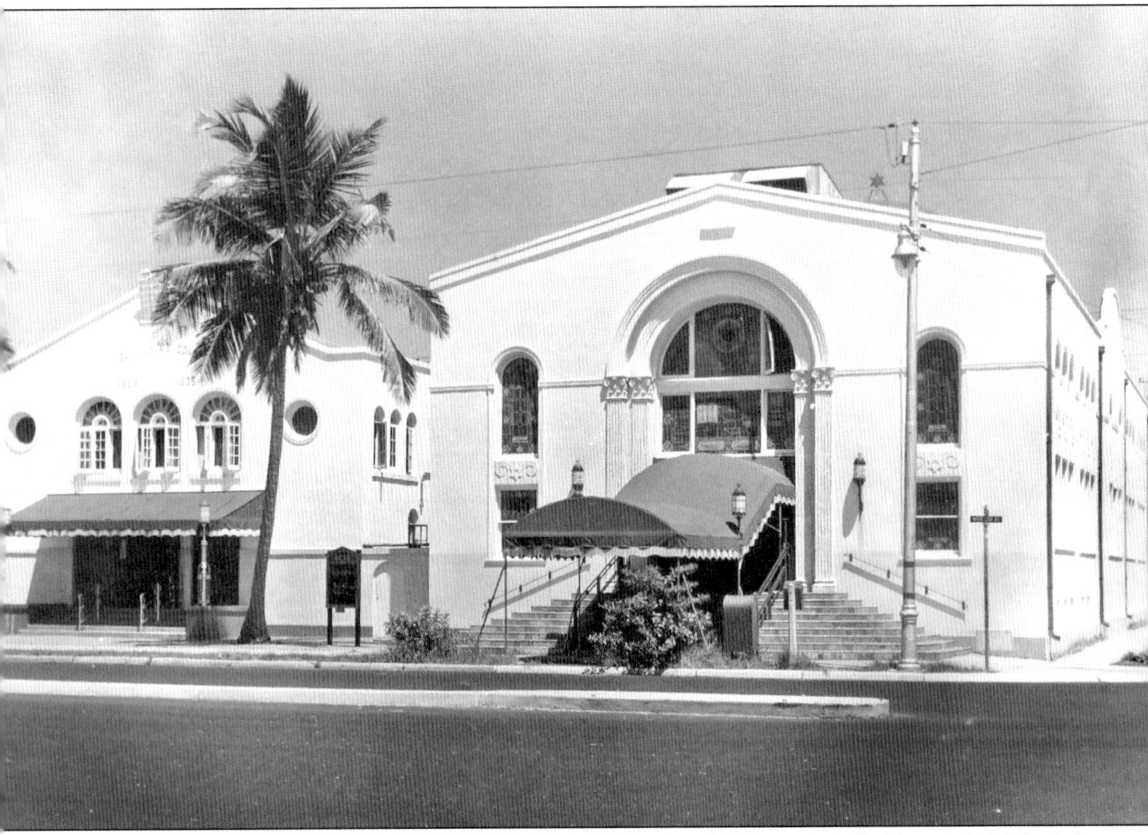

Congregation Beth Jacob, 1938. These synagogues, built in 1929 (left) and 1936 (right), served the first Jewish congregation on Miami Beach, which is locally referred to as the "Beach." When Jews moved out of the neighborhood, this became the home of the Jewish Museum of Florida after extensive restoration. Here is the place to collect, preserve, and interpret the material evidence of the Jewish experience in Florida—within walls that resonate with Jewish memories. (See museum on page 127.)

On the Cover: Ruth Zion and Leo Benjamin with Alligators, 1911. Ruth Belle Zion, daughter of Morris and Clara Zion, was born in New York City and settled with her family in Miami in 1911. Her father, for whom Leo Benjamin worked, founded many of the Jewish organizations. Her son, Murray Dubbin of Miami, was one of the first two Jewish representatives from South Florida to the Florida State Legislature in 1963. (Courtesy Murray Dubbin.)

IMAGES
of America

JEWS OF GREATER MIAMI

Marcia Jo Zerivitz
Founding Executive Director
Jewish Museum of Florida

ARCADIA
PUBLISHING

ISBN 978-0-7385-6719-8

Published by Arcadia Publishing
Charleston SC, Chicago IL, Portsmouth NH, San Francisco CA

Printed in the United States of America

Library of Congress Catalog Card Number: 2008937761

For all general information contact Arcadia Publishing at:
Telephone 843-853-2070
Fax 843-853-0044
E-mail sales@arcadiapublishing.com
For customer service and orders:
Toll-Free 1-888-313-2665

Visit us on the Internet at www.arcadiapublishing.com

This book is dedicated to the Jewish pioneers who settled in Greater Miami and who preserved their family photographs, so that we can tell this story. Their perseverance to tame the hostile environment and commitment to their traditions made it comfortable for more Jews to follow them and build a strong community that takes care of its own and continues to help all those in need. This documentation of our collective historic memory helps ensure Jewish continuity.

Contents

ACKNOWLEDGMENTS

For the past 23 years, I have been immersed in a passion—gathering "stuff" to document Jewish life in Florida. Beginning in 1985, I traveled 150,000 miles to 30 Florida cities over six years to conduct research and train hundreds of volunteers to collect family photographs, documents, and artifacts and to record oral histories. I was part of a team for the MOSAIC project to create a traveling exhibit to tell our story of how achievements trumped discrimination—how Jews contributed to the development of the state and maintained Jewish traditions while overcoming severe challenges.

As the exhibit traveled, enthusiasm mounted to create a permanent museum. A site was found on South Beach that had been an historic synagogue, on the verge of demolition. In 1992, I was selected as the founding executive director to create a strategic plan, lead the board of directors to raise the funds for restoration of the building, and execute the mission to continue to collect and preserve our stories to pass them on to the next generations. The Jewish Museum of Florida opened in 1995 to continue research, produce exhibitions based on the growing collections, and present cultural and educational programs for people of all ages and backgrounds.

This book is a testament to each member of the MOSAIC task forces throughout the state. One research area was Greater Miami.

Unless otherwise noted, the images in this photograph documentary are from the collections of the Jewish Museum of Florida. In addition to all the families who are part of this story, I want to recognize as contributors the Historical Museum of Southern Florida, Florida State Archives, Howard Kleinberg, and the *Miami Herald*. Michael Knoll, Ira Newman, and Philip Mitchell prepared the photographs for publication. My partner throughout this fabulous journey has been my husband, Elliott Zerivitz. He edits everything that I write, critiques the content, asks probing questions, chases leads, and supports my obsession in every way.

My deepest appreciation goes to all those who save photographs and label them. May this be an inspiration to each person who picks up this book to do the same for future generations.

INTRODUCTION

Florida, the first of the American territories to be discovered and settled, did not allow Jews to settle until 1763 and was among the last to develop a substantial Jewish population. The stereotyped image as the "destination of Jews settling in Florida" has been Miami. In reality, Miami was among the state's latest communities to develop a Jewish population at all. Miami-Dade County, on the southeast coast of Florida, is composed of 32 cities, with Miami as the county seat and the largest and oldest city. Miami was founded in 1896 when Henry Flagler's railroad was extended there—thus attracting Jews for the economic opportunity.

Where did these Jews come from? They came from other places in the United States (either New York or Key West) and were mostly immigrants from Russia and Romania. Romanian Jews had come to Key West in the 1880s and 1890s and left for reasons such as a result of a peddler's tax in 1891, the decline of the cigar industry, or the general decline of that city as the railroad arrived in Miami. Russian Jews who had come to New York began to migrate south with the railroad—first to Fort Pierce, West Palm Beach, and then Miami.

The first Jew to arrive was either Sam Singer or Jacob Schneidman. The City of Miami was incorporated July 28, 1896. There were about 350 male voters, of which one-third were black; women were not allowed to vote. Twenty-five of these residents were Jewish, including Singer, Schneidman, W. Wolfe, Jacob Schneider, M. Buholtz, Abe Safraneck, M. Seligman, Moe Haines, Julius Frank, Charles and Morris Kanner, David Singer, N. Goldenberg, and the Goldman brothers. According to Isidor Cohen, the earliest permanent Jewish settler and a signatory of the city's charter, Jews owned 12 of the 16 businesses in Miami.

These pioneer Jews had religious services beginning in 1896. There was no synagogue at the time, but a rabbi was brought from West Palm Beach to conduct High Holy Day services. After the great 1896 fire that destroyed most of the businesses and a yellow fever epidemic in 1899, the Jewish population declined by 1903 to only Isidor Cohen.

Miami remained a harsh environment for would-be settlers, but a fledgling tourist industry sustained optimism. In 1904, Cohen married widow Ida Schneidman, they had a daughter in 1906, and the first *bris* was celebrated in 1907 for their son Eddie. The death of a Jewish tourist in 1912 forced the small Jewish community to gather to discuss creating an organization and a cemetery. Meeting at the home of Mendel Rippa, the group of 35 Jews established the first congregation in Miami. By 1915, there were 55 Jews in Miami. In the 1920s, there was the Zionist Society, United Jewish Aid Association (eventually the Jewish Family Service), B'nai B'rith lodge, National Council of Jewish Women, Hadassah, Workmen's Circle, the *New Jewish Unity* newspaper (1926–1935), and the *Jewish Floridian* (1928–1990).

Tremendous advertising combined with abundant land, new roads, the automobile, and commercial aviation created a tourist and real estate boom. A population of 30,000 (100 Jewish families) exploded to more than 130,000 with 3,500 Jews by 1925. Jews founded Temple Israel, the first Reform Judaism congregation, and were among those who chartered the University of Miami, which today has a Center for Contemporary Jewish Studies and Hillel. The hurricane that swept Miami just as Kol Nidre services on Yom Kippur ended on September 18, 1926, brought the real estate boom to an abrupt halt. From 1926 to 1931, the city suffered a boom and bust, two hurricanes, the failure of five banks, and finally the stock market crash. Headlines read, "Miami is Wiped Out."

But the headlines were wrong. By the mid-1930s, Miami began a gradual recovery. New residents arrived by air, train, and the Mallory Steamship Line. Tourists were lured to boating, fishing, and tropical gardens. Miami became the "gateway to Latin America," a reputation that would increase dramatically as the century wore on. During the 1930s, approximately 4,500 Jews lived among a Miami population of more than 110,000. Satellite communities emerged. The hotel, banking, and construction industries escalated with greater participation by Jews, who also helped start Miami-Dade College and Florida International University, with a Judaic Studies program.

The perilous situation of European Jews evoked a response in Miami's small but active Jewish community, which founded the Greater Miami Jewish Federation in 1938. The Jewish Home for the Aged began in 1940.

When the Japanese bombed Pearl Harbor, local leaders, who were seeking to expand business and visibility, convinced the government that Miami was the ideal location for training military personnel. As a result, funding and soldiers poured into the area, particularly Miami Beach. Many of these soldiers were Jews, who returned after the war, when South Florida's image as a year-round resort reemerged.

The tourist industry was revitalized with the widespread use of air-conditioning, mosquito control, development of Miami International Airport, and Israeli businessman Ted Arison's expansion of the cruise ship business. The postwar economic boom brought additional tourists and settlers to Miami. Many were Jews who were attracted by the new jobs created from tourism. In 1950, the county had a population of 495,000 people, of which 55,000 were Jewish. For the next five years, approximately 650 Jews arrived each month. A new house was built every seven minutes—and many of the builders were Jews. In 1952, Abe Aronovitz became the first (and to date, the only) Jewish mayor of Miami.

Many Jews, horrified by news of the Holocaust, began to challenge antisemitism at home. The Anti-Defamation League organized in Miami in 1940. During the McCarthy era and the radical Right influence, bombings and desecration of area synagogues were prevalent. Following the communist takeover of Cuba in 1959, about 12,000 Cuban Jews immediately fled the country, finding refuge in Miami and its environs; their business acumen helped revitalize the city.

From the postwar period until the mid-1960s, most jobs were related to the tourist and building industries or real estate. Most Jews were involved in the services and retail trades but many were moving into medical and legal professions. In 1963, the first two Jews from South Florida were elected to the state legislature, and Florida had its second Jew in U.S. Congress. (The first was David Levy Yulee, who brought Florida into statehood in 1845.) In this period, Jews began to move to North Miami and North Miami Beach. Cuban Jews started their own congregations.

The 1973 Arab oil embargo plunged Miami into the worst recession since the 1930s. Yet, Jewish Miami continued to grow. By 1980, the Greater Miami Jewish population reached its all time peak of 230,000 and included a full array of Jewish organizations such as Jewish Federation Television and the *Miami Jewish Tribune* (1986–1993).

In the 1980s, Miami became the new Ellis Island for people fleeing troubled countries. The influx of Caribbean immigrants, as well as the growing Spanish-speaking Cuban population, alienated some people and many Jews moved north to Broward and Palm Beach counties. By 1985, the Jewish population had declined to 209,000. Many of the older Jews, who had lived on Miami Beach, had died. But the Greater Miami Jewish community has been reinvigorated by the arrival of Jews from Latin America, Russia, and Israel. In 2008, the Jewish population of the county decreased again to less than 120,000 but has retained its vibrancy. There are more than 60 congregations, 34 Jewish educational institutions, and 3 Jewish Community Centers. The highest percentage and increase in Jewish population is in North Dade, especially in Aventura. Greater Miami hosts Florida's third-largest Jewish population and the nation's 10th largest.

Miami Beach and Antisemitism

From the early 20th century, people visited the southern tip of Florida to picnic on its sandy beaches or to bathe in the warm waters of the Atlantic Ocean. In 1913, the Collins Bridge opened, joining the Beach to the mainland. That same year, New York Jews Joe and Jennie Weiss and their son Jesse relocated to Miami Beach. Joe and Jennie operated a snack bar at a popular bathing spot at the tip of the Beach—the only place Jews could settle. Several years later, the Weiss family opened Joe's Stone Crab Restaurant in a small wooden-framed house, which they continued to expand and today remains the site of this world famous restaurant. It is still run by descendents of the Weiss family.

Developers placed restrictive covenants in their land deeds that prohibited the sale of Miami Beach lots to Jews north of Fifth Street. However, the Lummus brothers, who bought properties at the southern end of Miami Beach, did not bar Jews from ownership. Several modest Jewish-owned hotels and apartments arose on property sold to Jews south of Fifth Street. For their chief source of income, these early Miami Beach Jews owned and lived in apartments and rented units to others.

Rose and Jeremiah Weiss and their children moved to Miami Beach in 1919. Rose Weiss, known as "the Mother of Miami Beach," attended every city commission meeting for nearly 40 years and created the city's flag. The first hotel to cater to kosher Jewish winter tourists opened in 1921. In the mid-1920s, the Jacobs family opened the first of three hotels. The Blackstone opened in 1929 and was built by Nathan Stone, the grandfather of future U.S. senator Richard Stone.

Despite this activity, the Jewish population of Miami Beach grew slowly in the first half of the 1920s. It was confined to an area from Fifth Street south to the tip of the peninsula until 1925 and then, until the end of the decade, a rapidly growing Jewish neighborhood moved north to Lincoln Road. The real estate boom led to the creation of hundreds of new subdivisions and communities in Greater Miami and to a sharp increase in the area's population.

This speculative era lured many "bigger-than-life" Jews, including bankers Leonard Abess and Baron de Hirsch Meyer and attorney, businessman, Zionist, and community builder Max Orovitz. Henri Levy, a French-born Jew, migrated with his family to Miami Beach, an area he characterized as "a lush tropical paradise." In 1922, Levy developed the smart boom-era communities of Normandy Isle and Normandy Beach North, which later became Surfside. The boom collapsed in 1926, when a hurricane hit. But many "boomers," whose ranks included a considerable number of Jews, remained in the area. In the 1930s, Miami Beach's Jewish population grew significantly, reaching at least several thousand of the city's 28,012 by decade's end, as Greater Miami replaced Jacksonville as the center of Florida Jewry.

Many of the new arrivals to Miami Beach came, initially as tourists, from the northeastern United States. Most hotels and apartments continued to exhibit "Gentiles Only" signs. Jewish builders erected many of the finest hotels on South Beach during the 1930s. Many bore the streamline or nautical moderne style of architecture designed by Henry Hohauser, who moved to Miami Beach in 1936. His initial project was to design a second sanctuary for Beth Jacob, Miami Beach's first Jewish congregation and the building that now houses the Jewish Museum of Florida.

The art deco buildings of the 1930s and 1940s are architectural treasures known throughout the world. In the 1980s, Barbara Baer Capitman, a Jew, launched the campaign that established the Miami Beach Art Deco District. Jews operated many of the hotels.

The 1930s also marked the dismantling of restrictive barriers to Jewish ownership of real estate throughout Miami Beach, as large numbers of Jews purchased commercial properties from debt-ridden owners only too happy to sell them. Jews also began buying residential lots whose restrictive covenants proved impossible to enforce after the property had changed owners a couple of times. While discrimination had by no means vanished, conditions were improving. But it was not until 1949 that a law was passed by the Florida Legislature that ended discrimination in real estate and hotels.

The Jewish retail, institutional, and residential presence was most strongly felt at the southern portion of the island. Small Jewish businesses dotted the streets, and Jewish tenants filled apartments. The Orthodox Congregation Beth Jacob was organized in 1927, and their synagogue was built in 1929. This historic building is now part of the Jewish Museum of Florida. In the 1930s, many members of Beth Jacob broke away and organized a Conservative congregation, Jacob Joseph, which became the Miami Beach Community Center in the 1940s and, finally, in 1954, Temple Emanu-El. As the Jewish population continued to move north, and many Jewish soldiers poured into the area for wartime training, Jews founded the Beth Sholom Center in a storefront on Forty-first Street in 1942 (it was renamed Temple Beth Sholom in 1945). Today there are more than 20 congregations on the Beach. Jewish education is abundant: The Hebrew Academy has been around since 1947, Lehrman Day School since 1960, and the Talmudic Academy since 1974.

There has been a *mikvah* since 1944 and an *eruv* since 1982. In 2005, Touro College opened in part of the Temple Emanu-El building.

Commensurate with their increase in numbers, Jews began to play increasingly more important civic roles. Baron de Hirsch Meyer was the first Jew to sit on the Miami Beach City Council (1934). Mitchell Wolfson, who migrated to Miami with his family from Key West, became Miami Beach's second Jewish councilman. In 1943, he was elected mayor, the first of 15 Jews who have served as mayor of Miami Beach (as of 2008). Mitchell Wolfson was very also important to business in Miami. With his brother-in-law Sidney Meyer, Wolfson formed WOMETCO (Wolfson-Meyer Theater Company) in 1949. WOMETCO became the first television station in Florida, WTVJ. Wolfson also built the Miami Seaquarium and left an endowment to create the Wolfson campus of Miami-Dade College.

By the mid-1940s, the Greater Miami Jewish Federation placed the number of Jews in Dade County at 29,325 in a county nearing 400,000 in population. Nearly one-half of these Jews lived on Miami Beach.

The tragedy of the Holocaust caused many Jews to turn to Zionism. Some South Florida Jews, led by Shepard Broad (who built the Broad Causeway), helped outfit boats and planes to transport Jews from Displaced Persons camps in Europe to Palestine. Inspired by firsthand experience in financing boatloads of Holocaust survivors and displaced persons to arrive in Palestine, Max Orovitz formed the Miami Group with fellow Jewish businessmen and created the Dan Hotel chain in Israel after statehood.

Following World War II, Jewish doctors could not get staff privileges at any area hospitals. In response, Jewish leaders in the community formed Mount Sinai Hospital on Miami Beach; Max Orovitz was the founding chairman for three decades. Today the 55-acre hospital, the city's largest employer, is renowned for its leadership in medicine, especially cardiac care.

As the social and cultural fabric of Miami Beach changed post World War II, so did the Beach's physical appearance. Hotels were built rapidly to satiate the desire of tourists. The hotel industry was greatly bolstered by Jews, including Ben Novack who, with Harry Mufson, built the Fontainebleau Hotel (1954). Designed by Morris Lapidus, the elegant hotel quickly became a trademark property. A year later, Mufson commissioned Lapidus to design the equally grandiose Eden Roc Hotel next door.

Larry King began his live talk show on Miami Beach in 1956. Sophie Tucker belted her songs in Yiddish during the 1950s and 1960s in the hotels. In 1967, Judy Drucker organized the first concert at Temple Beth Sholom and began bringing world-famous performers. Fifteen years later, Drucker formed the Concert Association of Florida. From Yiddish theater in the 1930s to Pavarotti on the Beach in the 1990s, from the Miss Universe Beauty Pageant at the Fontainebleau Hotel in 1960 to the opening of the Jewish Museum of Florida in 1995, Jews have been and are prominent in culture. Jews have played an active role in developing the arts and entertainment scene of Miami Beach to what it is today, and they continue to nurture it. Jews started the other museums, Bass Museum of Art and Wolfsonian, as well as the New World Symphony and Miami City Ballet. In 1990, Kenneth Treister designed the Miami Beach Holocaust Memorial.

In the 1970s, about 80 percent of the population on Miami Beach was Jewish. Today it is less than 20 percent. There is a resurgence of Orthodoxy, especially among younger families. The elderly Jews are gone, and Latin American and Israeli Jews have arrived. The increasing popularity of Miami Beach, rising real estate values, and a declining Jewish population have forced more synagogues to close their doors and become nightclubs and retail stores. The skyline of Miami Beach has changed from the day the first skyscraper went up in 1940. It continues to change, as some buildings come down and new higher ones go up. As architects, developers, and contractors, Jews have been involved in every aspect of these developments. Through their contributions to the physical appearance of Miami Beach, their roles in building the Beach are apparent and perpetual. The original developers did not want Greater Miami to become "a Jewish outfit." It did not, but the Jews have left an indelible footprint on the area's history.

One

In the Beginning
Jewish Pioneers

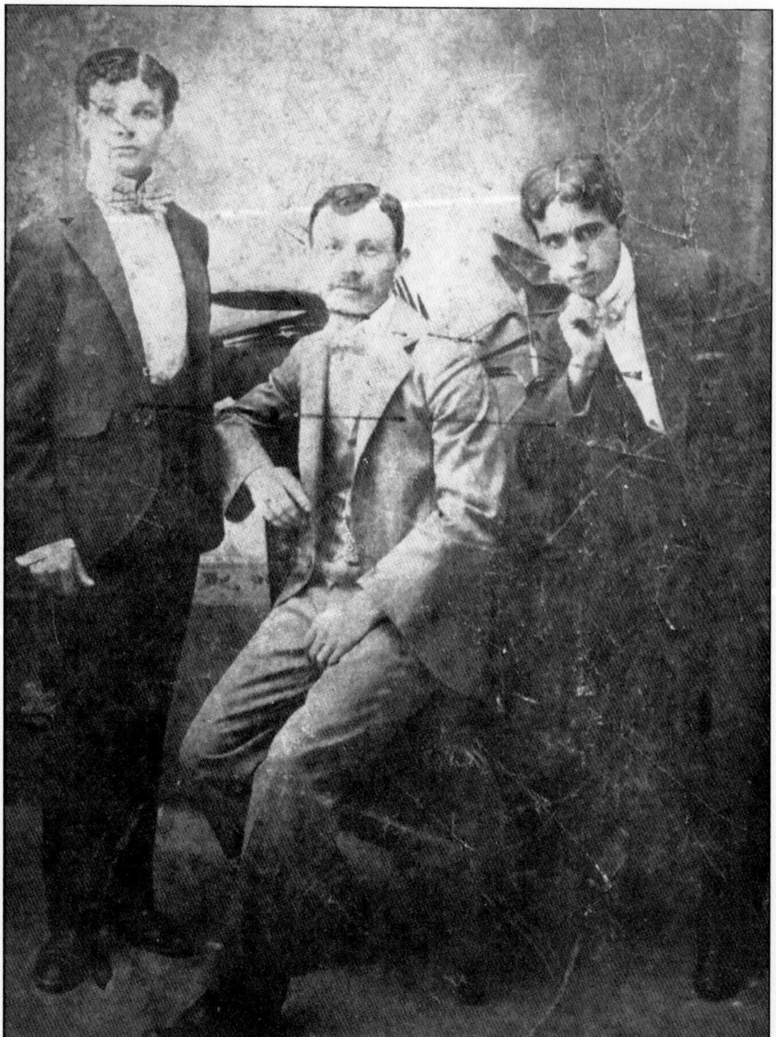

Pioneer Men of Miami, 1898. When Miami was founded in 1896, Jews owned 12 of the 16 businesses. Among them were Jacob Schneidman (left), Isidor Cohen (center), and Julius Frank, who died in 1896. Marcus Frank (right) was Julius's eldest son. By 1900, Schneidman; his wife, Ida; and Cohen were the only Jews in the city, and, shortly thereafter, Schneidman died.

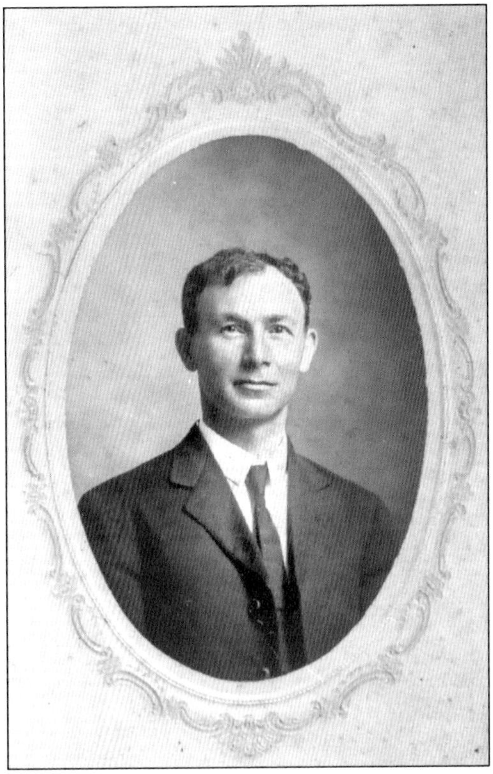

Isidor Cohen (1870–1951), 1904. Russian immigrant Isidor Cohen came to Florida in 1893. When he heard that Henry Flagler was bringing his railroad to Miami, he moved there. Cohen set up a store on the south side of the Miami River and brought his customers across in a rowboat. A true pioneer and the first known permanent Jewish settler in Miami, Isidor Cohen was a signatory of the city charter in 1896.

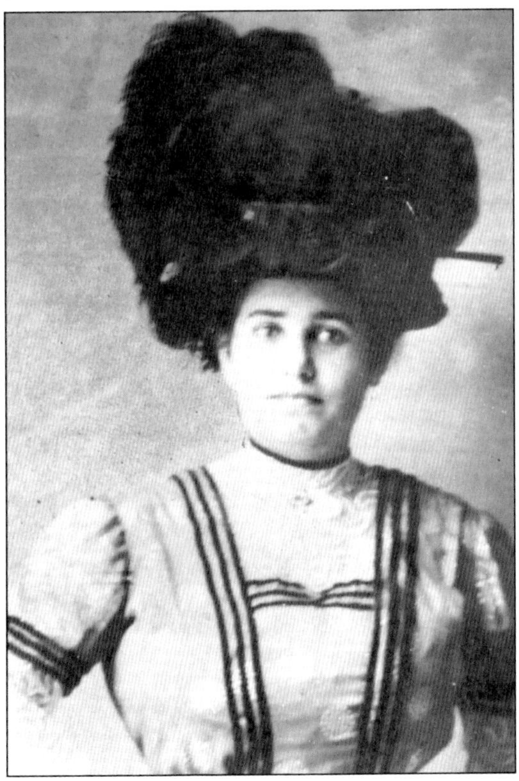

Ida Schneidman Cohen, 1904. Ida left Miami with son Murray upon the death of her husband, Jacob, and moved to New York. On a buying trip there in 1904, Isidor Cohen convinced Ida to marry him and return to Miami. Ida Cohen was a tireless leader, who was dubbed "Mother of Miami's Jewish community." She was founder of the Miami Jewish Home for the Aged and served as president of most Jewish women's organizations.

ISIDOR AND IDA COHEN, PROBABLY HIS SECOND STORE C. 1904. In his autobiography, Cohen writes, "Had an interview with Mrs. Tuttle . . . in regard to . . . a piece of ground for . . . a store building. Result disappointing. I was told to take a job clearing land, whereupon I tried to impress this naive lady that the last labor of this character my race had performed was in the land of Egypt, and that it would be a violation of my religious convictions to resume that condition of servitude."

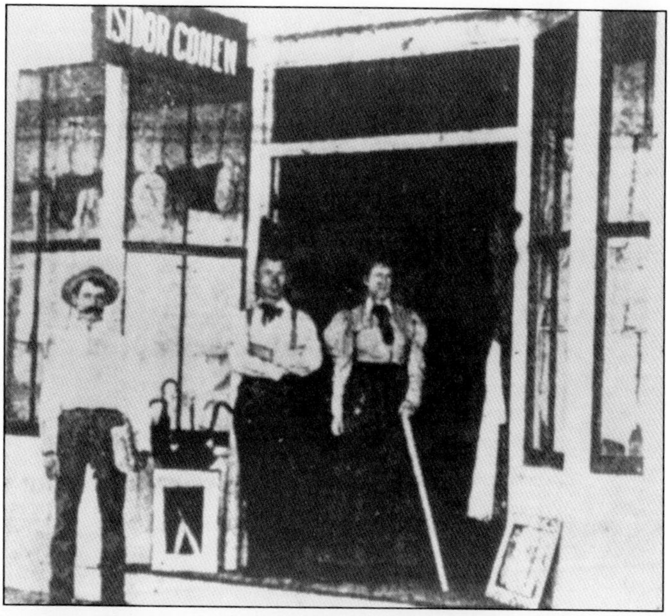

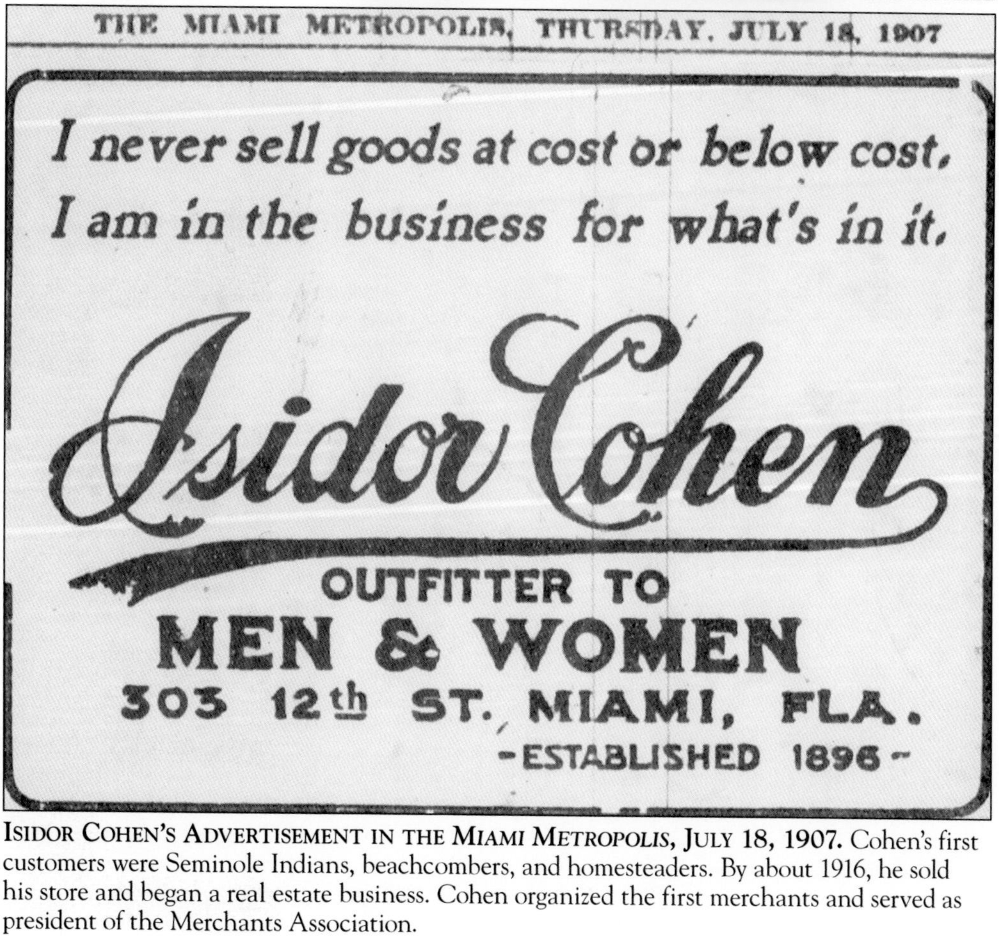

ISIDOR COHEN'S ADVERTISEMENT IN THE *MIAMI METROPOLIS*, JULY 18, 1907. Cohen's first customers were Seminole Indians, beachcombers, and homesteaders. By about 1916, he sold his store and began a real estate business. Cohen organized the first merchants and served as president of the Merchants Association.

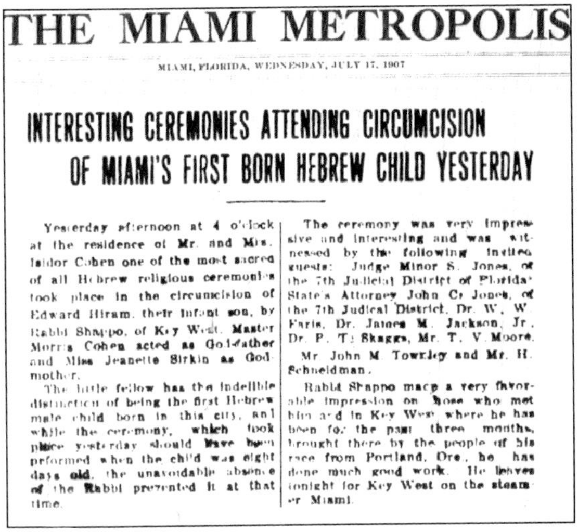

THE MIAMI METROPOLIS

MIAMI, FLORIDA, WEDNESDAY, JULY 17, 1907

INTERESTING CEREMONIES ATTENDING CIRCUMCISION OF MIAMI'S FIRST BORN HEBREW CHILD YESTERDAY

Yesterday afternoon at 4 o'clock at the residence of Mr. and Mrs. Isidor Cohen one of the most sacred of all Hebrew religious ceremonies took place in the circumcision of Edward Hiram, their infant son, by Rabbi Shappo, of Key West. Master Morris Cohen acted as God-father and Miss Jeanette Sirkin as God-mother.

The little fellow has the indelible distinction of being the first Hebrew male child born in this city, and while the ceremony, which took place yesterday should have been preformed when the child was eight days old, the unavoidable absence of the Rabbi prevented it at that time.

The ceremony was very impressive and interesting and was witnessed by the following invited guests: Judge Minor S. Jones, of the 7th Judicial District of Florida; State's Attorney John C. Jones, of the 7th Judical District, Dr. W. W. Faris, Dr. James M. Jackson, Jr., Dr. P. T. Skaggs, Mr. T. V. Moore.

Mr. John M. Townley and Mr. H. Schneidman.

Rabbi Shappo made a very favorable impression on those who met him and in Key West where he has been for the past three months, brought there by the people of his race from Portland, Ore., he has done much good work. He leaves tonight for Key West on the steamer Miami.

FIRST *BRIT* MILAH CEREMONY IN MIAMI, 1907. The *Miami Metropolis* reported on its front page the Jewish tradition for Edward, the infant son of Ida and Isidor Cohen: "Interesting ceremonies attending circumcision of Miami's first born Hebrew child yesterday." Normally the *brit* is held on the eighth day after birth, but it took three weeks for Rabbi Julian Shappo to arrive by boat from Key West to perform the ritual. Actually, Edward was the first born Jewish boy in Miami.

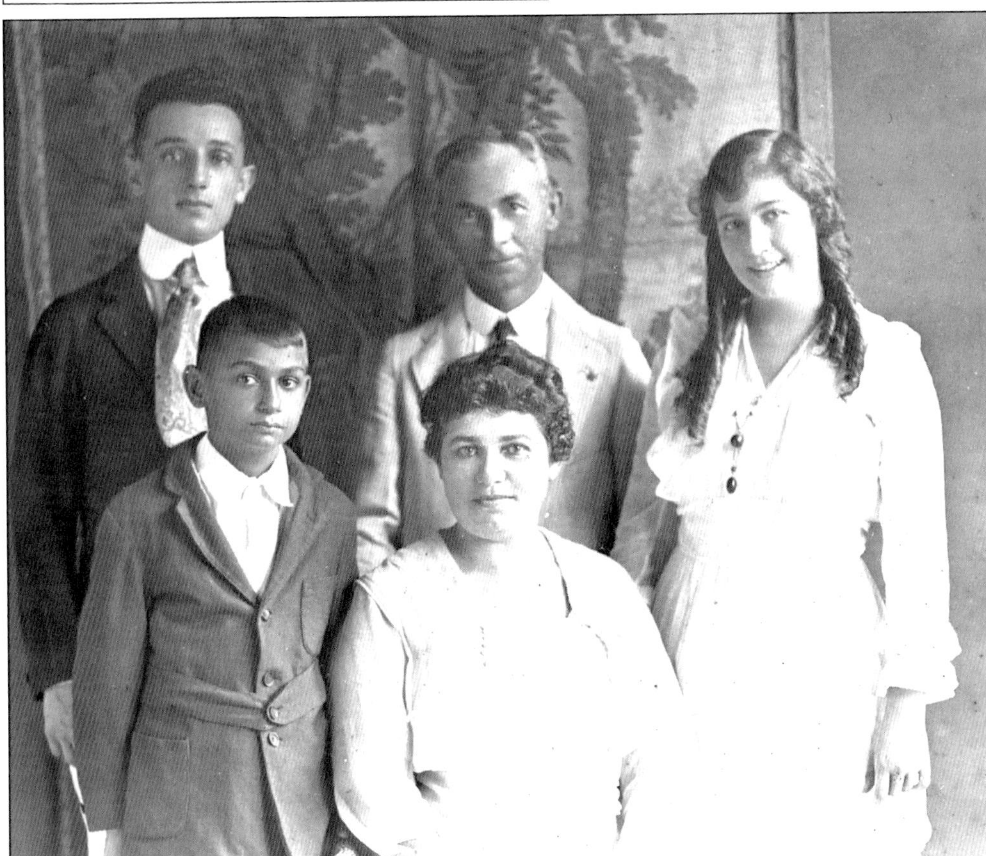

ISIDOR AND IDA COHEN FAMILY, MIAMI, 1919. Members of this blended family are, from left to right, as follows: (first row) Eddie and Ida; (second row) Murray, Isidor, and Claire. Murray was a president of Beth David, which his parents helped found. Claire (Weintraub), the first Jewish child born in Miami, was in the first graduating class from the University of Miami in 1928 and founded the Miami Museum of Science and the March of Dimes in Miami, as a result of her son Alfred's having polio in 1946.

JULIUS FRANK KILLED IN FIRE, 1896. Frank emigrated from Russia to New York and then followed Flagler's railroad down Florida's east coast, first to West Palm Beach then, finally, to Miami in 1896. He and his wife, Julia, had six children. On December 26 of that year, Frank was killed in an explosion caused by a fire that destroyed most of the stores. Miami's first store for women's apparel, which was owned by Julia (below), survived.

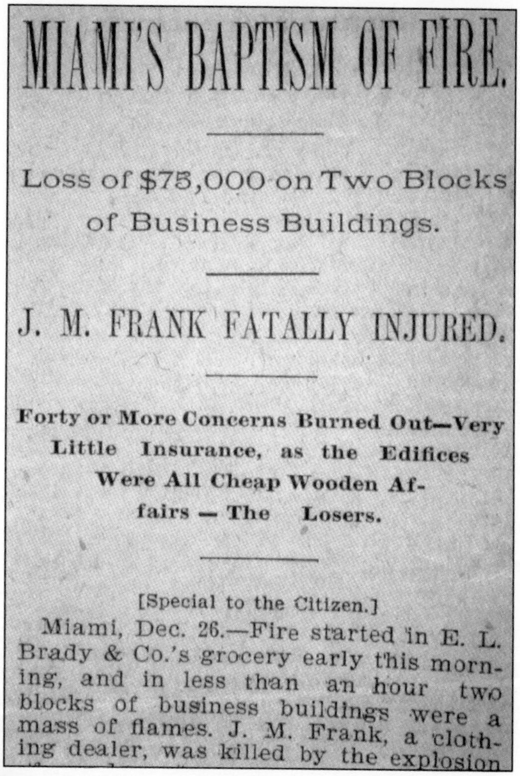
MIAMI'S BAPTISM OF FIRE.

Loss of $75,000 on Two Blocks of Business Buildings.

J. M. FRANK FATALLY INJURED.

Forty or More Concerns Burned Out—Very Little Insurance, as the Edifices Were All Cheap Wooden Affairs — The Losers.

[Special to the Citizen.]

Miami, Dec. 26.—Fire started in E. L. Brady & Co.'s grocery early this morning, and in less than an hour two blocks of business buildings were a mass of flames. J. M. Frank, a clothing dealer, was killed by the explosion

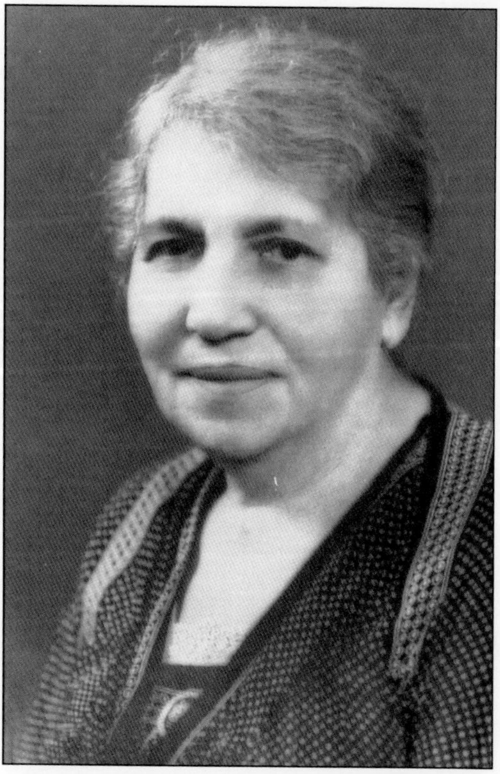

JULIA FRANK (1865–1934), 1898. A son of this widow was taken with the Spanish-American War soldiers as a mascot when they were shipped to Cuba. Julia wrote to Pres. William McKinley, appealing for her son's return. He was released, but another tragedy was yet to follow. A younger son, awaiting the arrival of his brother's ship, was killed when he fell out of a palm tree.

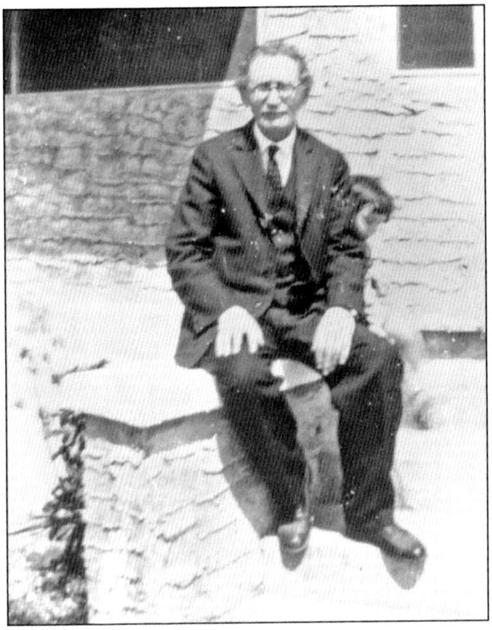

MORRIS ZION, C. 1919. Zion settled in Miami in 1911, after having founded a congregation, B'nai Zion, in Key West. He founded Miami's first Jewish congregation that was also named for him, but the name changed to Beth David in 1917 when David Afremow contributed $5,000. Zion, who was in the dry goods business, also served as founding president of the United Jewish Aid Association (1920).

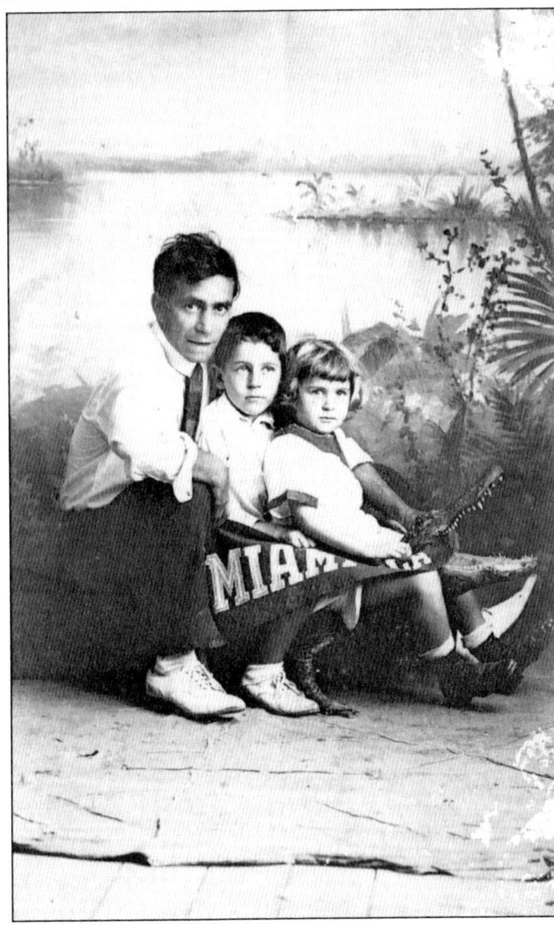

POSED ON AN ALLIGATOR. The children of Morris Zion, Ruth and Jack, are pictured here with Leo Benjamin in 1911. In 1920, Jack Zion was the first to have a Bar Mitzvah in Beth David, the congregation that his father founded. He grew up to be an educator and was principal of Hialeah High School. Leo Benjamin came down on a freight train and started making a living selling watches. At this time, he clerked for Morris Zion.

FIRST SYNAGOGUE, BETH DAVID, 1920. Founded in 1912, the congregation was established with 35 members. Services were held in various public halls until 1920, when Beth David acquired its first building. It was located at Northwest Third Avenue and Second Street, a highly desirable location in the center of town. The need for larger quarters brought the congregation to its present location on Coral Way in 1949.

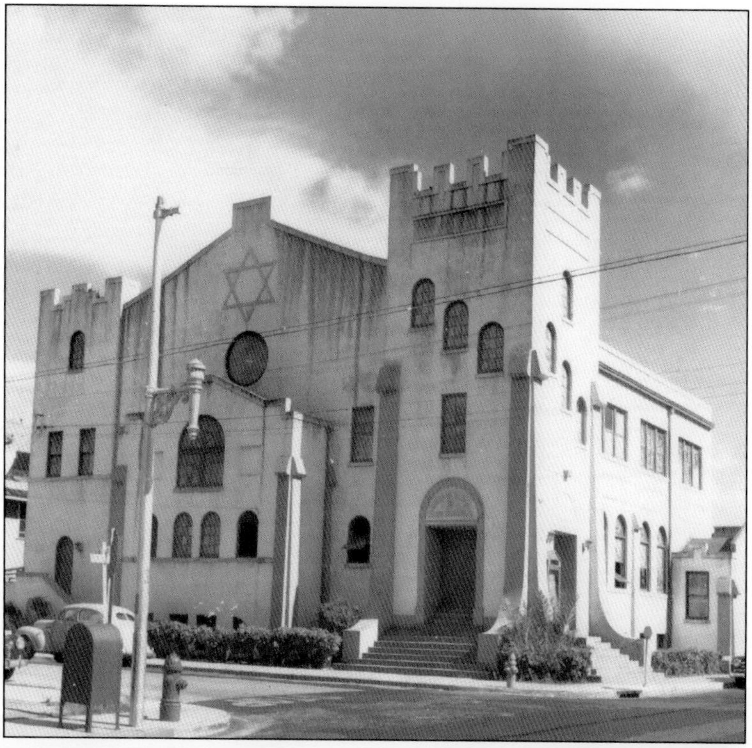

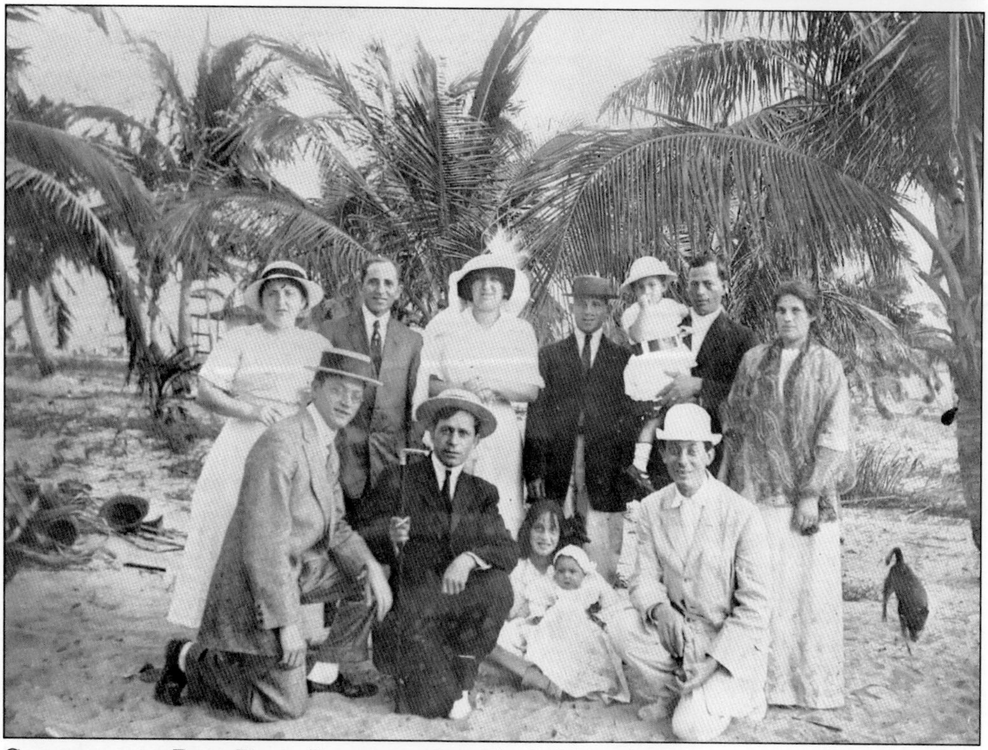

CONGREGATION BETH DAVID PIONEERS, 1914. The Dublers, Shaffs, Abensons, and Leo Benjamin got all dressed up for a picnic on Cape Florida, which is now Key Biscayne.

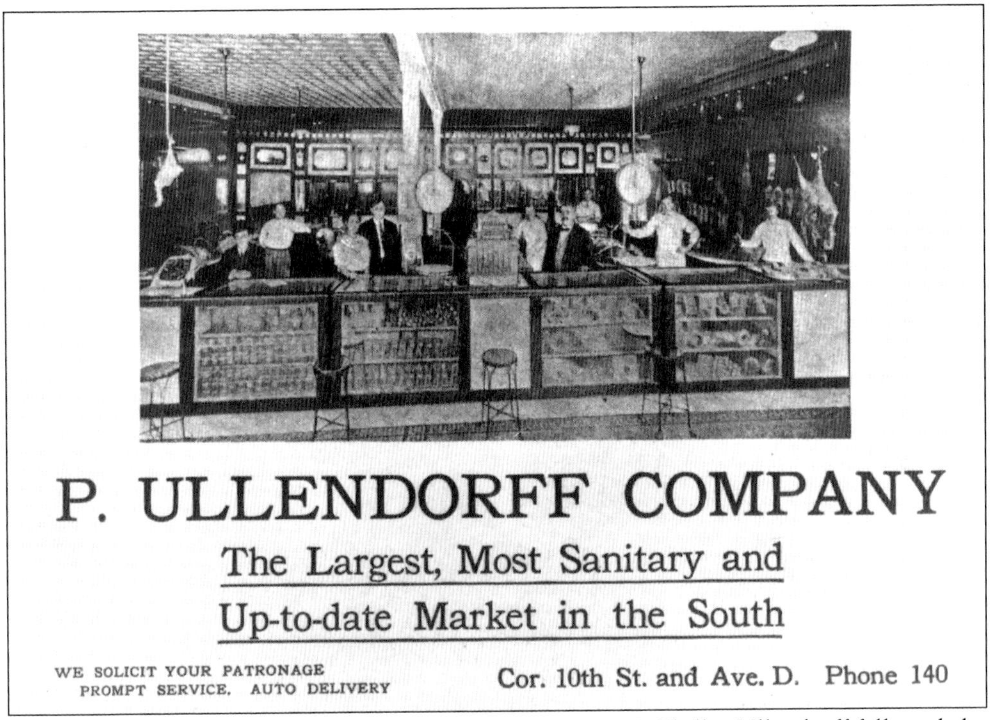

ADVERTISEMENT FOR P. ULLENDORFF COMPANY, C. 1906. Phillip Ullendorff followed the railroad to Miami in 1896. His first meat business was so successful that he expanded it into a corporation in 1911. A large land owner in several states, he formed a real estate company and made a large contribution to Miami's first Reform congregation, Temple Israel, which was named for his father.

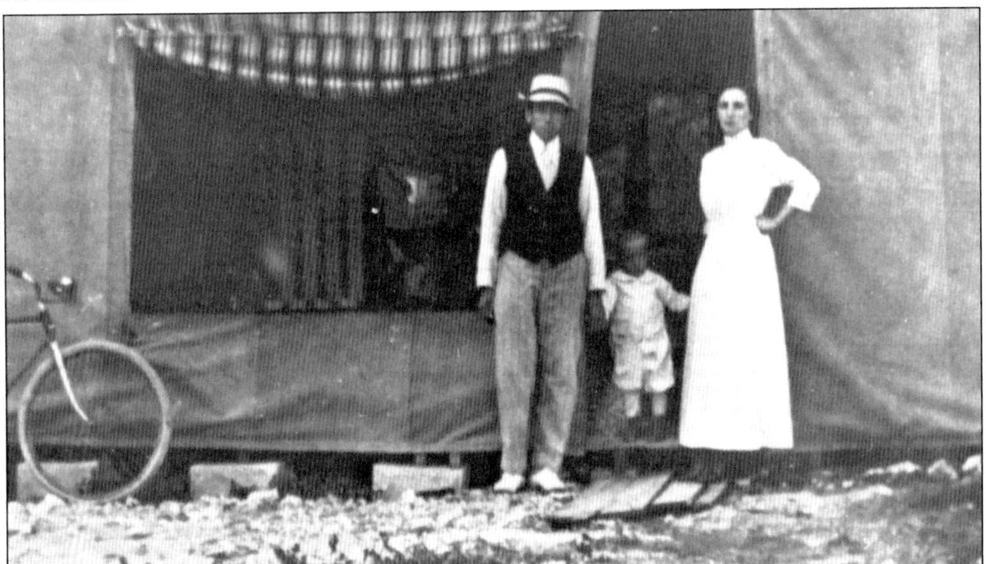

FIRST HOME FOR NEHAM FAMILY, 1906. The pace of settlers arriving overwhelmed the rate of erecting housing. Like many families when they first arrived, Sarah and J. Neham and their son Harry lived in this tent on Flagler Street and First Avenue.

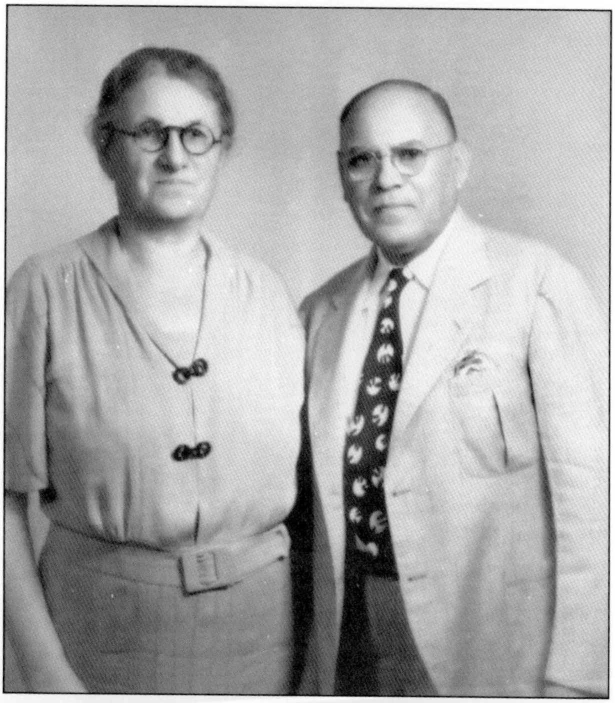

SARAH AND SOL SCHWARTZ, C. 1919. "In 1898, I developed a fever to enlist in the army to serve my new country," said Schwartz after he emigrated from Romania to New York. With his wife, Sarah, he moved to Key West to enlist and later became a peddler there. The Schwartz family moved around Florida until they settled in Miami in 1917. In 1920, they organized the *Chevra Kadisha* (burial society).

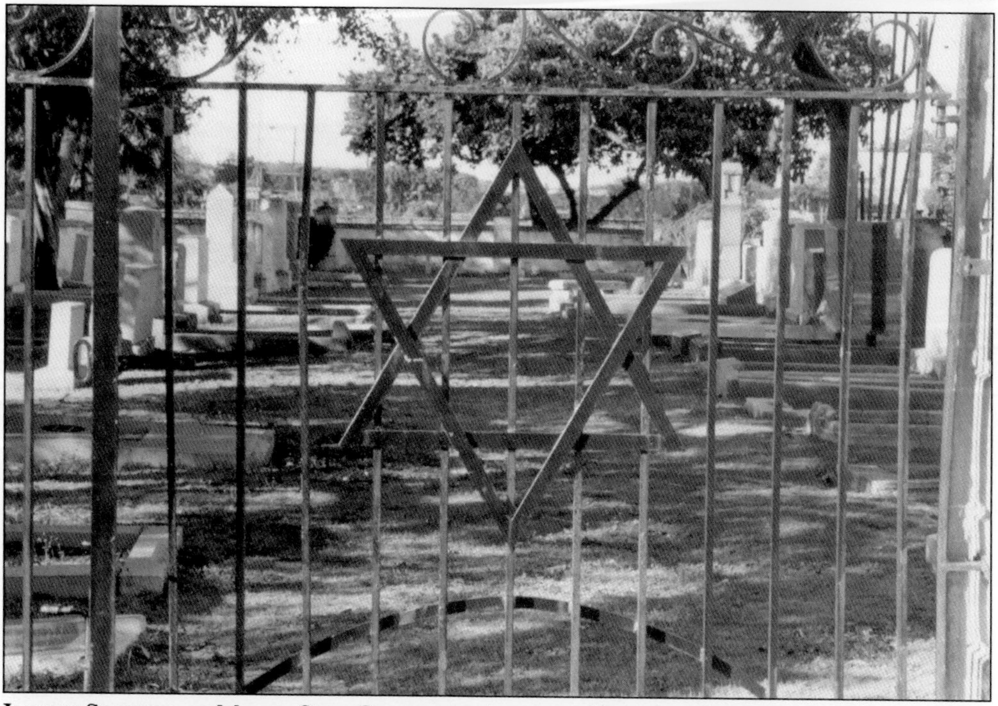

JEWISH SECTION OF MIAMI CITY CEMETERY. A group of Jews first designates land to bury their dead under Jewish laws and traditions. This cemetery opened in 1897. In 1912, the death of Morris Sack prompted action. Beth David bought two blocks from the Miami City Council for $400, walled it in, and had a rabbi consecrate it. The last Jew was buried there in 1964. Today there are five Jewish cemeteries in Miami.

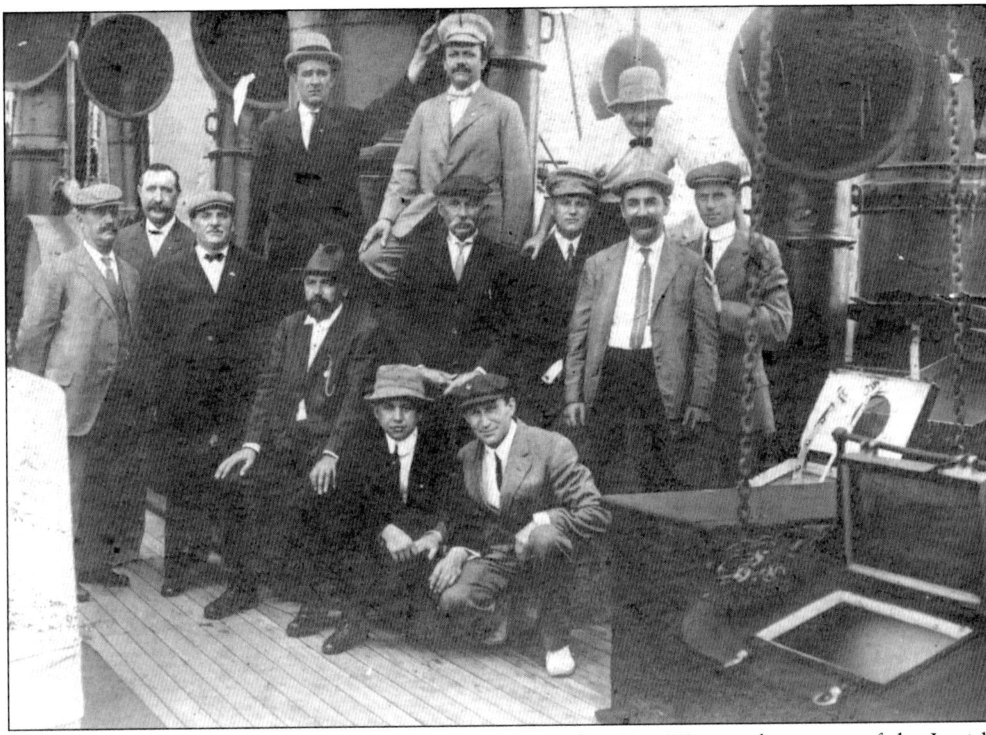

Louis Fine Sailing from Russia, 1896. Fine arrived in Key West and was one of the Jewish merchants who actively supported Cuba in its fight for independence. By 1908, he had moved to Miami.

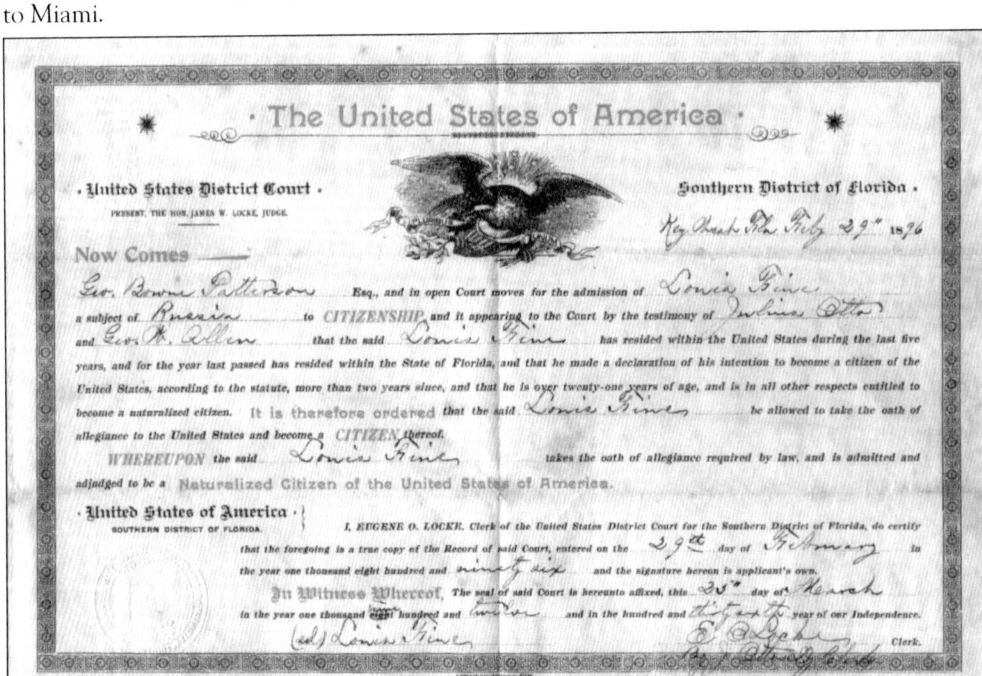

· The United States of America ·

· United States District Court ·

PRESENT, THE HON. JAMES W. LOCKE, JUDGE.

Southern District of Florida ·

Key West Fla Feby 29th 1896

Now Comes Geo. Bowne Patterson Esq., and in open Court moves for the admission of Louis Fine a subject of Russia to CITIZENSHIP and it appearing to the Court by the testimony of Julius Otto and Geo. R. Allen that the said Louis Fine has resided within the United States during the last five years, and for the year last passed has resided within the State of Florida, and that he made a declaration of his intention to become a citizen of the United States, according to the statute, more than two years since, and that he is over twenty-one years of age, and is in all other respects entitled to become a naturalized citizen. It is therefore ordered that the said Louis Fine be allowed to take the oath of allegiance to the United States and become a CITIZEN thereof.

WHEREUPON the said Louis Fine takes the oath of allegiance required by law, and is admitted and adjudged to be a Naturalized Citizen of the United States of America.

· United States of America ·
SOUTHERN DISTRICT OF FLORIDA.

I, EUGENE O. LOCKE, Clerk of the United States District Court for the Southern District of Florida, do certify that the foregoing is a true copy of the Record of said Court, entered on the 29th day of February in the year one thousand eight hundred and ninety six and the signature hereon is applicant's own.

In Witness Whereof, The seal of said Court is hereunto affixed, this 25th day of March in the year one thousand nine hundred and twelve and in the hundred and thirty sixth year of our Independence.

(sd) Louis Fine

E. O. Locke, Clerk.

Citizenship Certificate of Louis Fine (1866–1923). This documents Fine's arrival in Key West, Florida, in 1896 and of his becoming a citizen that same year.

LOUIS FINE, JEWISH MASTER OF MASONS, 1935. The Masonic orders have offered Jews a degree of social integration not always available by other routes. Louis Fine was the first Jewish master of the Biscayne Bay Lodge of Masons.

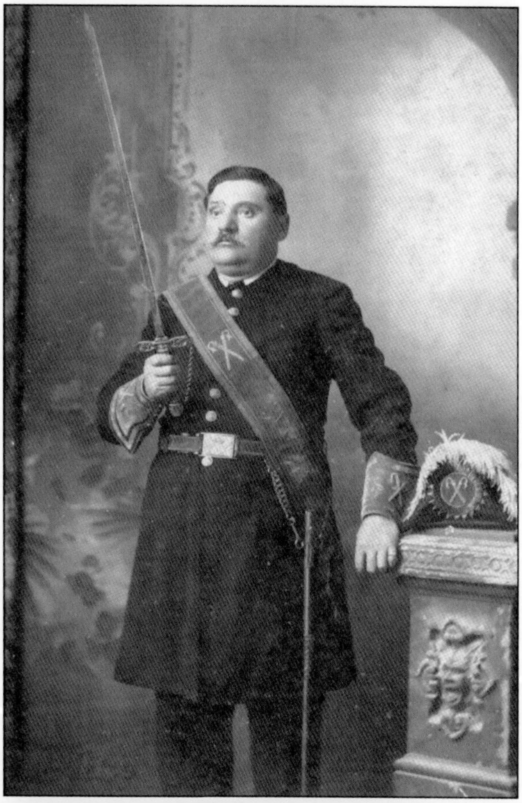

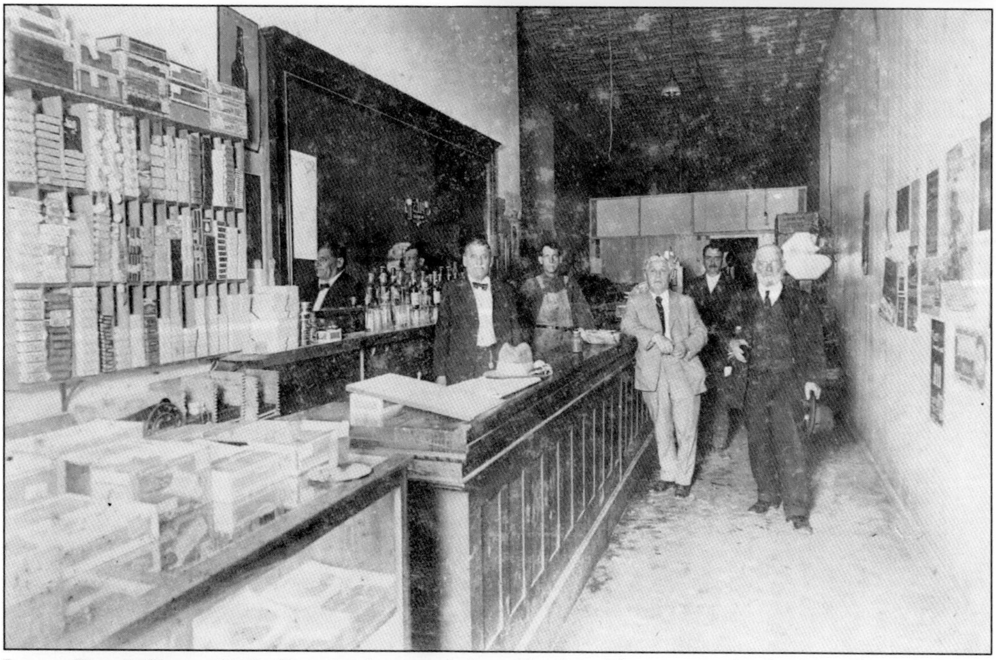

LOUIS FINE'S BAR, 1909. Fine (in bow tie behind bar) and his son Isador had a saloon. A prime mover in organizing the first congregation, he served for many years as its president. His friend David Afremow (with elbow on bar), owner of New York Bargain Store, had stopped in for a drink.

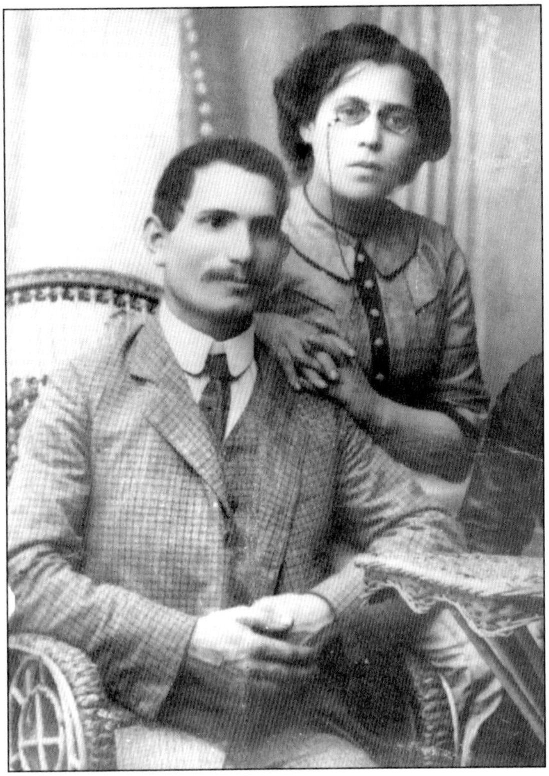

Henry and Jennie Seitlin, c. 1915. Russian immigrant Seitlin was an active Zionist, drawn in 1910 to a kibbutz training center in Homestead, Florida. In 1913, he moved to Miami where he was first a peddler and then opened the Boston Shoe Store. Henry sent for his wife, Jennie; son Sam; and brother Harry. The Seitlins, parents to four boys, were among the founders of Beth David, the Greater Miami Jewish Federation, Pioneer Women, and Hadassah.

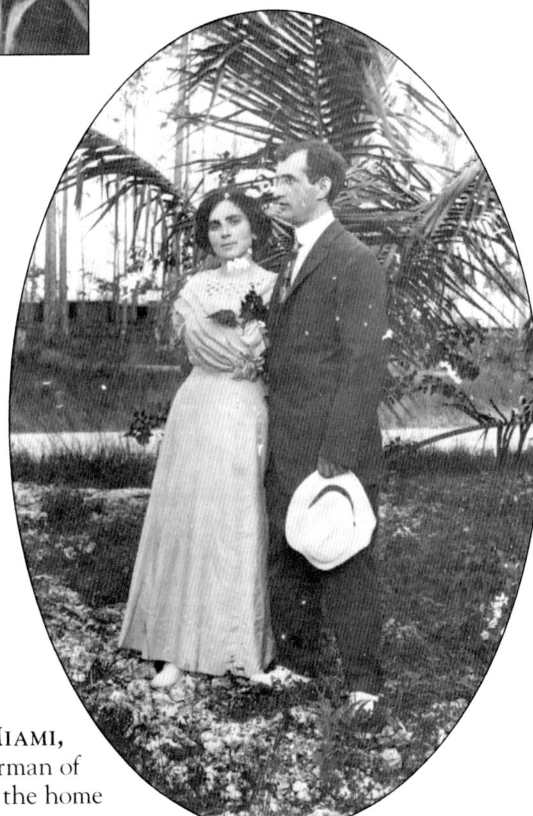

First Known Jewish Wedding in Miami, 1913. Rose Seitlin of Miami and Max Lehrman of Homestead were married June 13, 1913, in the home of Morris Zion.

NELL LEHRMAN, 1915. Nell Lehrman (Gibbs) was the second Jewish girl born in Miami, in 1914. In 1916, the family moved to Fort Lauderdale, where her father, Max, opened a department store. She married Louis Gibbs of Live Oak and settled in Tallahassee.

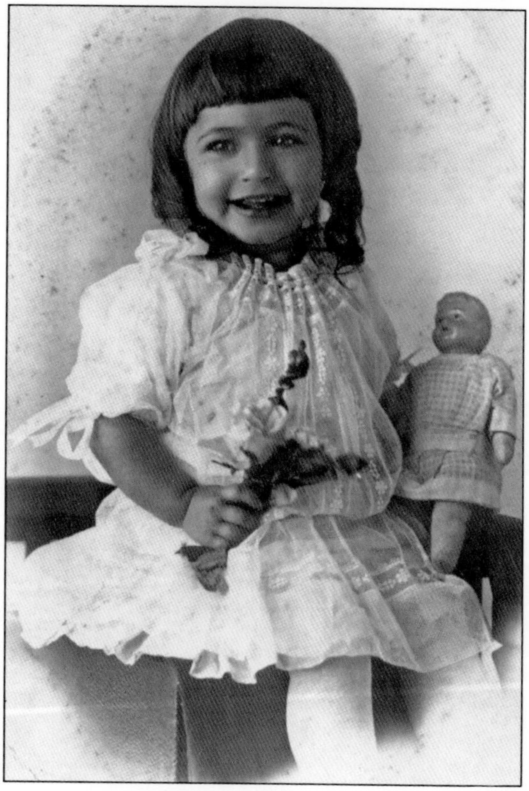

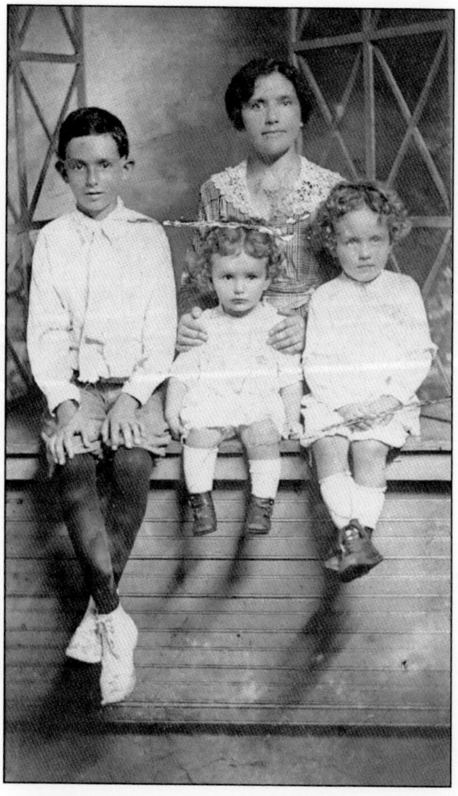

DUBBIN FAMILY, 1919. Rose Gerson Dubbin proudly poses with her children (from left to right) Albert, Daniel, and Henry. Reflecting on the early days, Albert said Miami was "primarily agricultural with streetcars and a ferry to Miami Beach." He married Ruth Zion (pictured on the cover) in 1927 and became a lawyer. Daniel and Henry took over the family business, Sanitary Mattress Works, founded by their father, Samuel, in 1917.

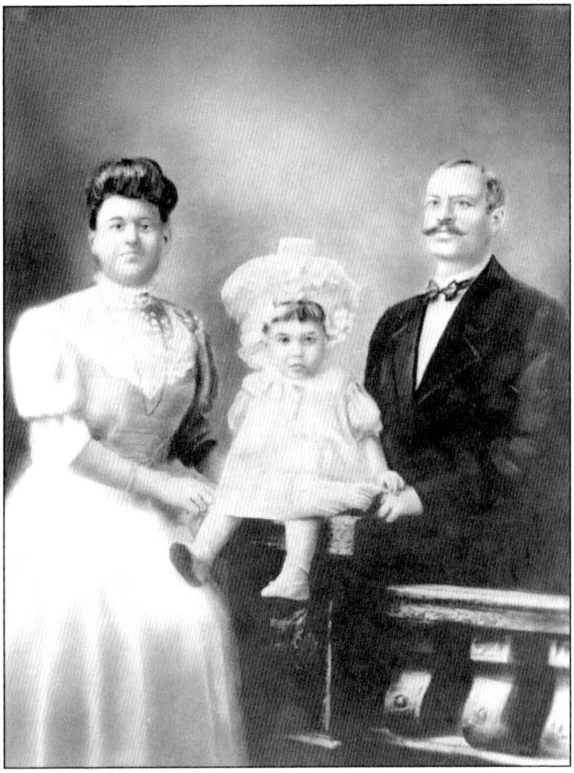

ENGLER FAMILY, 1911. Anna and Abram Engler brought their daughter Reba to live in Miami from Key West in 1911. Reba Engler (Daner) attended Miami schools and the University of Miami through law school, becoming the first known Jewish woman lawyer in South Florida. She practiced law from 1937 to 1992 and was president of Miami's first Hadassah chapter. Also, the law library at the University of Miami bears her name.

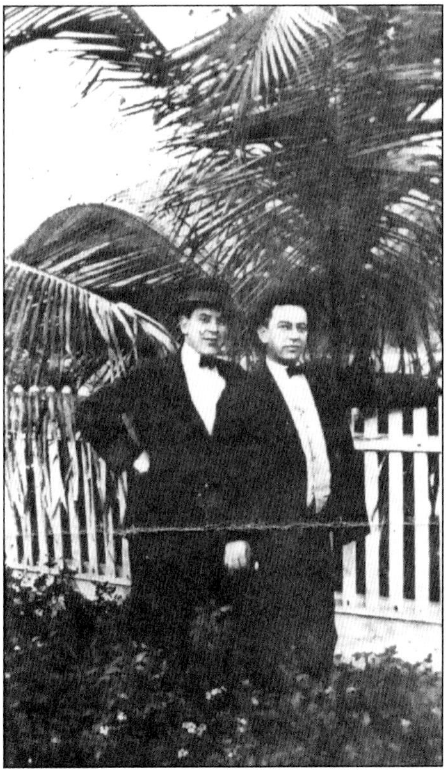

JOE AND JACK RIPPA, C. 1915. The Manuel Rippa family emigrated from Romania to Key West, where he was a successful cigar manufacturer. At the beginning of the 20th century, much of the Key West community moved to Miami, including the Rippas. The meeting to form the first congregation was in the home of Mendel Rippa and some descendants continue to live in the area.

JENNIE RIPPA AND PHILIP SEGALL, 1910. These cousins from Romania were engaged to marry. Jennie, however, broke off the match and married Philip G. Blanck. Their children, Adele (Faske) and Sidney, both served as judges for the Circuit Court of Miami. There have been more than 100 Jewish judges in Greater Miami.

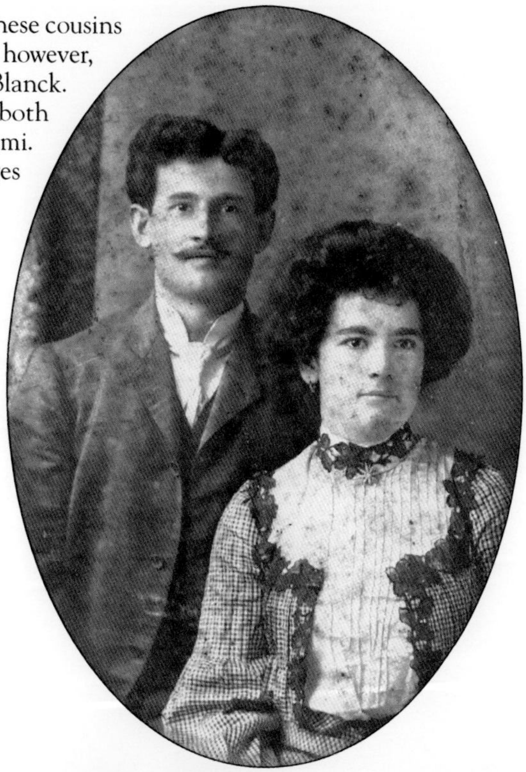

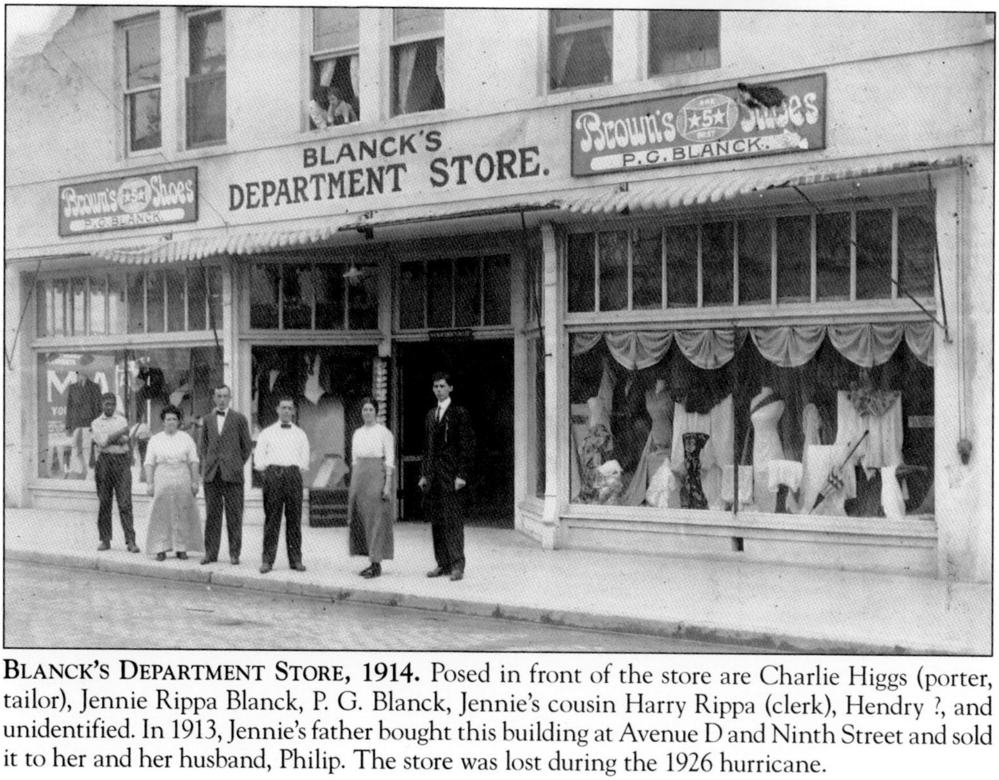

BLANCK'S DEPARTMENT STORE, 1914. Posed in front of the store are Charlie Higgs (porter, tailor), Jennie Rippa Blanck, P. G. Blanck, Jennie's cousin Harry Rippa (clerk), Hendry ?, and unidentified. In 1913, Jennie's father bought this building at Avenue D and Ninth Street and sold it to her and her husband, Philip. The store was lost during the 1926 hurricane.

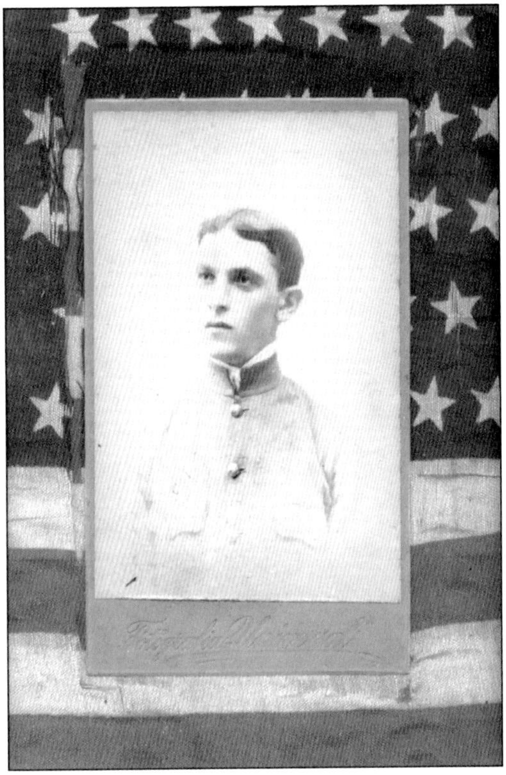

HARRY DAVID RIPPA, SPANISH-AMERICAN WAR SOLDIER, 1898. To demonstrate his patriotism as a new American, Harry enlisted at the age of 17.

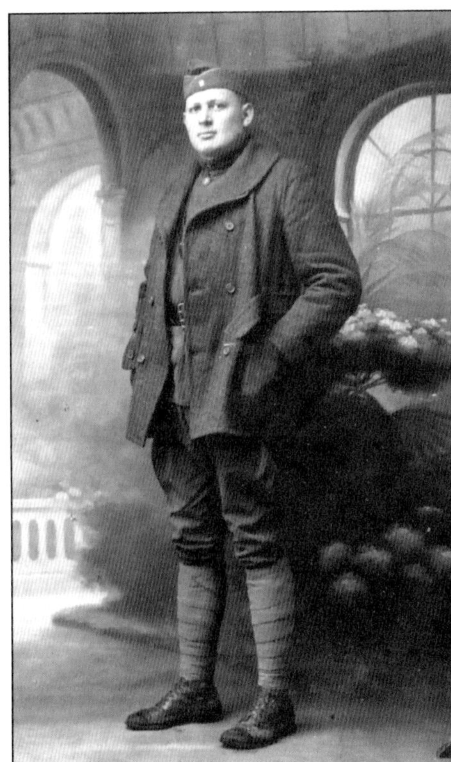

WILLIAM WOLFSON, WORLD WAR I, 1917. William had attended Virginia Military Institute in 1902, where his father, Louis Wolfson, allotted him $5 per month for pocket money. The first Wolfson to land in Florida from Europe was Joseph, who came into Key West in 1884 in the aftermath of a shipwreck. His brother Louis and Louis's wife, Rosa, joined him a few years later. Louis moved his family to Miami in 1915.

Two

Developing a Community on the Mainland

Post 1920s

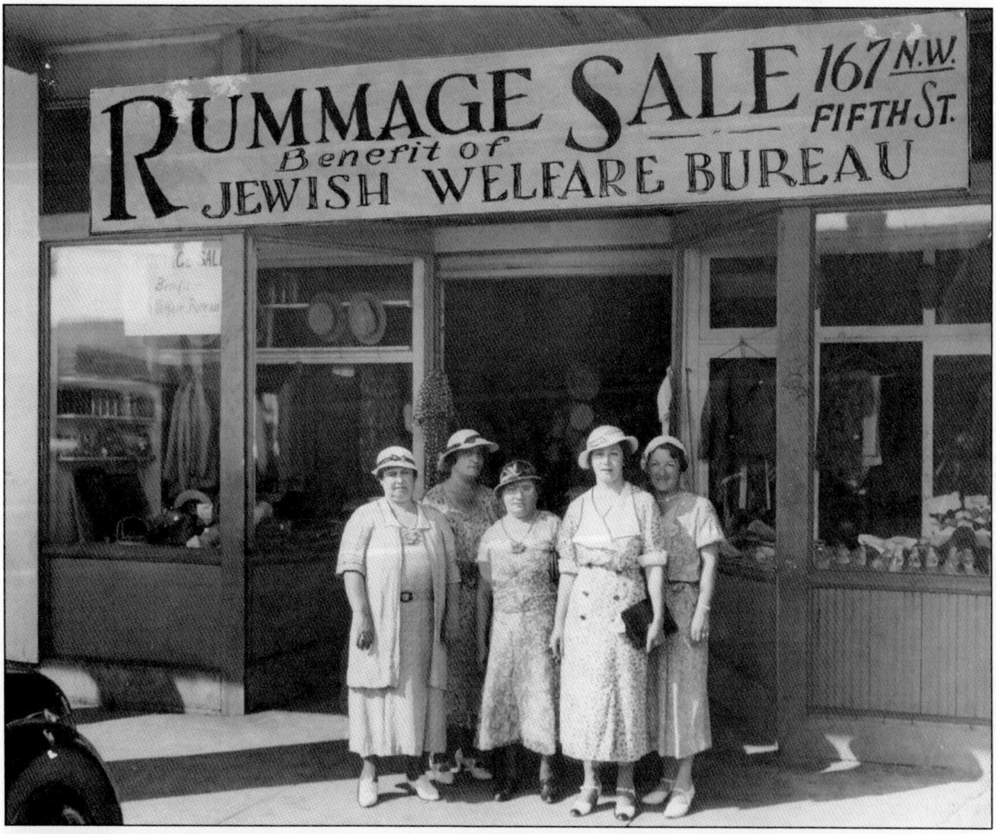

Jewish Welfare Bureau, 1920s. As the community developed, more organizations were created for business networking, to meet humanitarian needs, and for social connections, as Jews were excluded from other clubs. The women of the Jewish Welfare Bureau held rummage sales to raise funds. Morris Zion was the founder and first president of the Jewish Welfare Bureau, which was originally called the United Jewish Aid Association. His wife, Clara, is shown on the left.

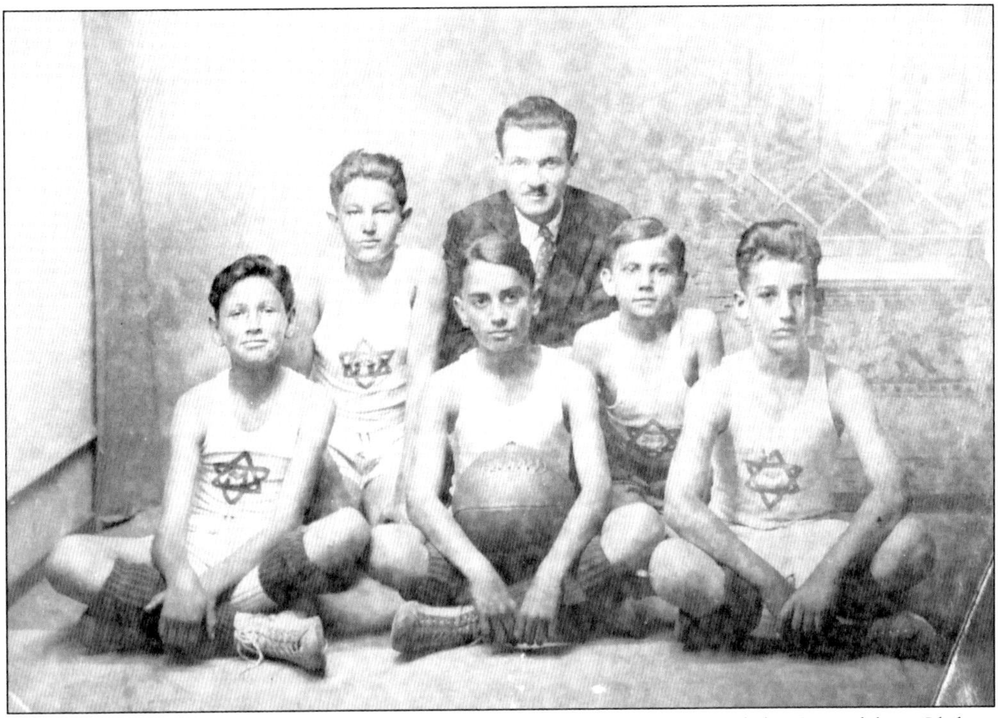

JEWISH SOCCER TEAM, 1920S. This team might have been a part of the Friendship Club, a Jewish social club.

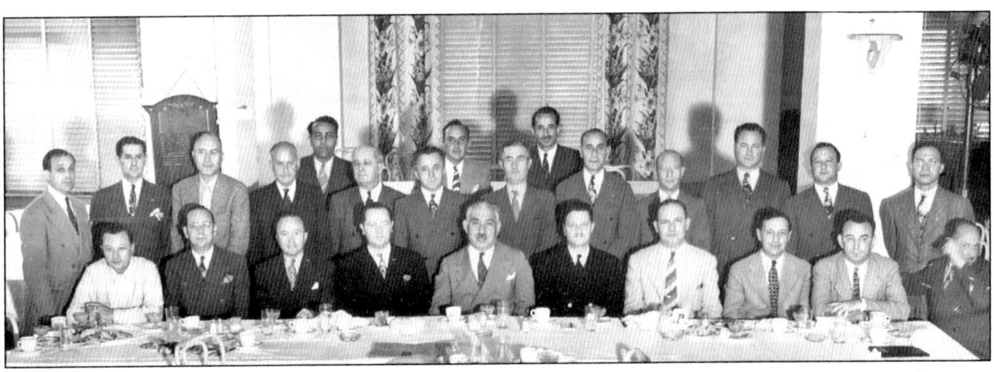

PRO-BUS CLUB, 1943. This was a group of Jewish professionals and businessmen who met for lunch and social events. Leonard Wien (second row, eighth from left) is among the community leaders.

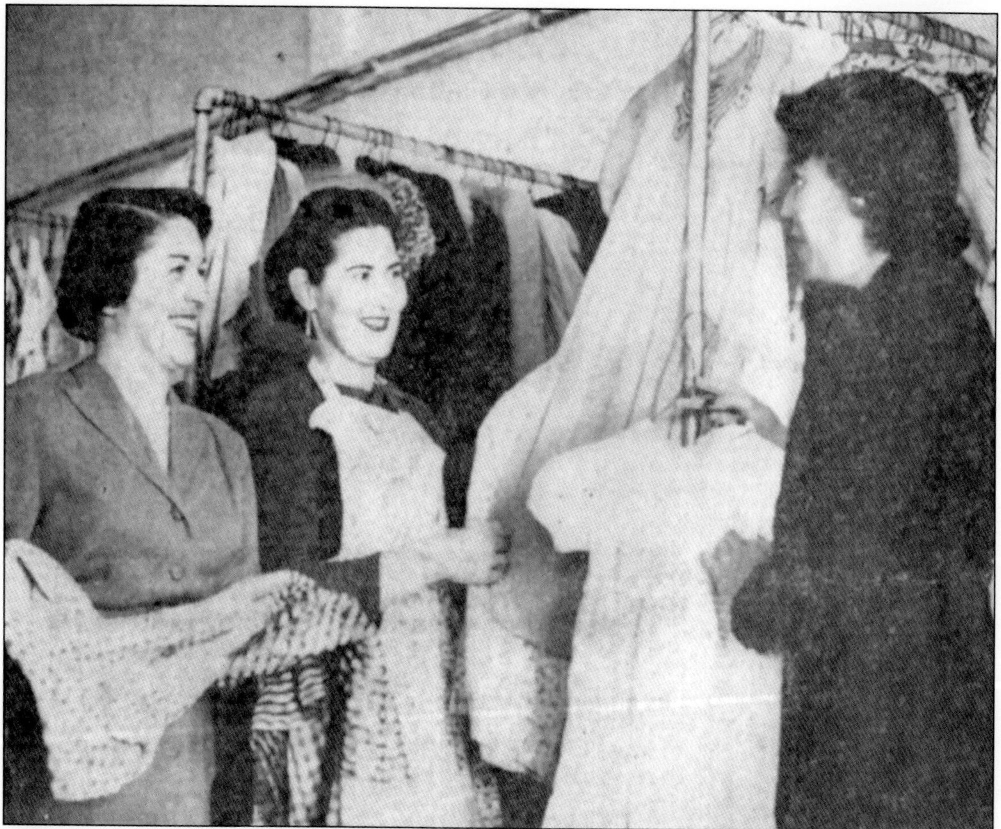

NATIONAL COUNCIL OF JEWISH WOMEN, 1950. The Miami section of this national organization was founded in 1921 and assists women, children, and families. One way to raise funds was opening a thrift shop, which was the first in the area and was located in downtown Miami. Regina Stahl (center) shows the founder and chairman Myra Farr (left) and Juliet Oshlag how she promotes a sale. Farr has been active on the national level for 50 years.

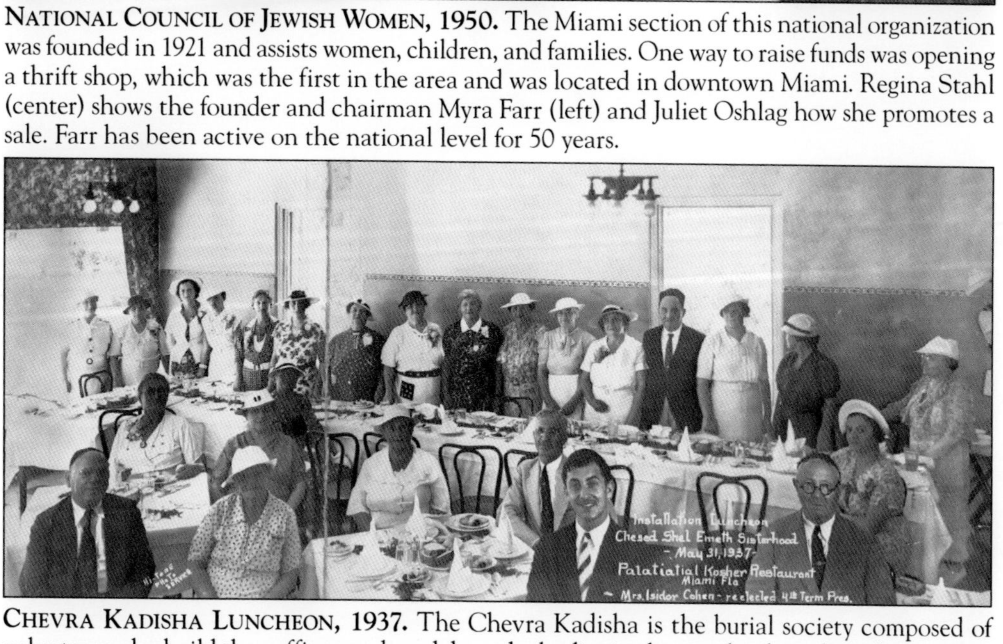

CHEVRA KADISHA LUNCHEON, 1937. The Chevra Kadisha is the burial society composed of volunteers who build the coffins, wash and dress the bodies in the simple white shroud prescribed by Jewish law, and who keep vigil until the burial. Identified at this event are Ida Cohen, Sarah Stone, Minnie Engler, and Dora Rosengarten.

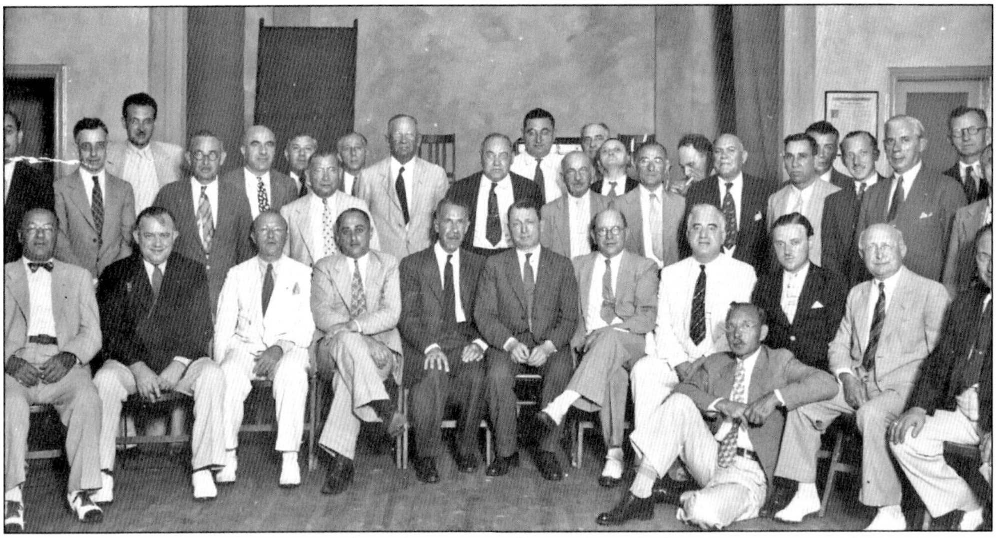

B'NAI B'RITH, 1928. Sholem Lodge of B'nai B'rith was founded in Miami in 1925. In 1941, the lodge was so large (1,500 members) that the national organization adopted a policy to split lodges on the basis of location and size. Today, with chapters throughout the state, this organization works to educate its members and to support Jewish causes.

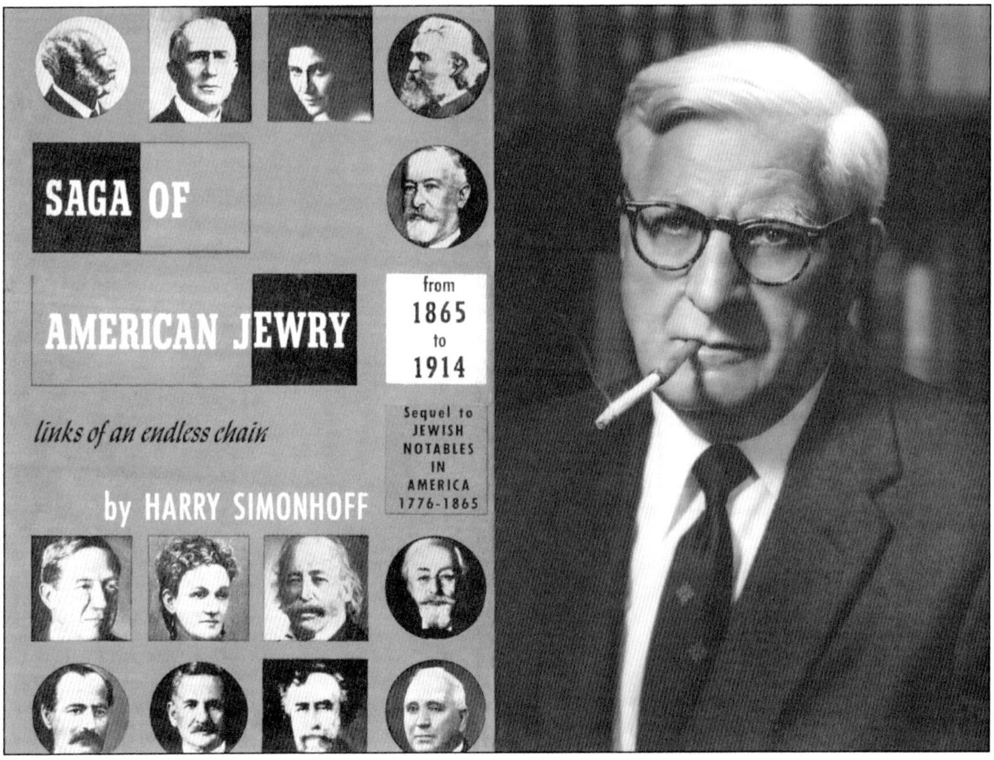

HARRY SIMONOFF. Ardent Zionist Harry Simonoff founded the Miami chapter of the Zionist Organization of America in 1926, aided in the formation of B'nai B'rith, and was a leader in the Anti-Defamation League. He authored several books, including *Saga of American Jewry*.

GROUNDBREAKING OF TEMPLE ISRAEL, 1927. In 1922, Rabbi Salo Stein and discontent members of Beth David broke off to form a Reform congregation. Miami's city manager, Frank Wharton, was the main speaker at this event. Also pictured are Herbert Feibelman, D. J. Apte, Herman Wolkowsky, Bernard Wolkowsky (Wall), and Joe Richter. Erected in 1927 at Northeast Nineteenth Street and Second Avenue, Temple Israel of Greater Miami remains the "downtown" temple, as it is locally referred.

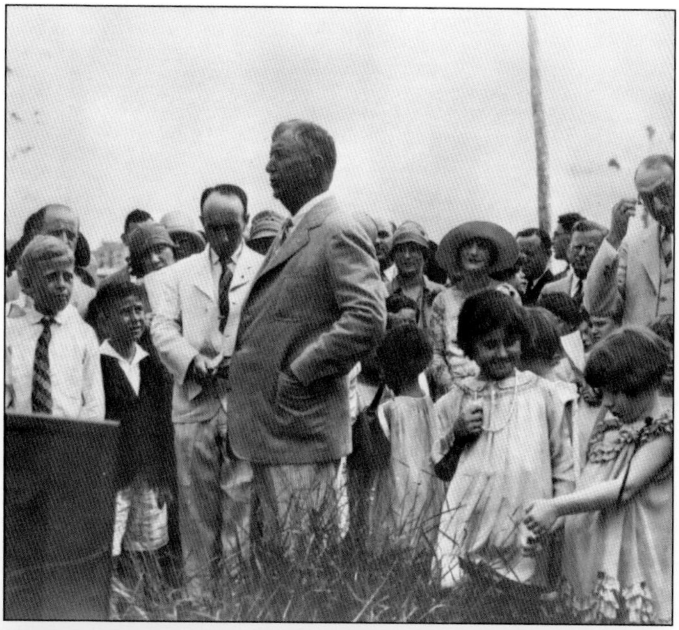

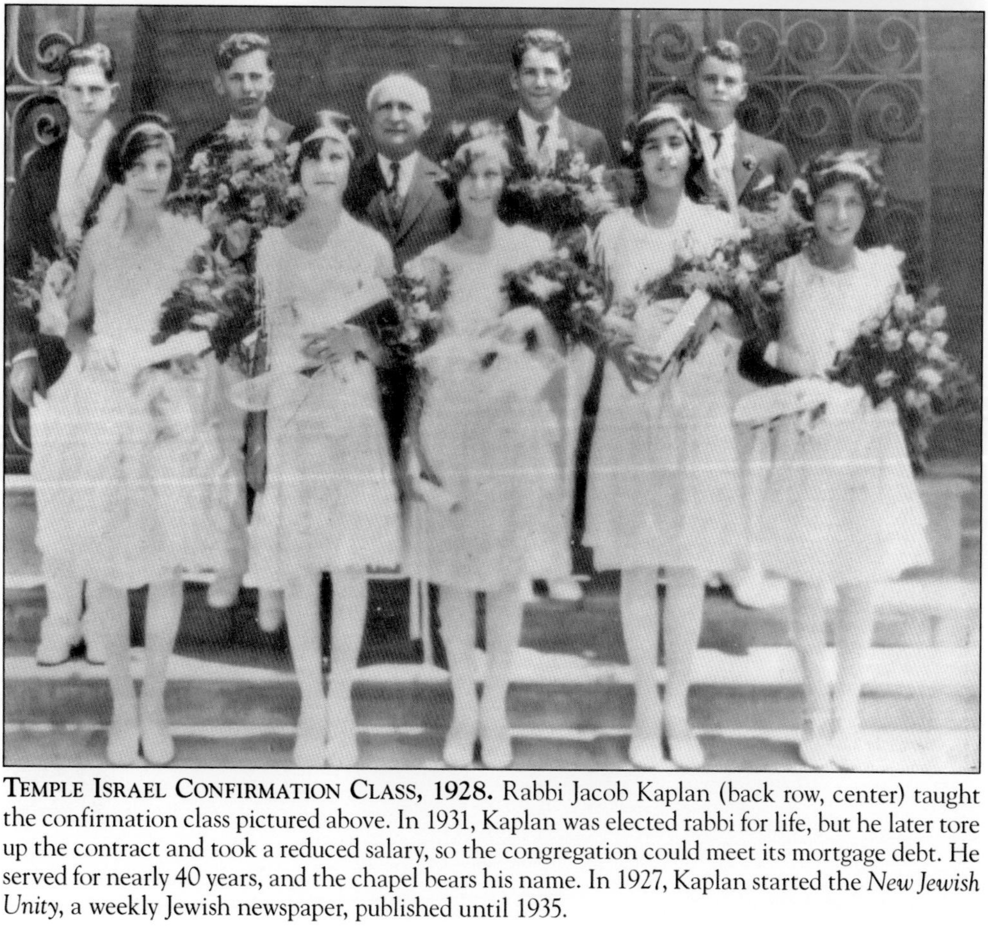

TEMPLE ISRAEL CONFIRMATION CLASS, 1928. Rabbi Jacob Kaplan (back row, center) taught the confirmation class pictured above. In 1931, Kaplan was elected rabbi for life, but he later tore up the contract and took a reduced salary, so the congregation could meet its mortgage debt. He served for nearly 40 years, and the chapel bears his name. In 1927, Kaplan started the *New Jewish Unity*, a weekly Jewish newspaper, published until 1935.

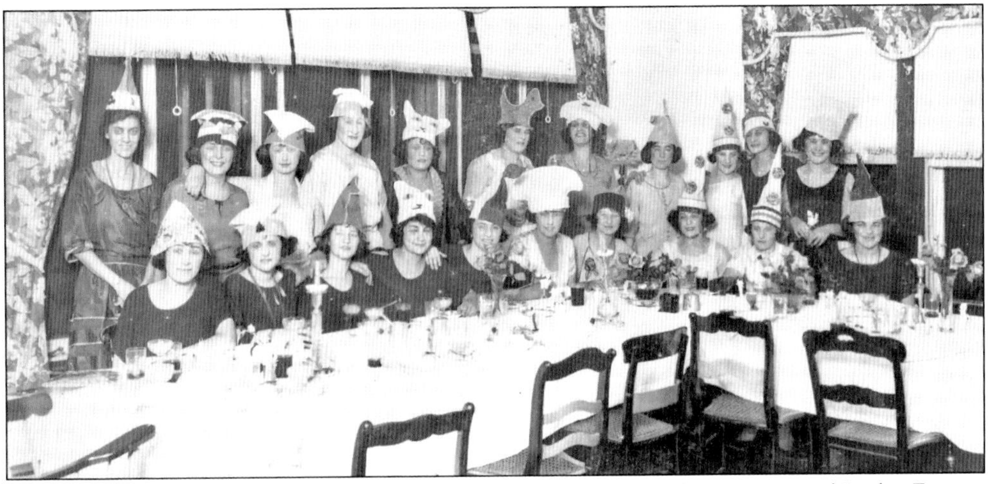

CLARA SCHWARTZ'S WEDDING SHOWER, 1922. When Clara Schwartz married Isador Fine, it was a merging of two pioneer Key West families who had moved to Miami. Her wedding shower at the El Commodore Hotel was a grand affair for all the young Jewish ladies in town.

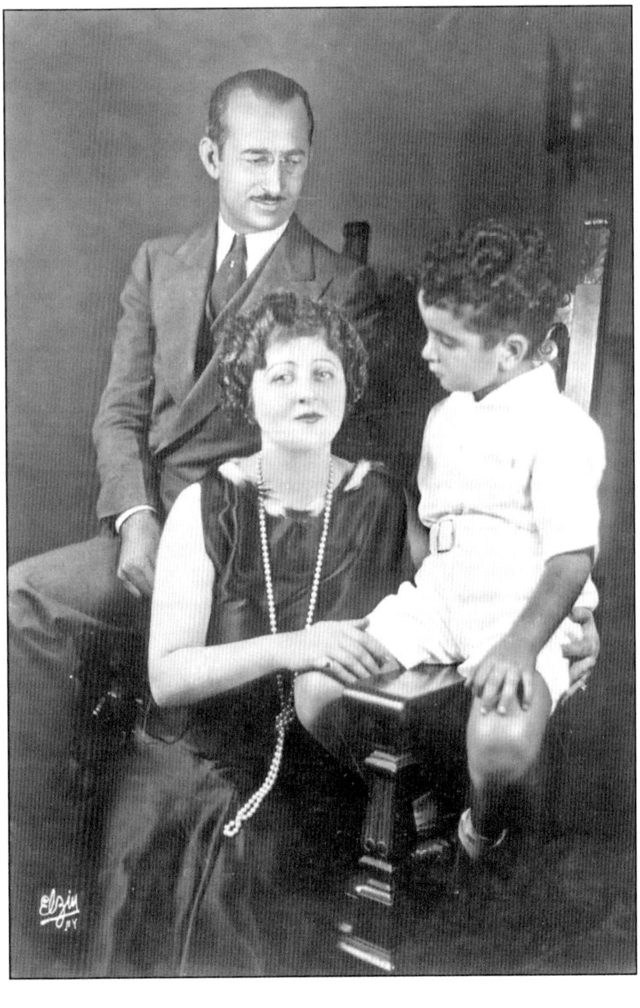

IRWIN CASSEL WITH HIS WIFE, MANA-ZUCCA, AND SON MARWIN, 1926. Irwin was the first president of Miami's first symphony, which drew on talented local musicians, such as his wife. Mana-Zucca, who composed music, held piano concerts in her living room each Tuesday.

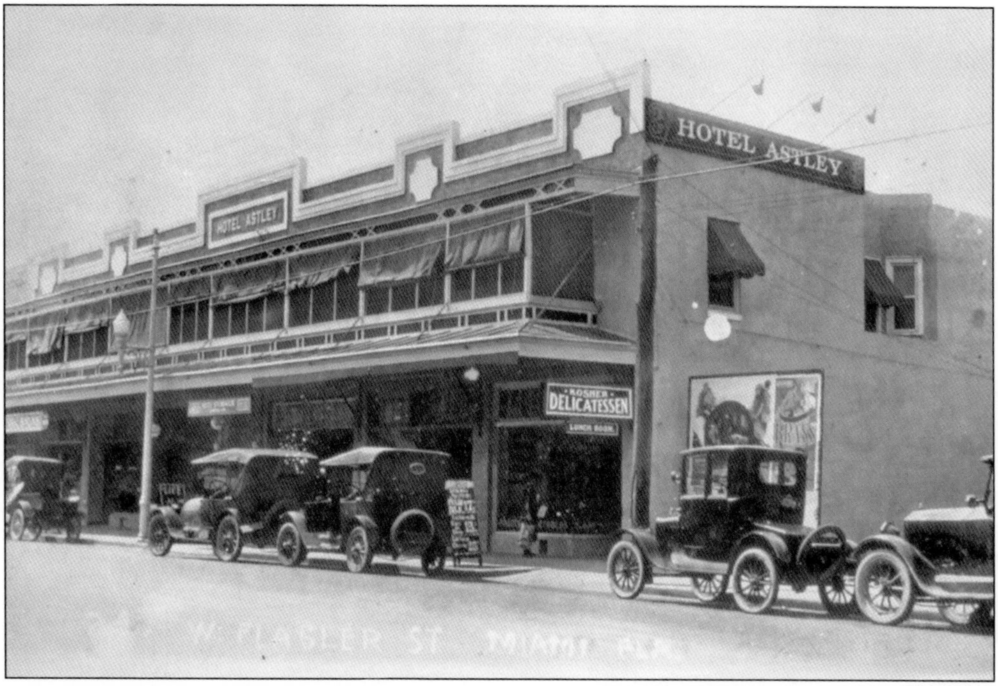

SAUL COHEN DELI, 1923. Saul Cohen left Philadelphia in 1920 when he was offered a free ride on a freight ship bringing produce down to Miami. He liked what he saw and decided to remain. That same year, Saul opened the first delicatessen in Miami, on Flagler Street.

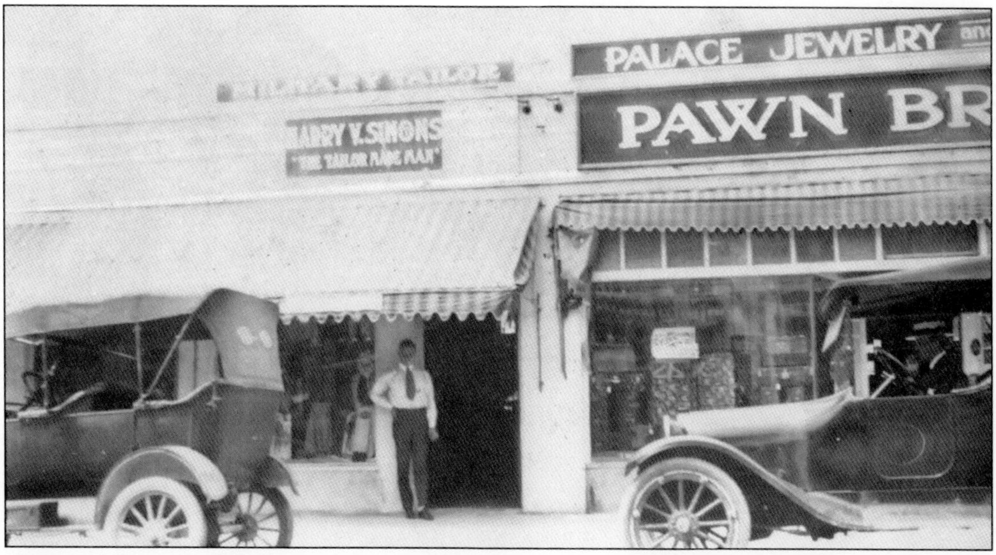

HARRY V. SIMONS IN FRONT OF STORE ON FLAGLER STREET, 1922. Simons had been a president of Beth David and was then the first president of the earliest Reform congregation, Temple Israel.

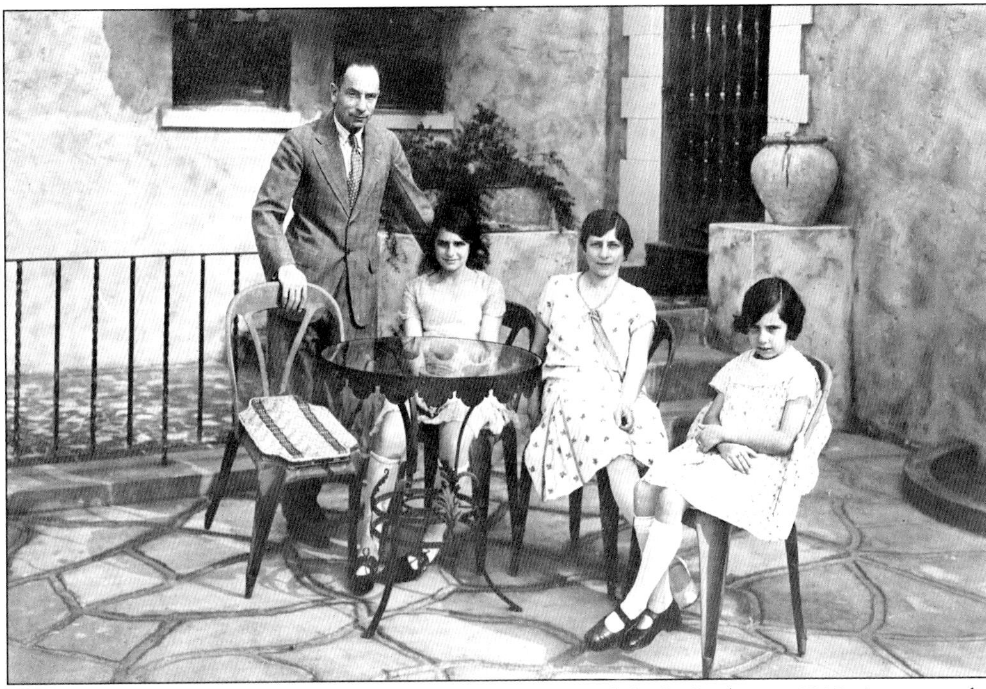

ARTHUR UNGAR FAMILY, 1919. Ungar started an automobile dealership in 1918. Active in the community, he assisted in making Mount Sinai Hospital a reality, was a founder of Temple Israel, and, as a University of Miami trustee, helped keep it financially stable in the early years of the Depression. Here he is shown with his wife, Marcella, and daughters Bertha (Abess), seated beside her father, and Marcella (Werblow), at right.

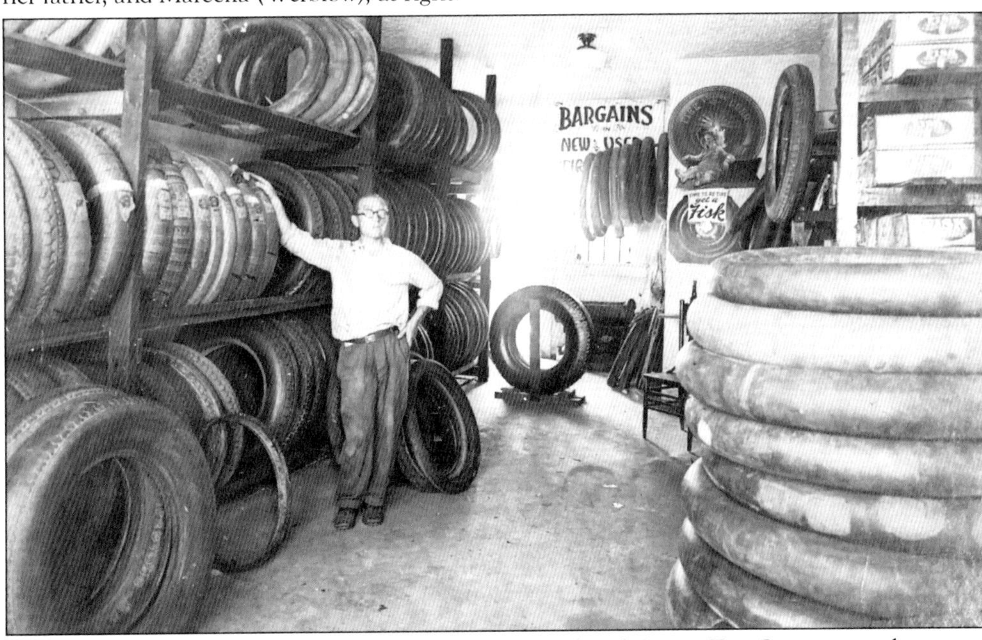

LOUIS PALLOT, 1924. Russian immigrant Pallot was founder of Norton Tire Company in downtown Miami, which was named for his and Gertrude's son, Norton. By 1958, the company became B. F. Goodrich Company's largest tire dealer in the state of Florida.

MITCHELL WOLFSON, 1926. A son of Louis and Rosa Wolfson, Mitchell came to Miami in 1917 and then founded WOMETCO (Wolfson-Meyer Theater Company) theaters with his brother-in-law Sidney Meyer. He was the first Jewish mayor of Miami Beach (1943). He often said that helping to build Miami Dade Community College was his proudest achievement; 80 percent of his foundation goes there.

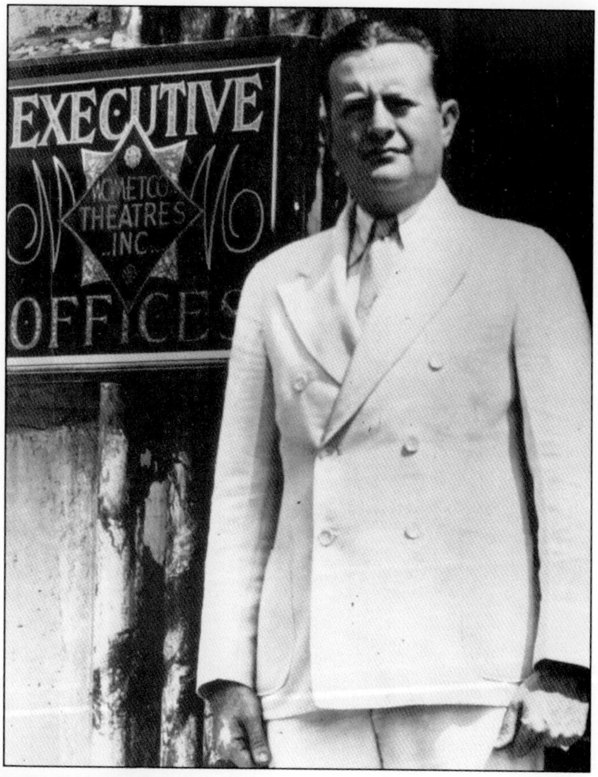

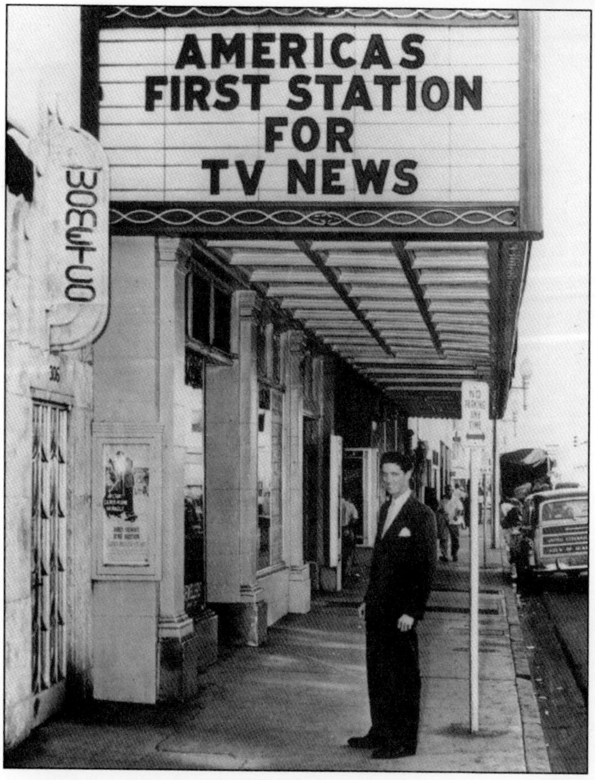

FIRST WOMETCO THEATER, THIRD STREET AND NORTH MIAMI AVENUE, 1926. In 1949, this theater was converted to a studio for Florida's first television station, WTVJ. Sidney Meyer was a 20th Century Fox moving picture representative in Florida, and married Mitchell Wolfson's sister Zenia. Wolfson and Meyer's company grew to include other theaters, radio and television stations, the Miami Seaquarium, and other industries, which have helped make Florida a leisure capital.

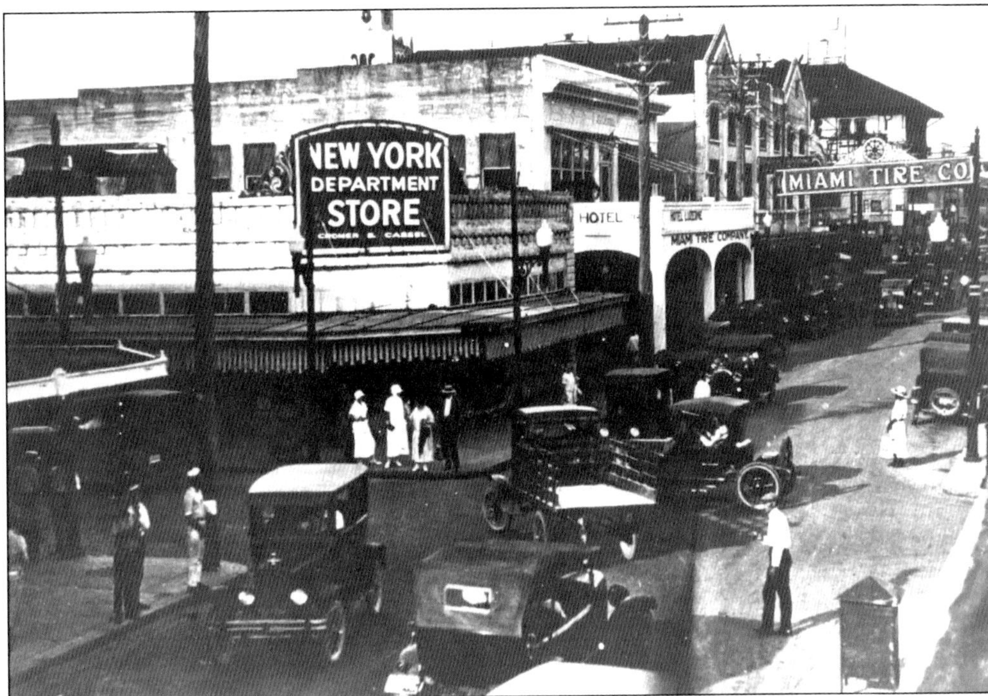

NEW YORK DEPARTMENT STORE, 1921. This popular business site was first David Afremow's store at Miami Avenue and Northeast First Street. It was purchased in 1913 by Daniel Cromer, who was joined by Irwin Cassel, and then rebuilt as Cromer-Cassel's in 1926. Later this became the site of a major chain, Richard's Department Store.

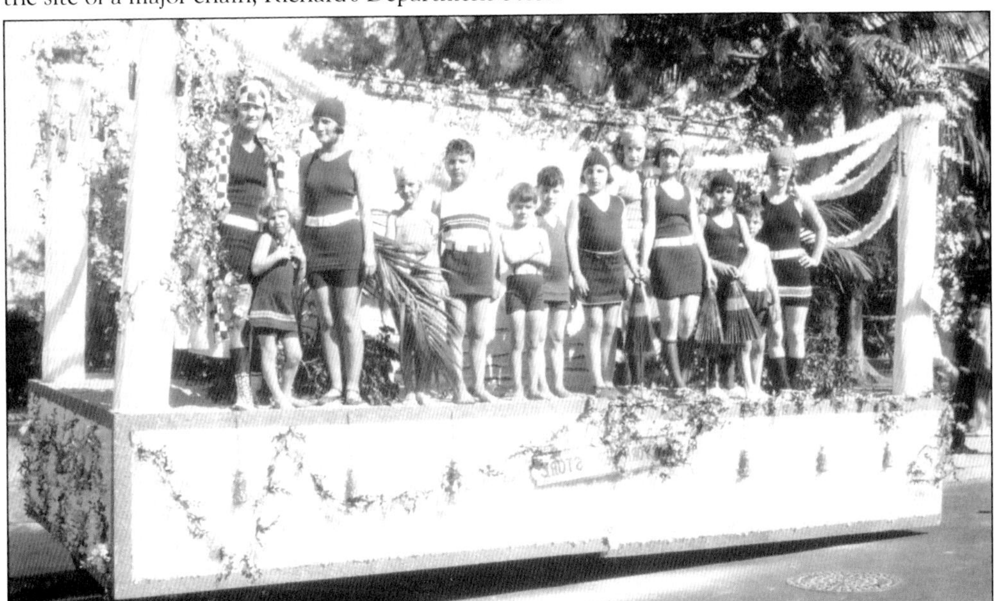

NEW YORK DEPARTMENT STORE FRUIT AND FLOWER PAGEANT FLOAT, 1924. The store had its own float in the 1924 Fruit and Flower pageant (predecessor to the Orange Bowl Parade). Those on the float include Chester Cassel, Doris Cromer, Maurice Cromer, Alvin Cassel, and Flossie Cassel (Alvin's mother).

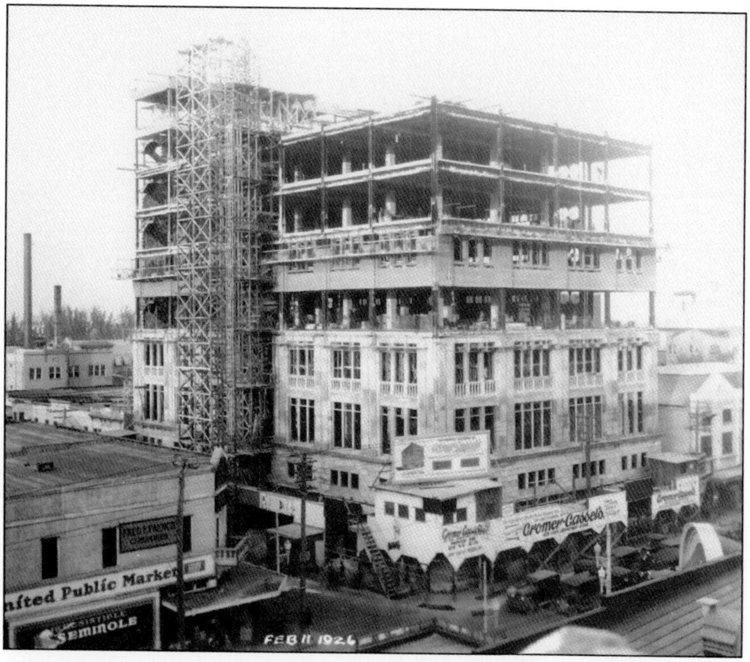

CROMER-CASSEL'S DEPARTMENT STORE UNDER CONSTRUCTION, 1926. After purchasing Afremow's New York Department Store, Cromer and Cassel had unbounded faith in the future of Miami and, on May 28, 1926, opened a nine-story, $5-million department store, the most modern in the South. It was severely damaged in the hurricane four months later and never recovered.

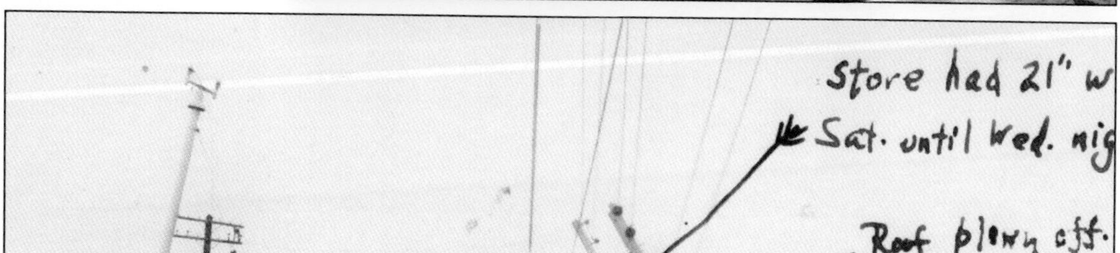

FINE-GOLDMAN STORE AFTER HURRICANE, 1926. During the 1920s, imagination, drive, and confidence propelled a fever of prosperity in Miami. Then, more quickly than it developed, the boom was blown away by the 1926 hurricane, which swept into the city just as the Kol Nidre service on Yom Kippur ended. The disaster brought the real estate boom to an abrupt halt, and most businesses were destroyed. National headlines stated, "Miami is Wiped Out."

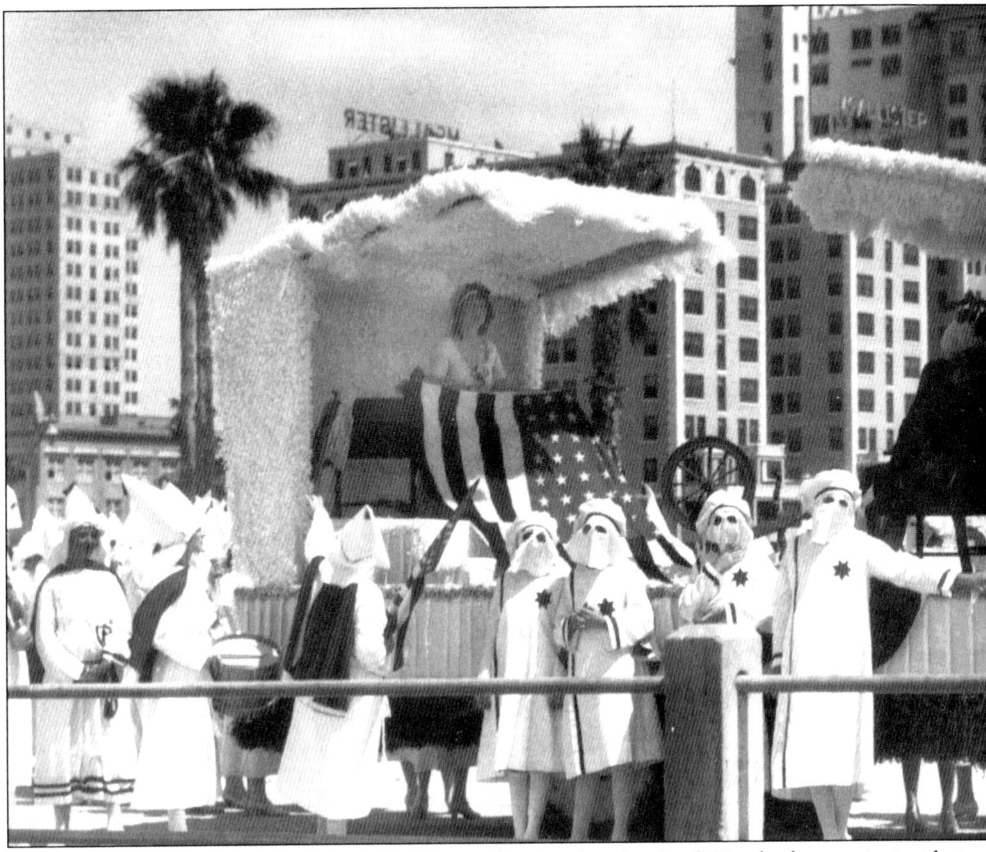

KU KLUX KLAN PARADE, 1927. The racist KKK, begun after the Civil War, had a very intimidating, antisemitic attitude, participating in many community events, such as this Fourth of July parade. Today the Klan is one of the most active groups on the far Right in Florida, often sponsoring rallies, and has become integrated with the newer elements of the fringe Right, including neo-Nazis and skinheads.

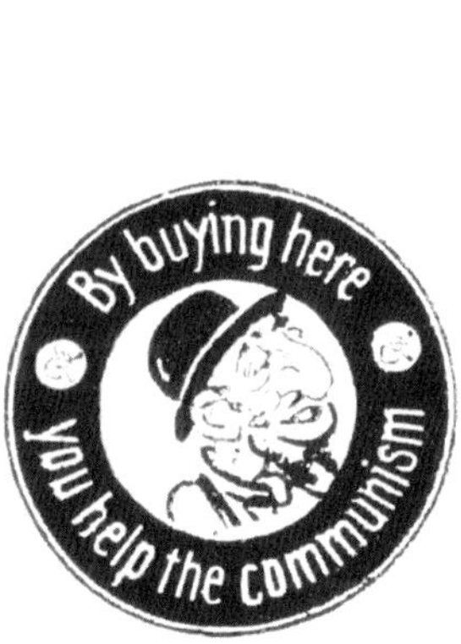

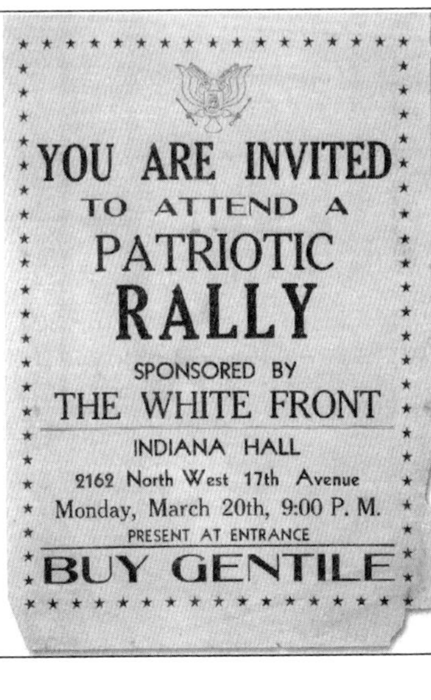

YOU ARE INVITED
TO ATTEND A
PATRIOTIC
RALLY
SPONSORED BY
THE WHITE FRONT
INDIANA HALL
2162 North West 17th Avenue
Monday, March 20th, 9:00 P. M.
PRESENT AT ENTRANCE
BUY GENTILE

NAZISM IN MIAMI, LATE 1930S. In an attempt to boycott Jewish businesses in downtown Miami, this type of signage (shown far left) was put on storefronts owned by Jews. The antisemitic artwork was taken directly from European Nazi sources, with a mangled English-language translation of the original German text. The White Front publicized a rally in 1939 (shown left). Burnett Roth collected thousands of documents like these for the Anti-Defamation League.

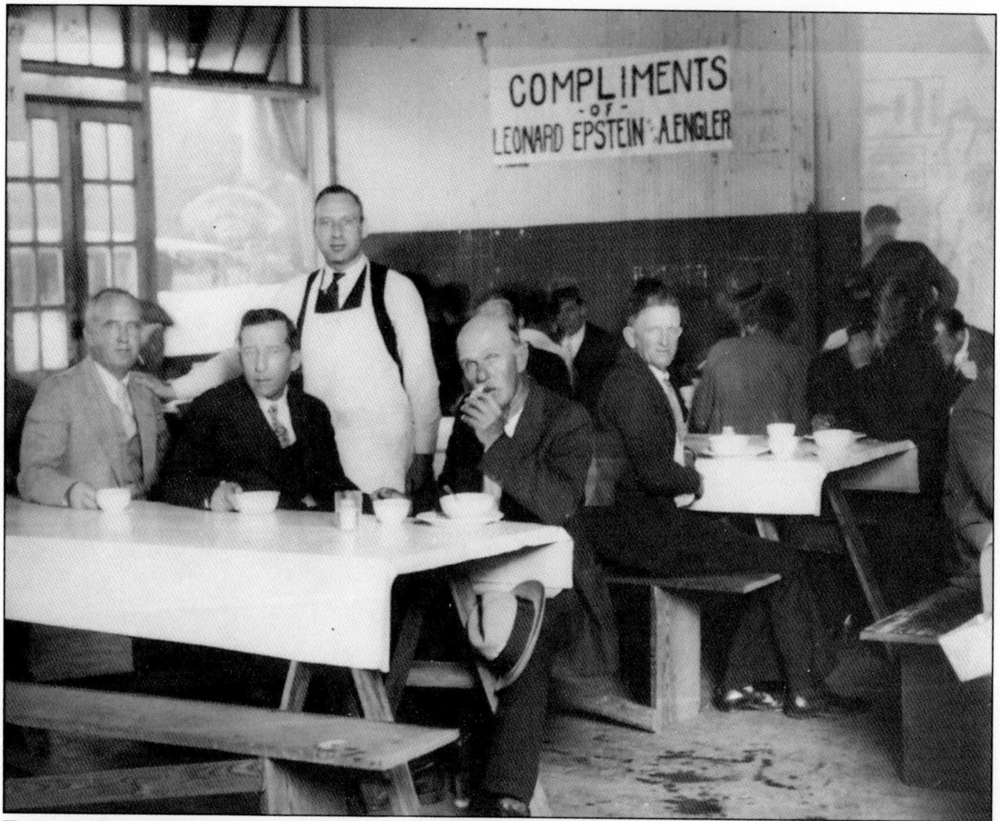

ENGLER SOUP KITCHEN, 1929. The Depression affected many lives in Miami, both Jewish and non-Jewish. Abram Engler and his son-in-law Louis Epstein ran a soup kitchen for the unemployed. Engler donated all the food as a charitable gesture.

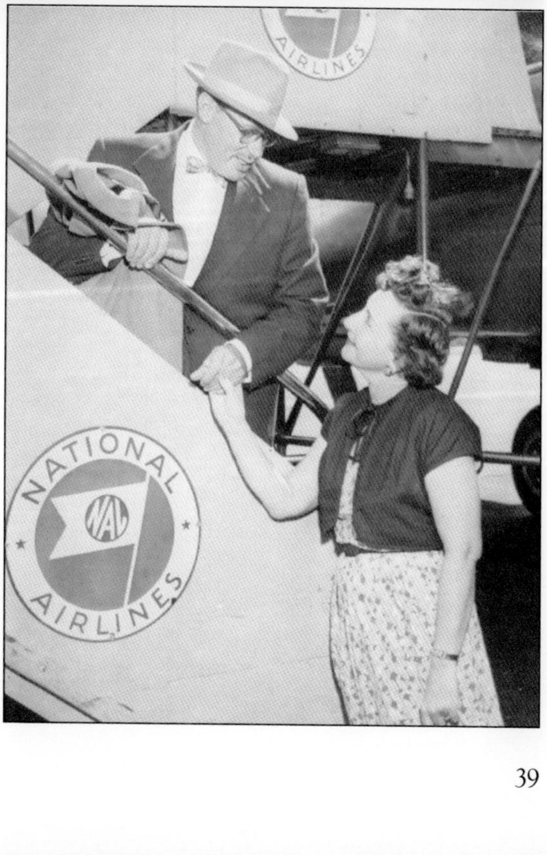

MOLLIE AND DAN RUSKIN, C. 1938. During the 1930s, new residents arrived by air, train, and the Mallory Steamship Line. Tourists were lured to boating, fishing, and tropical gardens attractions. Miami's reputation began as the "gateway to Latin America." Satellite communities emerged. The hotel, building, and banking industries escalated with greater participation by Jews. In this publicity shot for National Airlines, Dan is saying goodbye to his wife.

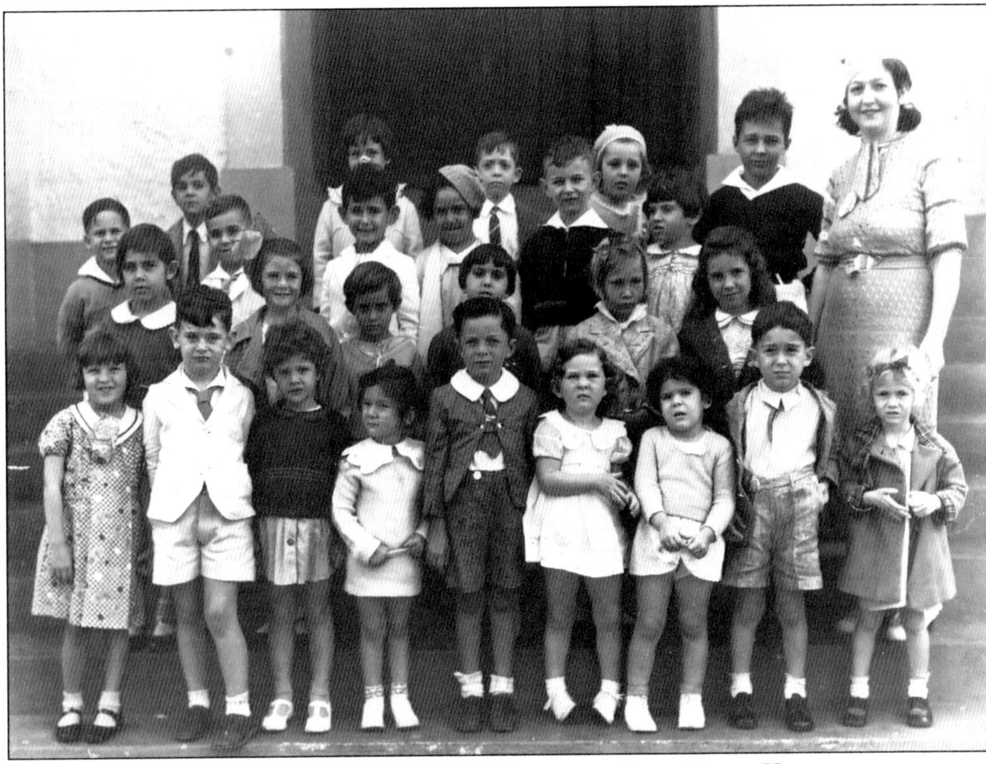

Beth David Kindergarten Class, 1933. More Jewish families resulted in the growth of the congregations and more children to educate. Identified are Joyce Rosengarten, Ida Engler, Miriam Shaff Weinkle, Eli Argintar, and Sonia Zalka.

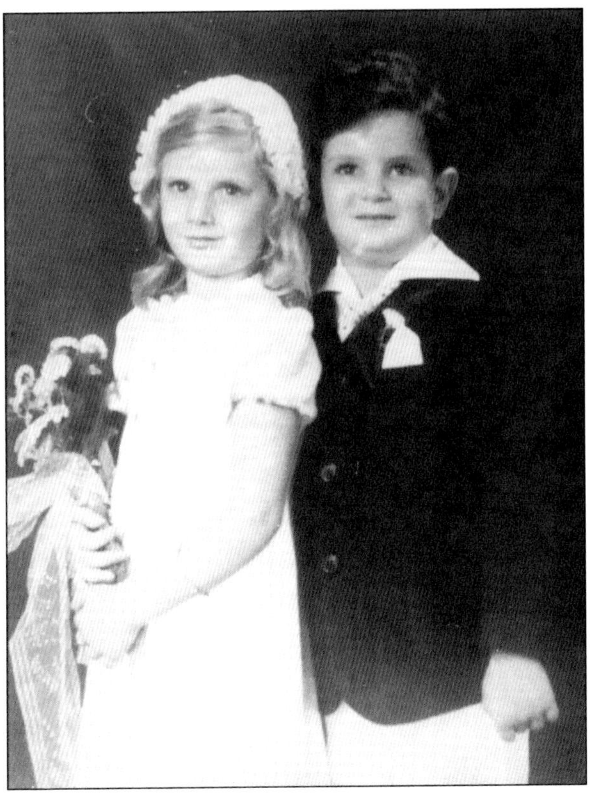

Tom Thumb Wedding, 1935. These events were held as fund-raisers for the congregations. At Beth David, Gloria Goodman (Scharlin), age three and a half, and her cousin Buddy Weissel, age four, charmed the audience to make contributions.

SAMUEL AND BEATRICE BLANK, 1964. The Blanks moved to Miami in 1925. Sam established the Florida Sugar Distributors, which later became National Brands. They expanded to a wholesale grocery business and beer distributor. Sam and Bea held leading roles in the Jewish community, including starting the Israel Bond Campaign in Miami. Here they were the first to receive a Medallion of Honor, an award from the Israel Bond organization for outstanding leadership and selling and promoting the bonds.

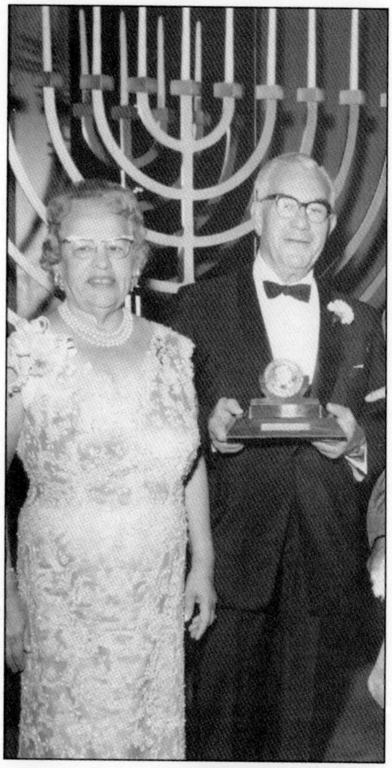

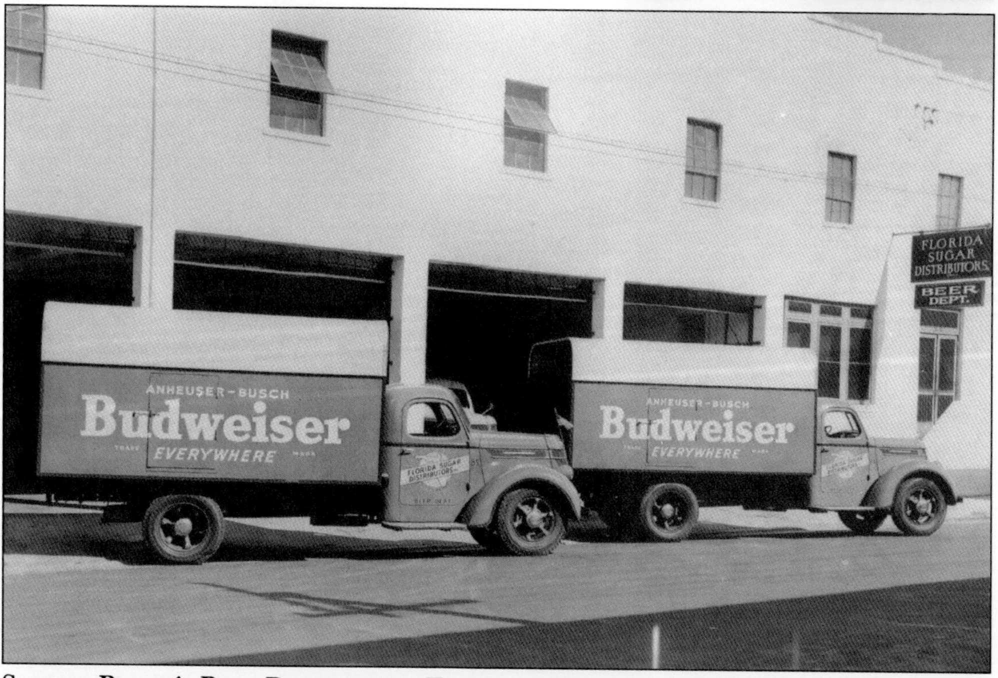

SAMUEL BLANK'S BEER DISTRIBUTOR TRUCKS, 1936. Most of the early residents of Miami were devout churchgoers who voted dry in 1913. When the law was repealed in 1933, Sam Blank quickly saw an opportunity and started his beer distributorship, which included Anheuser-Busch and Michelob. Sam was president of the Greater Miami Jewish Federation, which was founded in his home in 1938, and a member of the Miami Group that helped develop Israel.

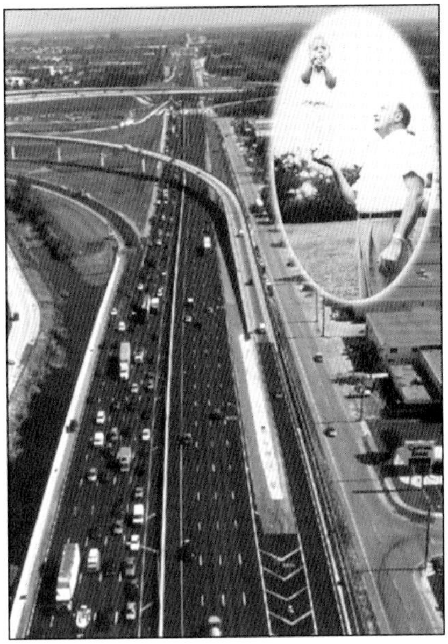

WILLIAM SINGER. Singer (inset) was looking for a Depression-proof business when he opened a 5¢ hamburger stand in 1938, Royal Castle. Son Larry (inset; shown in his dad's hand) joined his dad in 1947 and propelled its expansion to 175 restaurants. William Singer, best known for his service on the Florida Road Board (1957–1960), was instrumental in developing the state's highway system. The portion of Interstate 95 going through Miami-Dade County is named for William Singer.

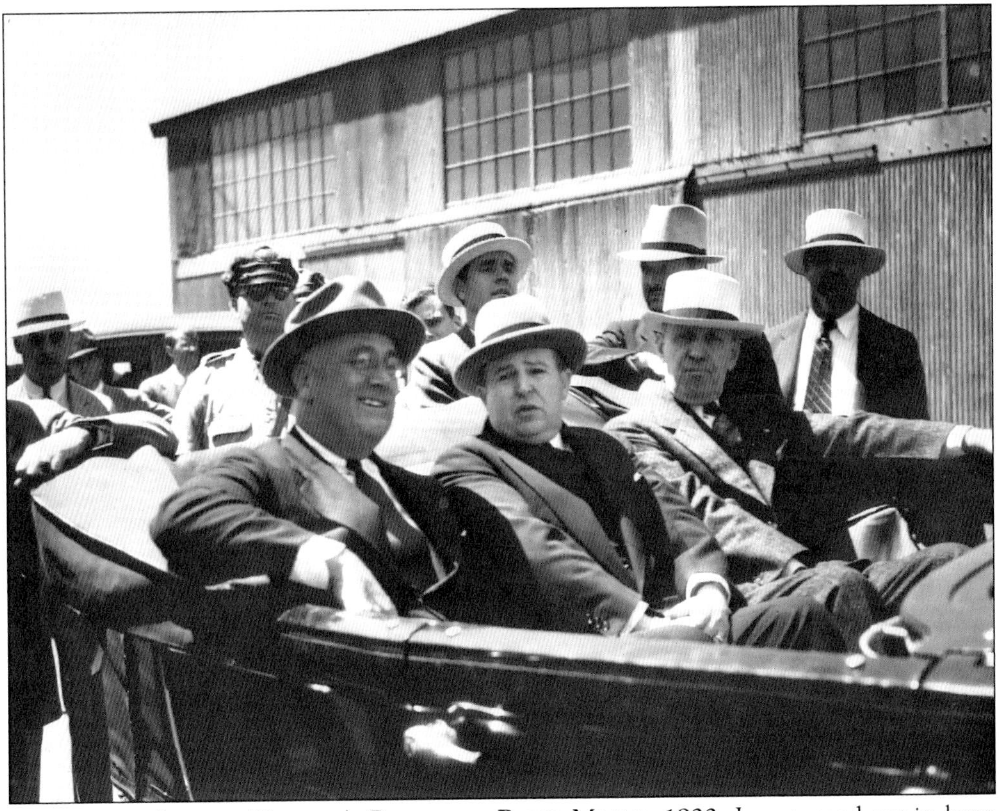

GOV. DAVID SHOLTZ (CENTER), BAYFRONT PARK, MIAMI, 1933. Jews turned out in large numbers to greet their Jewish governor and president-elect Franklin Roosevelt (left). Chicago mayor Anton Cermak (right) was killed in the attempted assassination of Roosevelt. Giuseppe Zangara was swiftly convicted of murder and executed in the electric chair in perhaps one of the shortest periods of time between crime and execution (32 days).

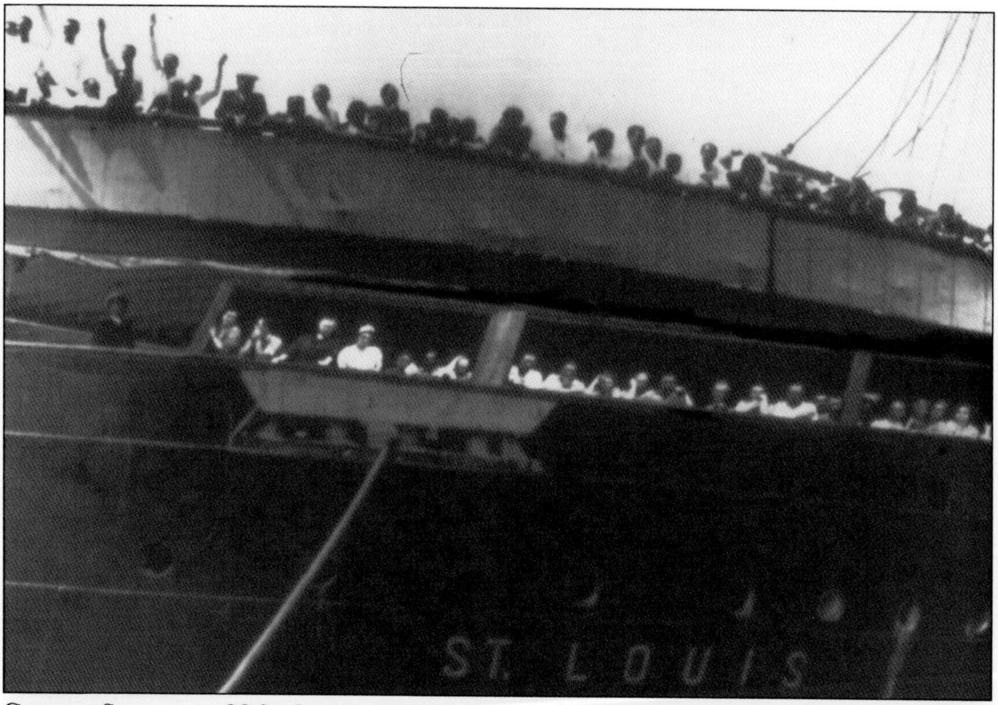

GERMAN STEAMSHIP SS *ST. LOUIS*, 1939. As the decade closed, the Jewish community confronted Hitler's solution to what he called the "Jewish problem." This ship arrived off Miami Beach on June 4, 1939, looking for a Florida port to accept its 937 passengers. A rally was held in Bayfront Park to allow the Jews on the ship refuge, but Pres. Franklin Roosevelt refused them. They were sent back to Germany, where most perished in the Holocaust.

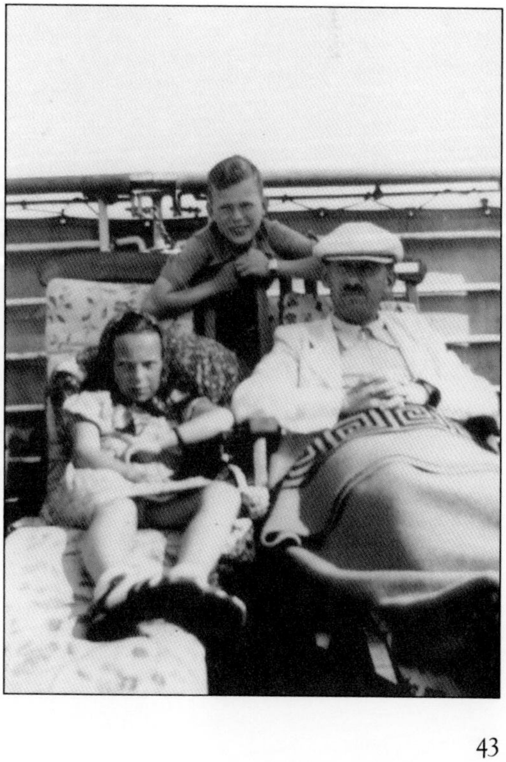

HERBERT KARLINER ON DECK OF THE SS *ST. LOUIS*, 1939. Ten-year-old Herbert Karliner saw the beautiful palm trees and hotels on Miami Beach from the ship and vowed to return, if he survived. Of the six members of his family, he and one brother were the only survivors. Herbert settled on Miami Beach in 1954. Shown here are Herbert (center), sister Ruth, and father Josef.

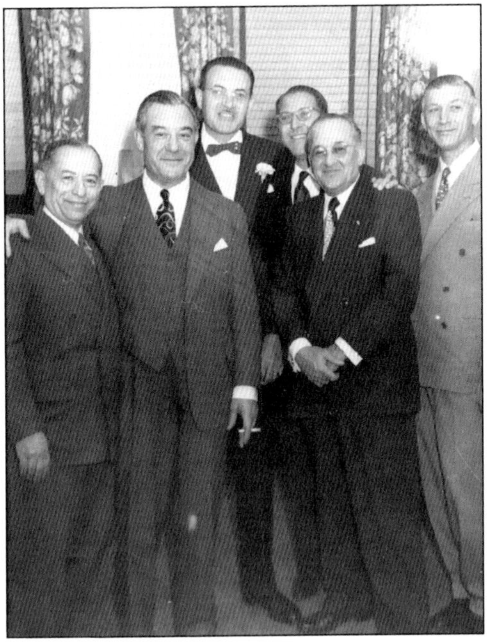

GREATER MIAMI JEWISH FEDERATION LEADERS, 1945. The terror building in Europe for Jews evoked a response in Miami's Jewish community as they organized for support, founding the Greater Miami Jewish Federation in 1938. Funds are raised to support Jewish local needs, as well as those overseas and in Palestine, and to provide services and programs through agencies. The leaders pictured from left to right are Moses Ginsberg, Samuel Blank, Stanley Myers, Herb Sher, Jake Sher, and Carl Weinkle.

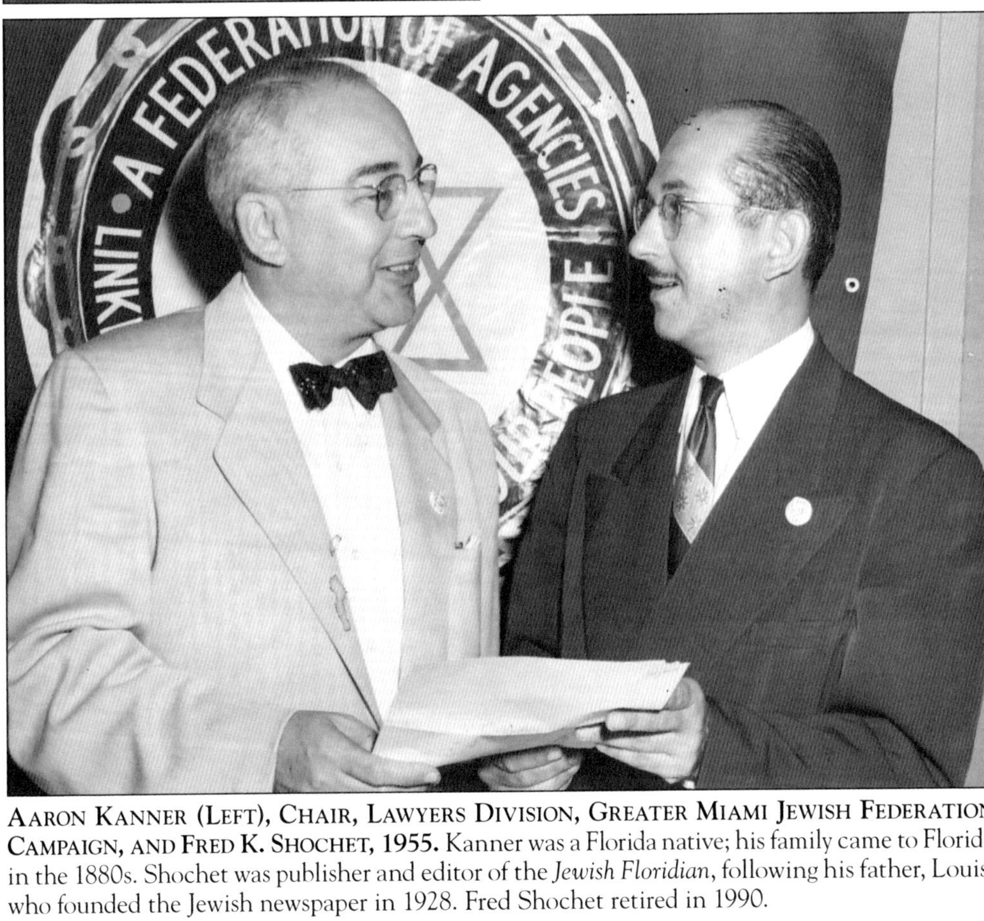

AARON KANNER (LEFT), CHAIR, LAWYERS DIVISION, GREATER MIAMI JEWISH FEDERATION CAMPAIGN, AND FRED K. SHOCHET, 1955. Kanner was a Florida native; his family came to Florida in the 1880s. Shochet was publisher and editor of the *Jewish Floridian*, following his father, Louis, who founded the Jewish newspaper in 1928. Fred Shochet retired in 1990.

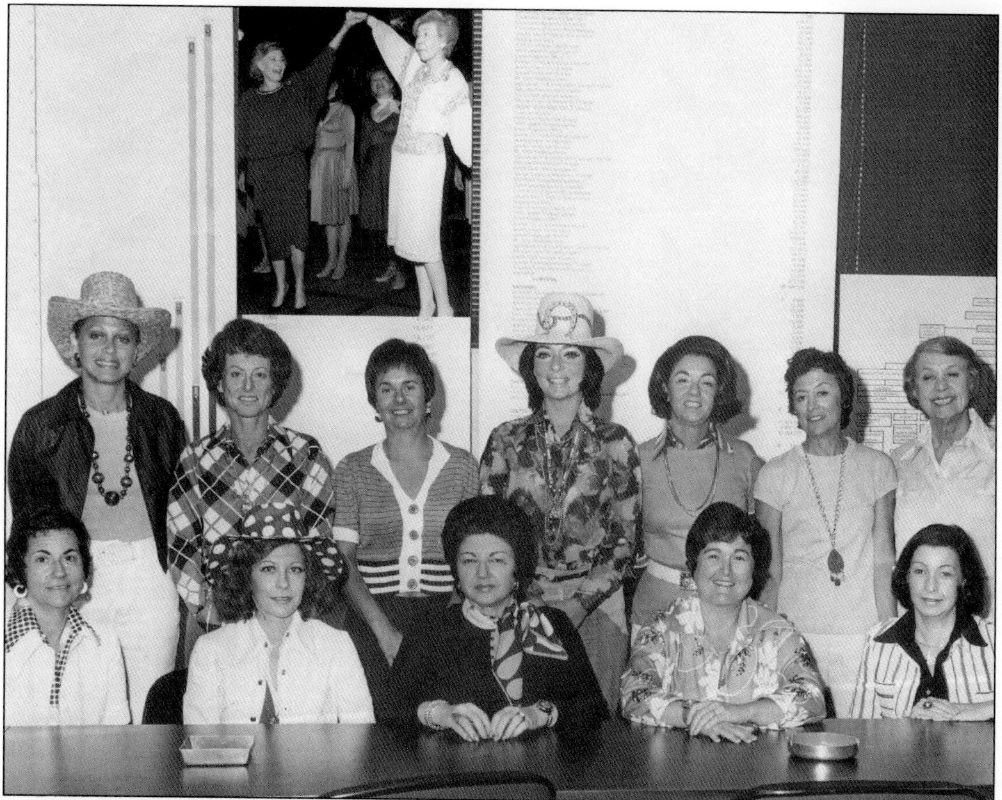

GREATER MIAMI JEWISH FEDERATION WOMEN'S DIVISION CAMPAIGN LEADERSHIP, 1974. From left to right are (seated) Gwen Weinberger, Maxine Schwartz, Goldie Goldstein, Bluma Marcus, and Jackie Traurig; (standing) Marilyn Smith, Bea Levy, Marlene Marks, Marcy Lefton, Val Silverman, Joyce Sumberg, and Reva Wexler. In 1972, Norma Kipnis-Wilson and Toby Friedland (both shown inset) initiated the Lion of Judah, now a national symbol of Jewish women's philanthropic commitment to the worldwide Jewish community.

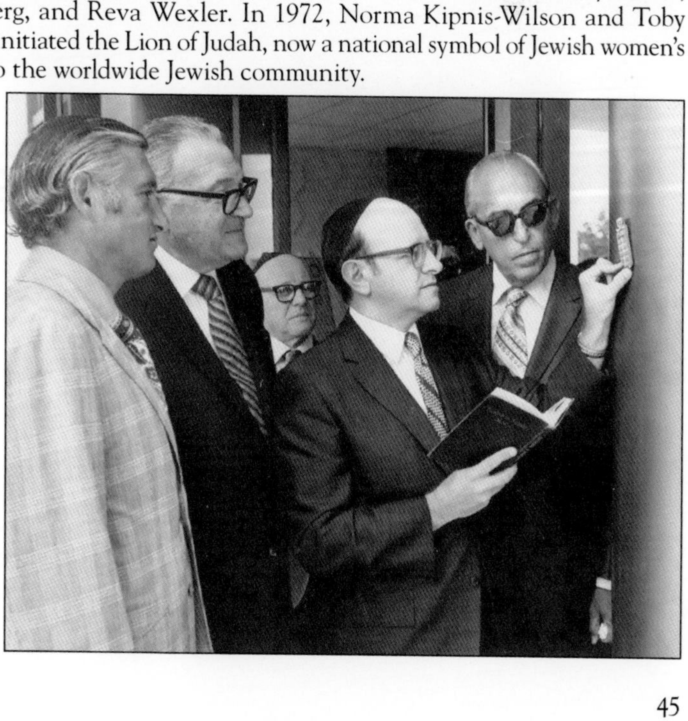

DEDICATION OF THE GREATER MIAMI JEWISH FEDERATION BUILDING AT 4200 BISCAYNE BOULEVARD, 1971. From left to right are Joseph H. Kanter; Stanley C. Myers (first president); unidentified; Rabbi Solomon Schiff (director, Community Chaplaincy Service); and Milton Weiss (then president of the Greater Miami Jewish Federation).

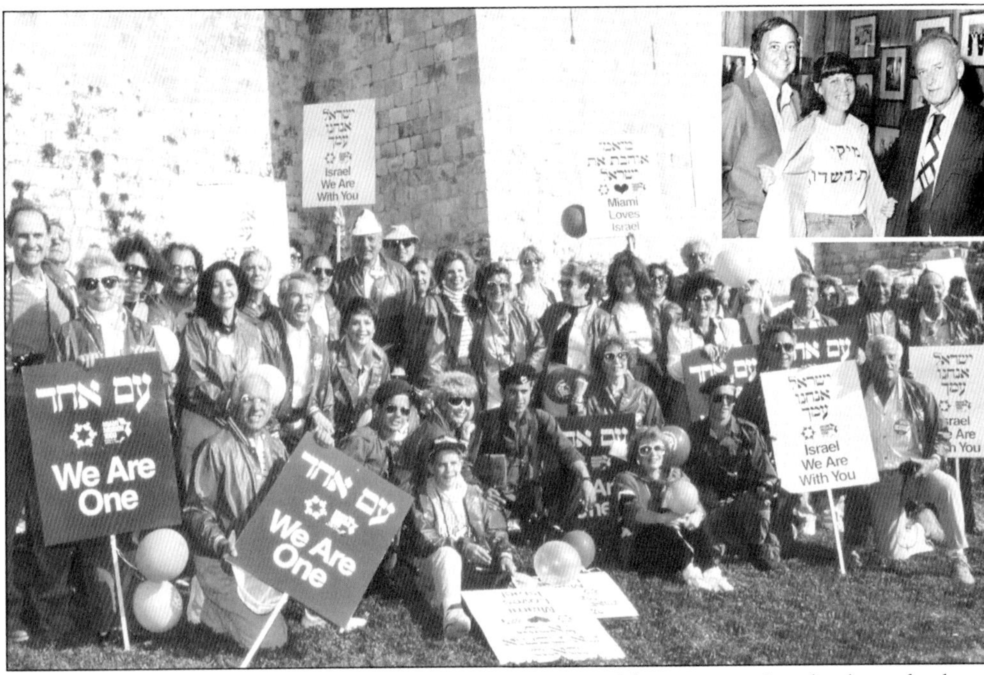

GREATER MIAMI JEWISH FEDERATION MISSION TO ISRAEL. Volunteers visit Israel to learn firsthand the human needs so they can return home to tell the stories and motivate fund-raising. Mikki and Morris Futernick (inset) have been longtime mission leaders and supporters of the Greater Miami Jewish Federation, shown here in 1978 with Yitzhak Rabin, the then prime minister of Israel.

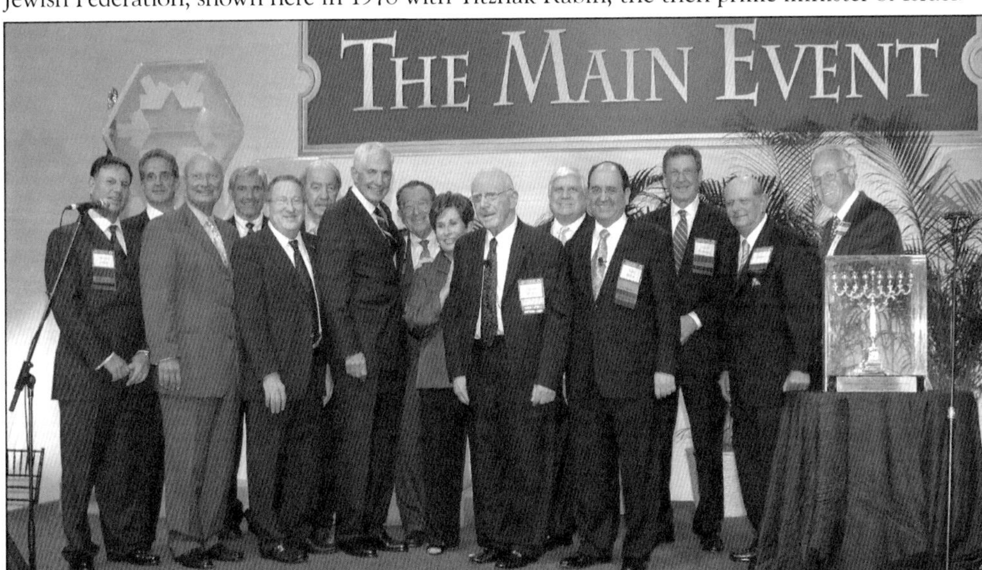

PAST PRESIDENTS, GREATER MIAMI JEWISH FEDERATION, 2008. Myron J. "Mike" Brodie received the federation's Friend of Israel Humanitarian Award for his lifetime of service to the Jewish community. Pictured from left to right are Michael M. Adler, Michael Scheck, Ezra Katz, executive vice president Jacob Solomon, Steven J. Kravitz, Isaac Zelcer, Norman Lipoff, Harry B. Smith, Nedra Oren, Brodie, Donald E. Lefton, Saby Behar, Aaron Podhurst, Harry "Hap" Levy, and Norman Braman.

Three

Building a Place in the Sun

Miami Beach

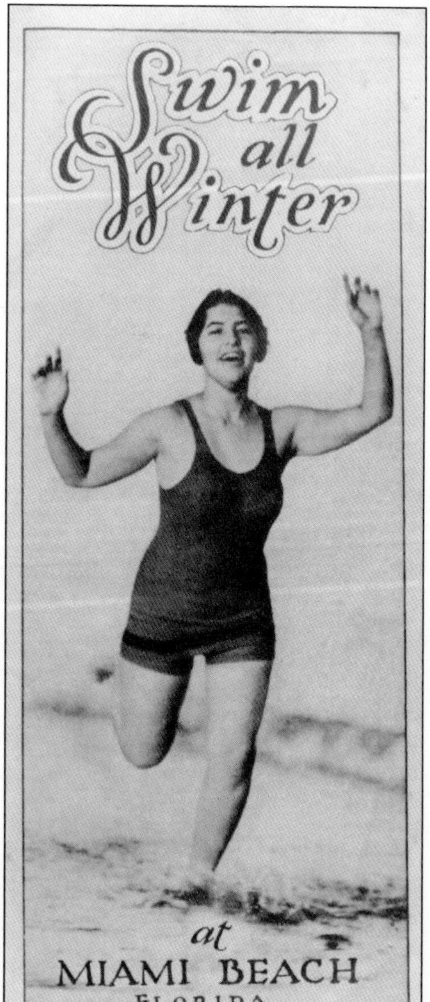

Miami Beach Tourism Brochure, 1925. Malvina Weiss, daughter of Rose and Jeremiah Weiss, was the cover girl promoting Miami Beach as a winter resort. Malvina taught in elementary school and was the first Sunday school teacher at Congregation Beth Jacob, the first Jewish congregation on Miami Beach.

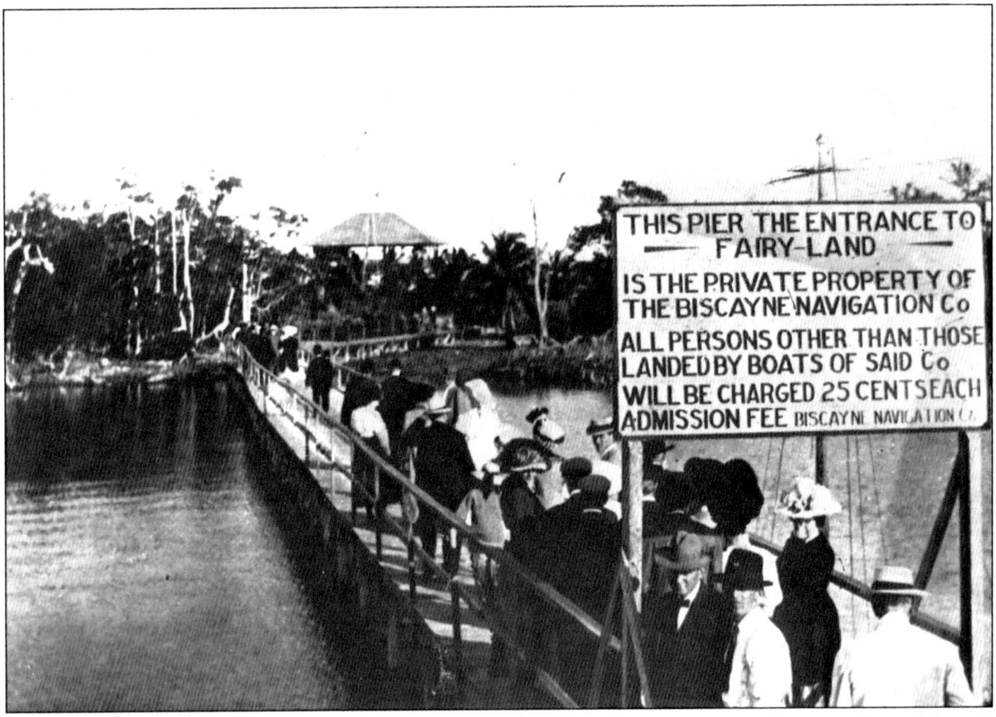

FERRY TO MIAMI BEACH, 1909. Before there was a bridge, a ferry transported visitors from Miami's bay front. Passengers were dropped off on the west side of the tip of Miami Beach. From there, they proceeded east across swampland to the ocean to visit such attractions as Smith's Casino, which appears in the background. In 1913, the Collins Bridge, the first roadway connecting Miami with Miami Beach, opened.

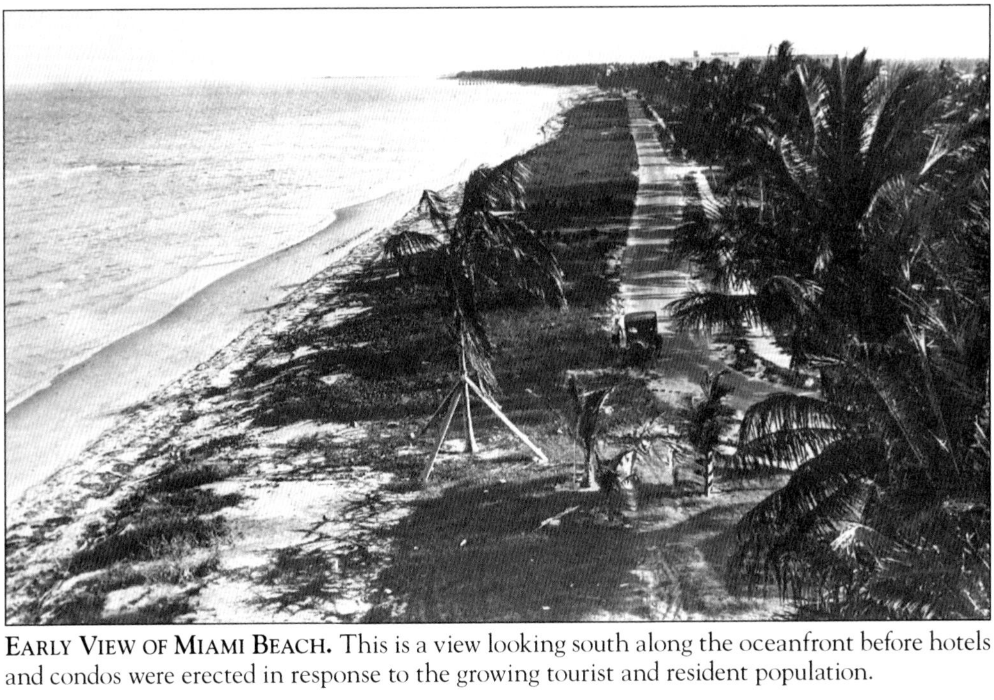

EARLY VIEW OF MIAMI BEACH. This is a view looking south along the oceanfront before hotels and condos were erected in response to the growing tourist and resident population.

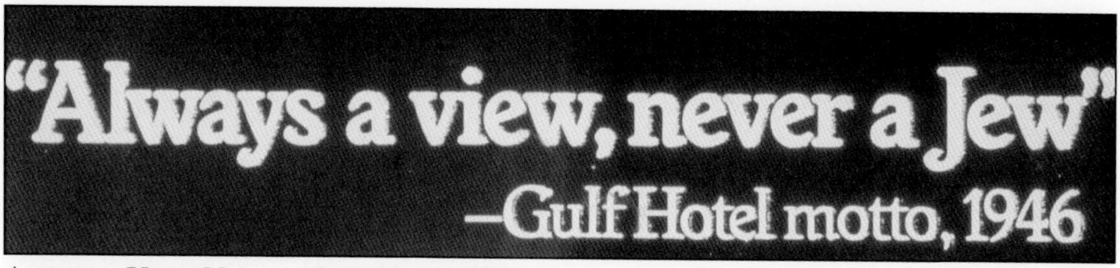

Always a View, Never a Jew. This Gulf Hotel motto revealed the discrimination policies of the hotels as well as the restrictions in land deeds that confined Jews to live south of Fifth Street.

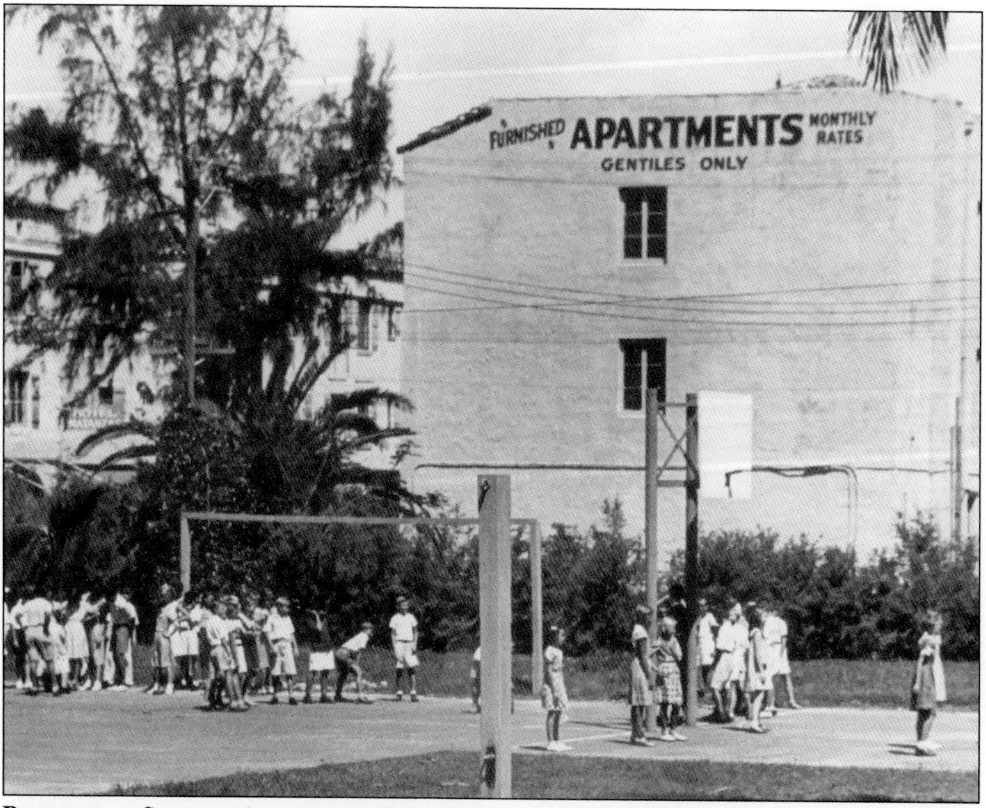

Restricted Sign on Apartment Building, c. 1915. Carl Fisher owned the lots on Miami Beach north of Fifth Street and his land deeds barred Jews. The first Jews to arrive in this tiny sun-splashed community were puzzled over the discriminatory barriers that confined them to live in a ghetto-style environment.

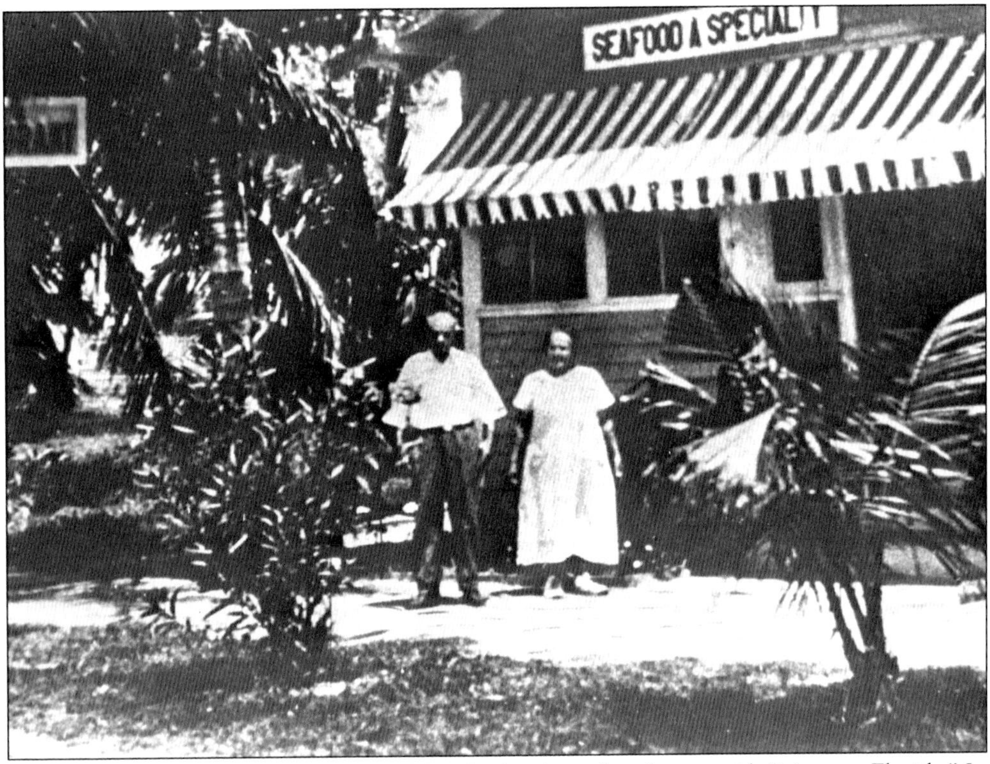

Joe and Jennie Weiss, c. 1917. Joe Weiss had asthma; his doctor said, "Move to Florida." In 1913, these Hungarian immigrants were the first Jews to settle on Miami Beach. They purchased this house to open a restaurant. In 1921, a Harvard scientist asked Joe to cook stone crabs as an experiment—they were great. Joe's Stone Crab Restaurant, in the original location, serves more than 350,000 pounds of crab annually.

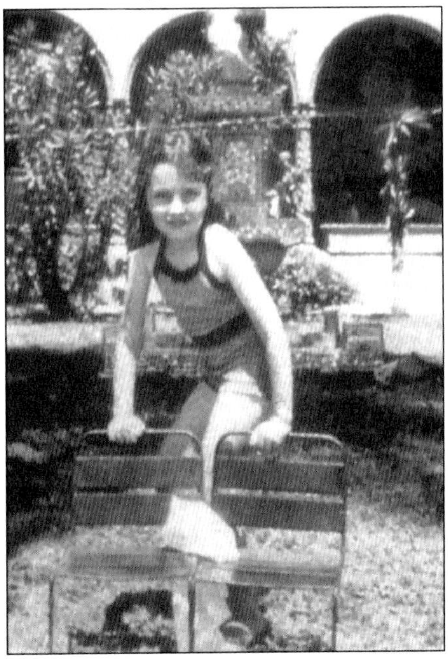

JoAnn Weiss in Courtyard of Her Family's Business, 1938. Named after her grandfather, the founder of Joe's Stone Crab Restaurant, JoAnn has spent nearly every day at the business, which is still in the family. She passed her business acumen to daughter Jodi and son Steve and authored a cookbook, *Eat at Joe's*.

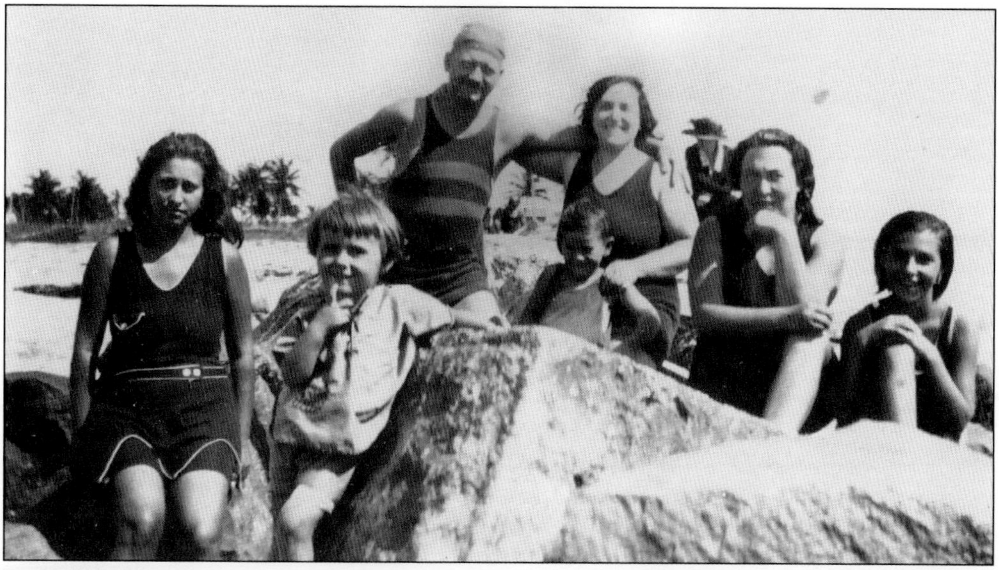

ROSE AND JEREMIAH "ABE" WEISS FAMILY, BEACH AT GOVERNMENT CUT, 1920. With their children Milton, Malvina, and Eugene, these Weisses (unrelated to the Joe Weisses) settled on Miami Beach in 1919 and were the second Jewish family there. Milton, a banker, was chairman of the Miami-Dade County Board of Education (1940s) and president of the Greater Miami Jewish Federation (1970s). Eugene, president of the high school, earned a Purple Heart during World War II.

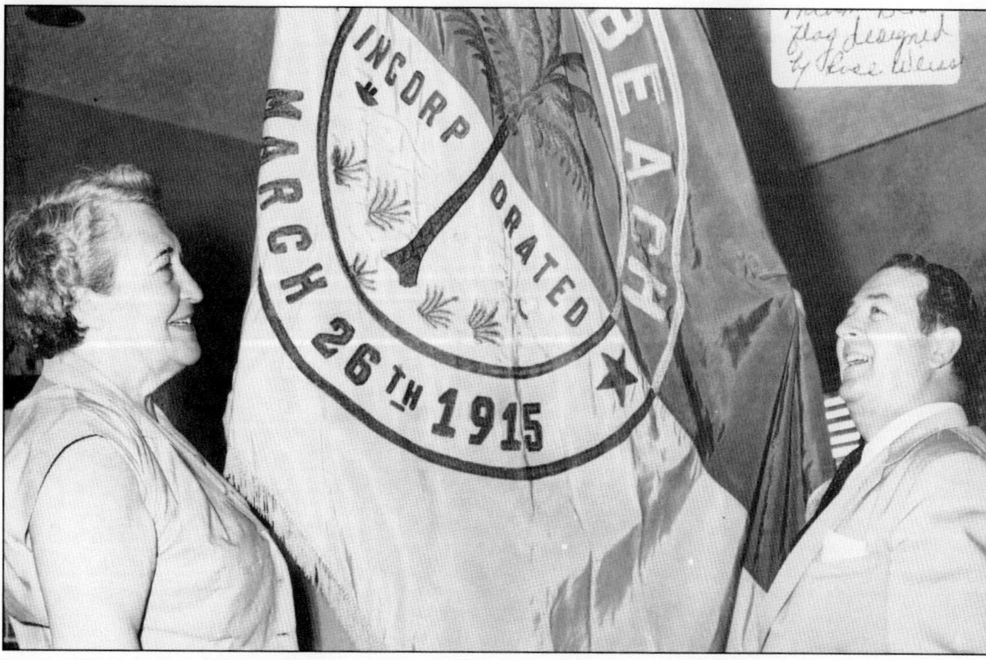

ROSE WEISS WITH MIAMI BEACH MAYOR HAROLD SHAPIRO, 1955. Known as the "Mother of Miami Beach" because of her civic roles, including perfect attendance at every city council meeting, Rosie designed and crafted the flag that is being displayed here on the city's 40th birthday. During the 1926 hurricane, her home became an American Red Cross emergency station, and for World War II, she sold $1 million in war bonds—more than any other woman in Florida.

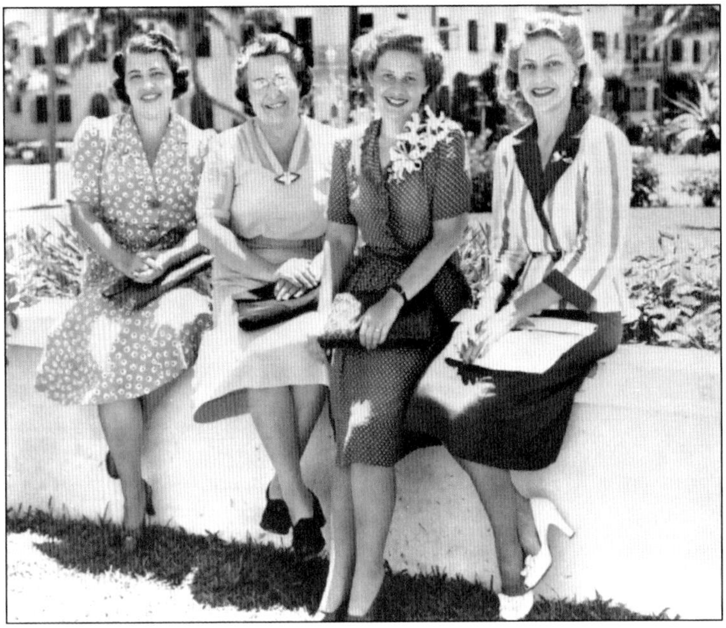

THE WEISS WOMEN, 1940. Rose is on an outing with, from left right, daughter Malvina and daughters-in-law Ruth Weiss, who is married to Eugene, and Ceci, who is married to Milton. Rose fought prejudice and founded nearly every Miami Beach organization. This entire family was deeply involved in civic and Jewish life. In 1975, Rose Weiss Park was dedicated on the land that she convinced the city to set aside for the public.

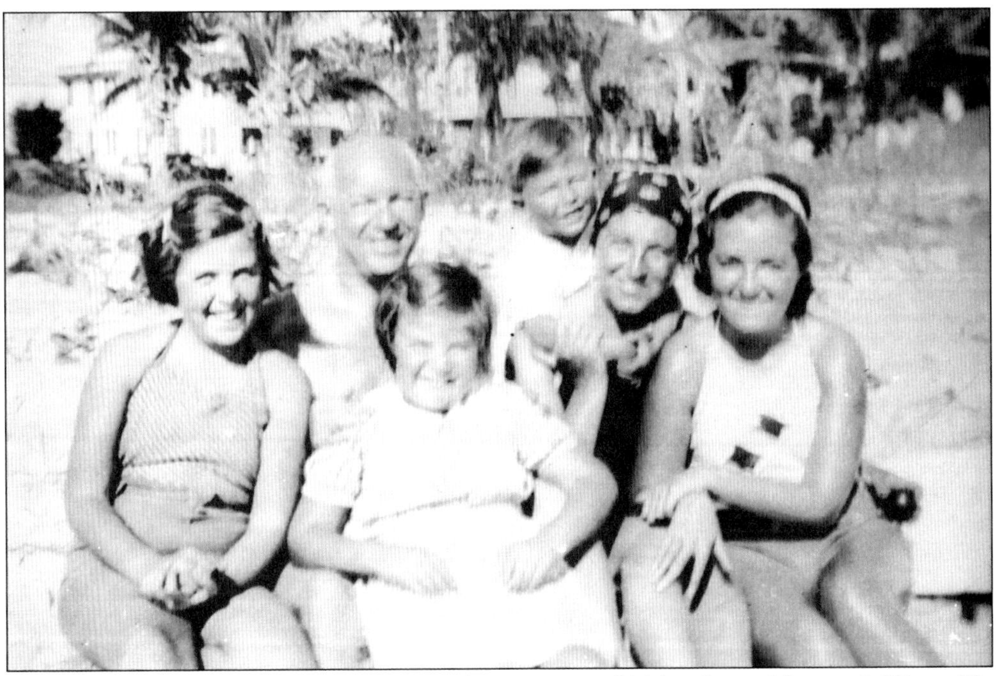

MORRIS WEISS FAMILY, 1934. Morris was the youngest of 11 brothers of Jeremiah Weiss. His family loved the beach and lived on Ocean Avenue at Tenth Street. Shown here are, from left to right, (first row) MariLyn (Potash), Audrey, Rose (mom), and Leila (Appelbaum); (second row) Morris (dad) and Warren. MariLyn and Leila have been major participants and philanthropists in the Jewish community.

ARTHUR (LEFT) AND JACK COURSHON, 1925. This image is prescient because Arthur and Jack were aerial aces in World War II as bomber pilot and bombardier. Jack Courshon flew one of the last bombing missions over Japan on the eve of its surrender. After the war, the brothers opened a law firm on the beach. Arthur, also a banker, was deeply involved in politics.

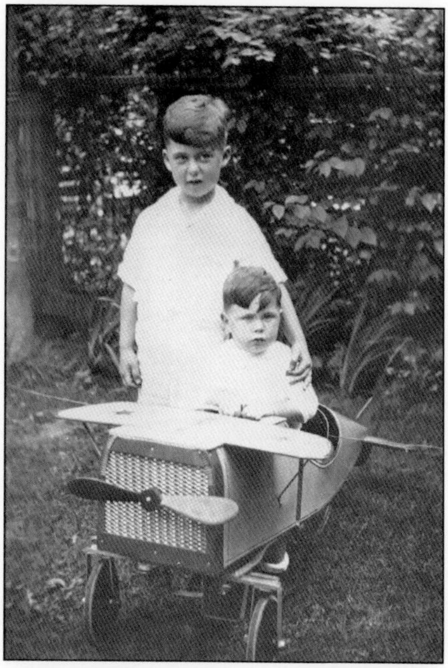

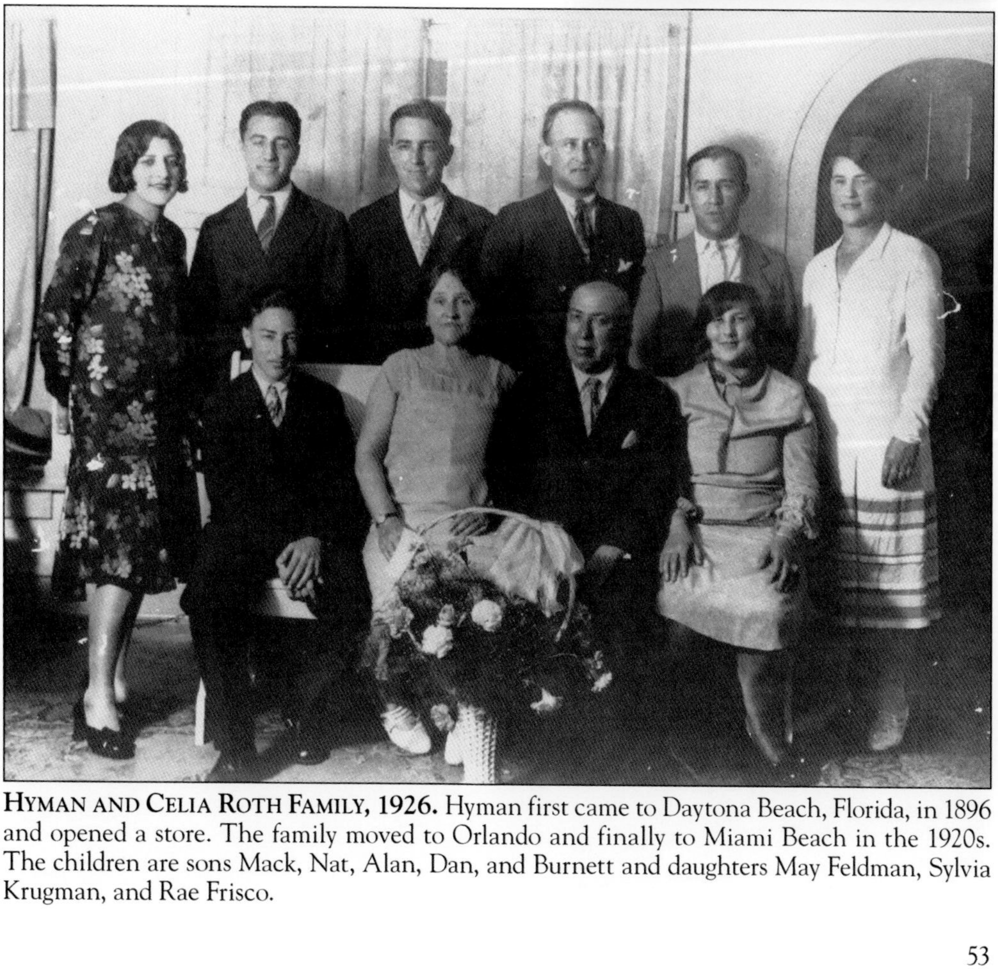

HYMAN AND CELIA ROTH FAMILY, 1926. Hyman first came to Daytona Beach, Florida, in 1896 and opened a store. The family moved to Orlando and finally to Miami Beach in the 1920s. The children are sons Mack, Nat, Alan, Dan, and Burnett and daughters May Feldman, Sylvia Krugman, and Rae Frisco.

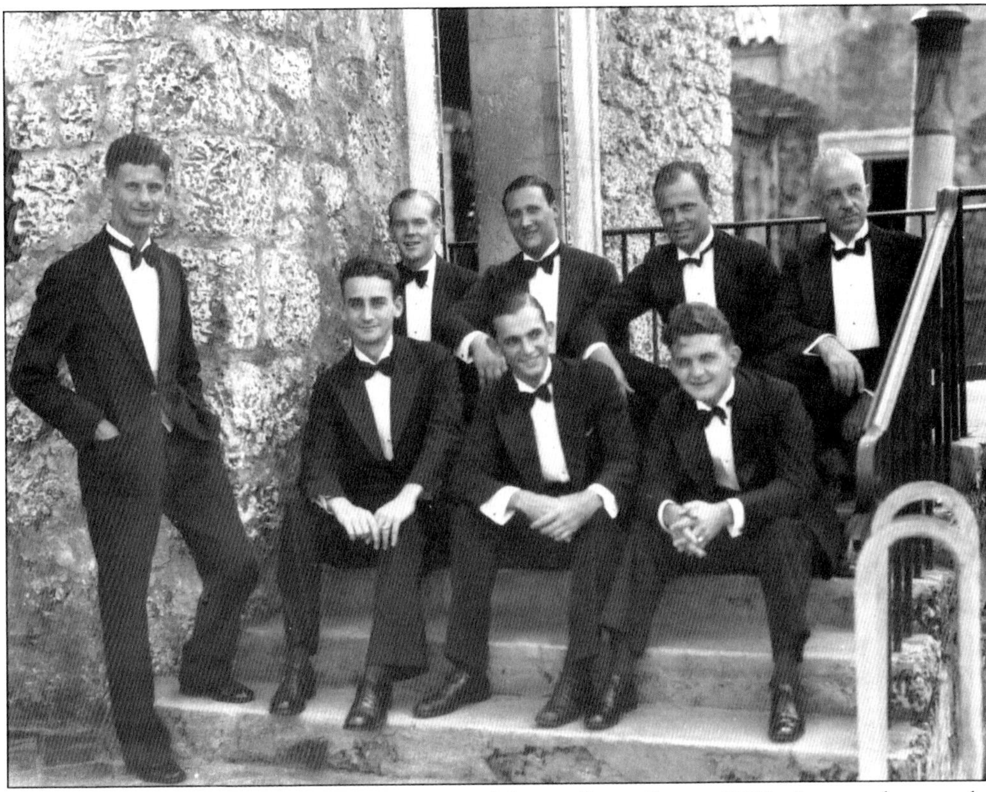

AARON FARR (LEFT) WITH UNIVERSITY OF MIAMI GLEE CLUB, 1927. As a student at the University of Miami, Aaron organized the first men's glee club then played with many of the nation's outstanding orchestras. Offered a position in Hollywood (California), he responded that he was perfectly satisfied to stay in Miami Beach. By 1939, he had written more than 400 songs. Aaron's father, H. H., opened Farr Tours travel agency in 1927.

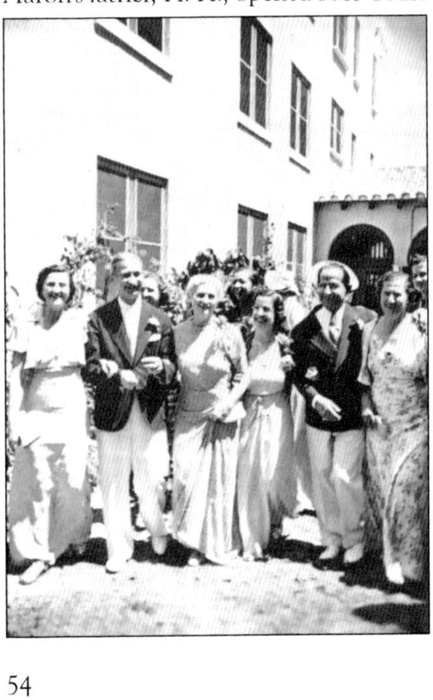

WEDDING OF MYRA GOODKOWSKY AND AARON FARR, 1938. The ceremony was held at the Nemo Hotel, which was built by Myra's family. Shown from left to right are Anna Magid, H. H. Farr, Helen Farr, Jeanette Goodkowsky, and Sam and Rose Magid. Myra and Aaron met when the latter rescued Myra as she was slipping off a horse. They have been deeply involved in both the Jewish and civic communities and are role models and mentors to many.

MIAMI BEACH DEVELOPER CARL FISHER AND "GENTILES ONLY" POLICIES. On the property owned by Carl Fisher, restrictive deed covenants stated, "Homes will not be sold to any individual who has one-quarter Hebrew or Syrian blood" or "property shall not be sold, leased or rented to any person other than of the Caucasian Race." Jews were considered Semites, not Caucasian, therefore this property was not available to them. Fisher did make exceptions for the "right kind" of Jews—those who were wealthy. Most of the hotels were restricted to Gentiles only. It was only after World War II that these restrictions began to weaken. Although the civil rights laws have made many changes, religious prejudice still exists. Subtle discrimination may occur in the form of restrictions at clubs or housing facilities.

Mr. Carl Fisher:

Enclosed find clipping which speaks for itself. Mr. John Hertz is a Jew, I don't believe he denies it. Evidently you are the type of man who has a prejudice against the Jew if [he. is not rich] enough. Christ, who was a friend of the poor and lowly and not the rich, could not buy at your end of Miami Beach, nor would he be allowed to play golf, because he was a poor Jew. I [, who] employ about two hundred Christians and have always been considered by them a friend, was denied the privilege of playing golf on your links because I did not deny I was a Jew. . . . This was my first trip to Miami Beach and my first experience in that form of prejudice. A bit out of date don't you think—simply not of a true Christian spirit. Your Glenn Adams told me he was sorry. I told him that I would not care to play where Jesus Christ, St. Paul and St. John would not be allowed to play because they were Jews.

Regretfully Yours
Harry Klein
c/o Klein's
Peoria, Ill.

October 10th, 1921.

Mr. Eugene C. Stahl,
121 Northeast First Street,
Miami - Florida.

Dear Sir :

I have your letter of October 6th and copy of the booklet. I don't think it is necessary for you to enclose a card which states "Hebrew Patronage is not Solicited". You can usually tell by the names of the people applying for apartments and their occupation whether they are desirable or not - and I would advise if you haven't sent these cards out with the booklets that you omit them. There are some Hebrews who are very high class people, and it does seem a shame to injure their feelings unnecessarily if it can be avoided. The average run of Hebrew trade at a Hotel is not desirable, particularly at a resort hotel, and it is quite a question of knowing just how to handle the undesirable ones best.

I think you have made one serious mistake in showing on the back cover the location of the Helene as being on the Ocean front. You might find this very serious if some of your guests arrive expecting to be on the Ocean front and find they are several blocks away from the Ocean. I think it would have been better to have had a picture of the Casino and Bath-House on the back cover with a memorandum that its only a few blocks distant to the Beach. However, it is probably too late now for you to make any change, but in your correspondence I would particularly call attention to the fact that the apartments are not located right on the Beach.

Yours very truly,

CGF;R

Carl G. Fisher

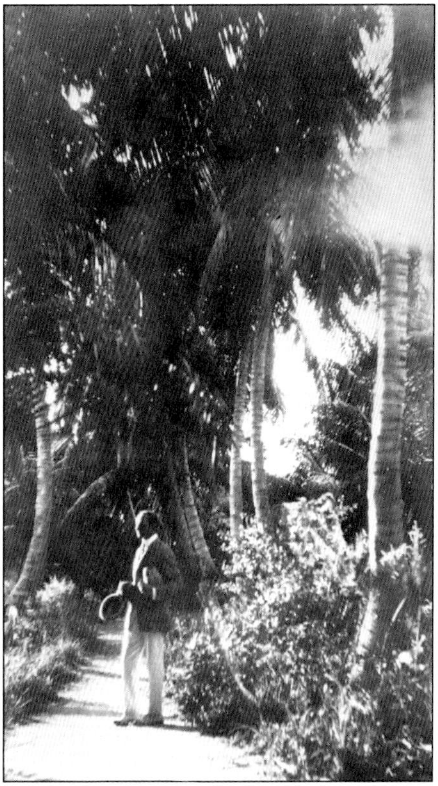

Henri Levy, Developer of Normandy Isle and Surfside, 1924. Levy said Miami Beach was "a lush tropical paradise" in a letter to his wife, and he moved his family there because a daughter of his had whooping cough. During a rainstorm, he ducked into the office of a real estate broker and emerged with enough land to develop into two communities. This was north of Carl Fisher's property where, as a Jew, he was allowed to make the purchase.

Sol Goldstrom's Bakery, 1925. German immigrant Sol Goldstrom came to Miami Beach as a widower with two children. He opened a bakery that supplied most of Miami Beach's hotels and restaurants. During World War II, Sol also supplied the U.S. Army on the Beach. He remarried, and both he and his wife, Josie, were deeply involved in every Jewish organization. Sol was also a member of the Elks and Masons.

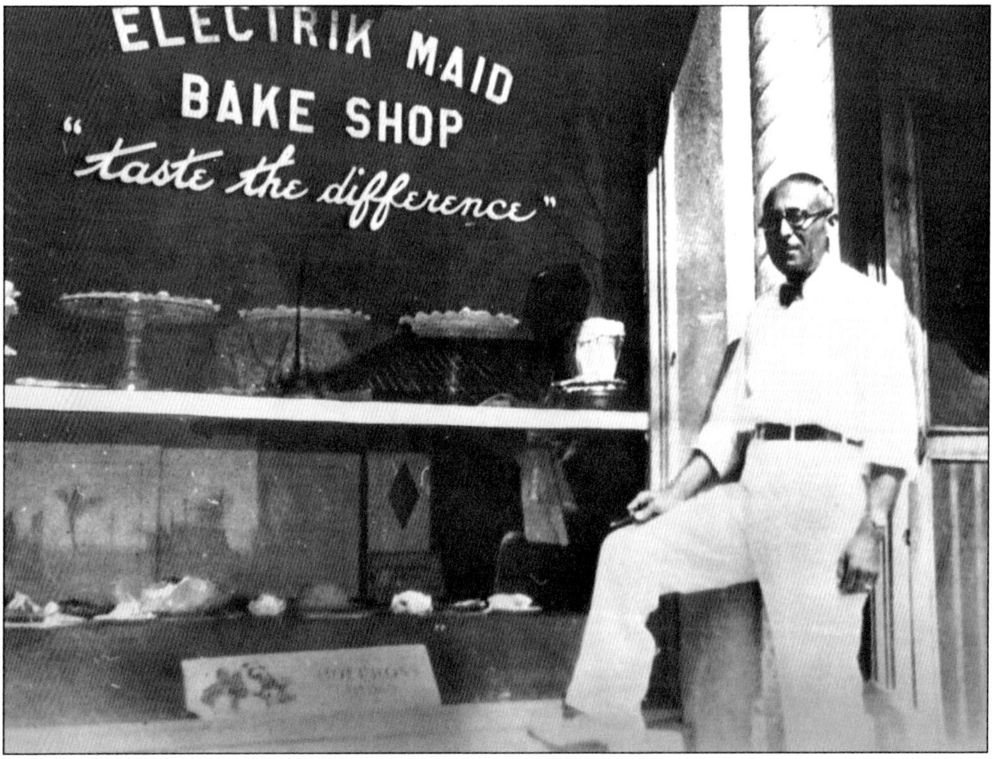

SOPHIA TENDRICH AND MAL ENGLANDER, 1940. Joseph and Bessie Tendrich settled on Miami Beach in 1929 and opened a grocery store. In 1930, Anna Englander arrived with her son Malvin. Mal and a Tendrich daughter, Sophia, met at a sorority party. They married and reared their six children on Miami Beach; all have been politically active. Mal was a city councilman. Sophia served as the first elected Jewish Democratic state committeewoman.

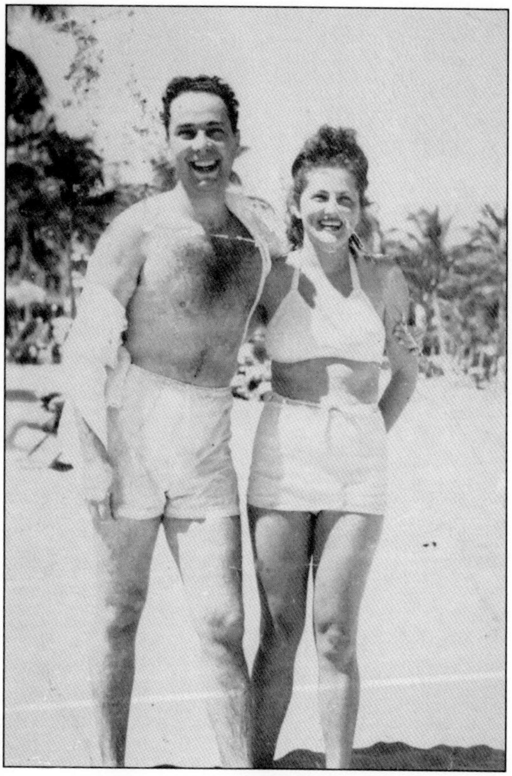

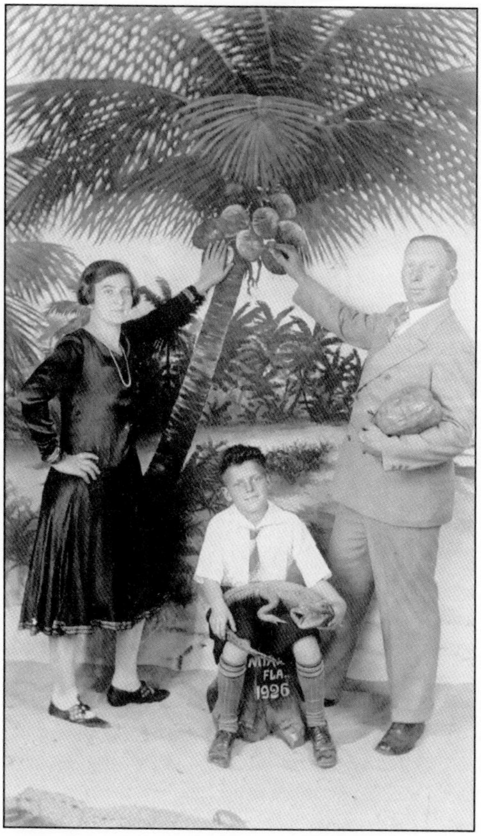

BESSIE, ISIDORE, AND MILTON GAYNOR, CONTRIVED TOURIST SET, 1926. The Gaynors moved to Miami in 1924, and following the 1926 hurricane, they settled on Miami Beach. Isidore drove a jitney to support his family.

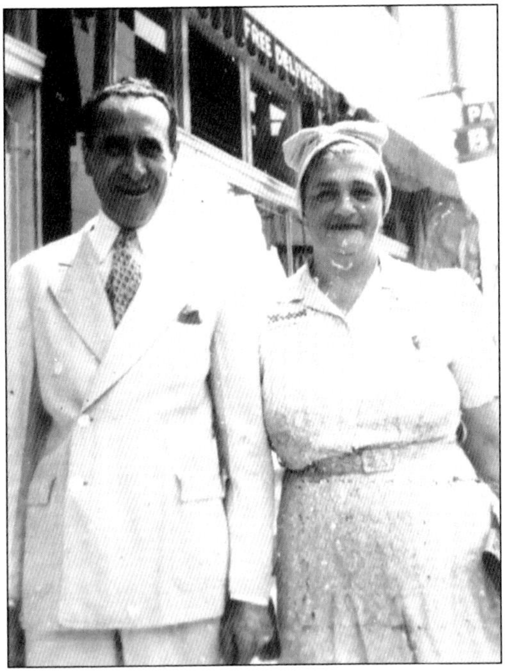

ABRAHAM "AL" AND BESSIE GALBUT, 1934. The Galbut family came to Miami Beach after the 1926 hurricane and rented an apartment for $300 per year. Al sold newspapers before entering the restaurant business. Bessie worked closely with him while rearing Paul, Hyman, and Miriam. The third generation of the Galbut family are professionals and operators of a large condominium conversion company—and there are 33 members of a fifth generation.

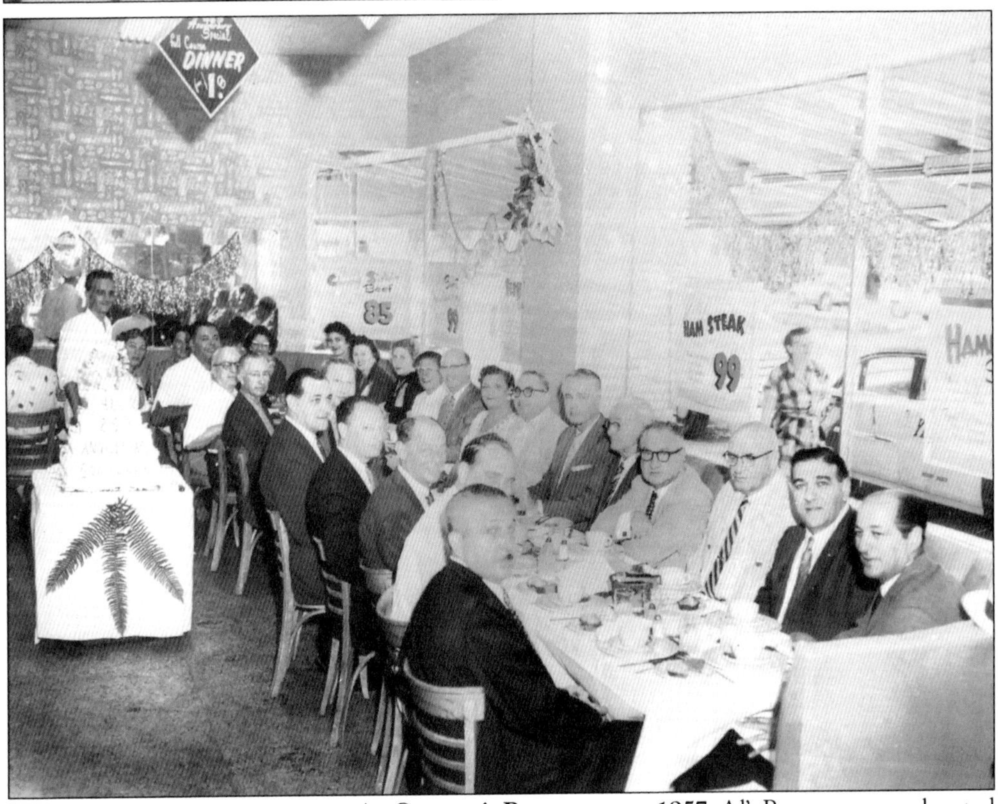

TWENTY-FIFTH ANNIVERSARY OF AL GALBUT'S RESTAURANT, 1957. Al's Restaurant was located at Fifth Street and Washington Avenue. Galbut was widely noted over the years for his generosity (serving ample amounts of food) and for providing for the poor as well as prison inmates.

SECOND-GENERATION GALBUTS, 1954. Hyman, who was a U.S. Navy captain during World War II and who served on the city council, also married a Bessie, the same name as his mother. This family portrait includes (seated) Hyman and Bessie, with children (from left to right) Robert, today a medical doctor; Abraham, an attorney; Russell, a developer; and David, a medical doctor; (standing) mother Bessie Galbut.

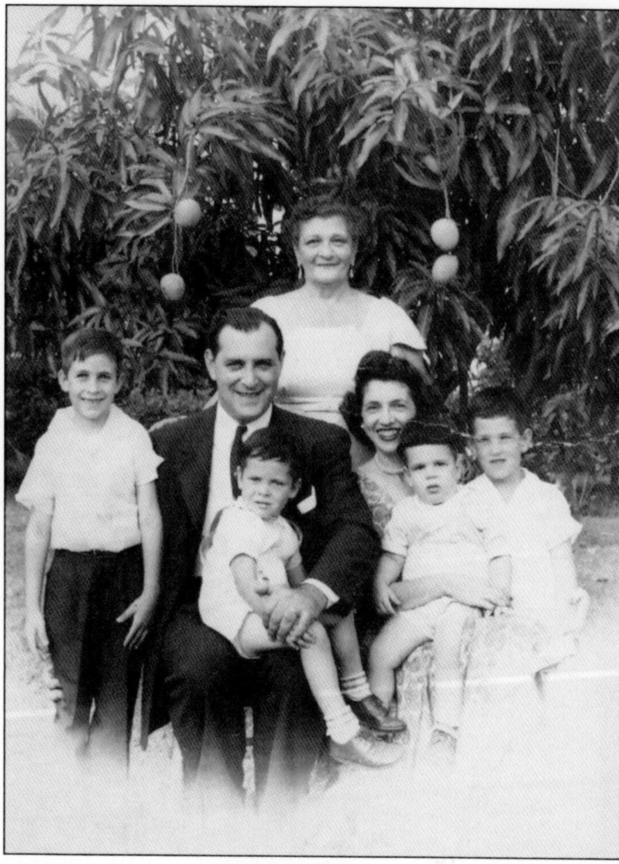

RABBI TIBOR STERN AND BESSIE GALBUT, 1956. Hyman Galbut made and installed these Ten Commandments tablets for Congregation Beth Jacob. They were dedicated in memory of Abraham Galbut, who was affectionately known as the "Mayor of South Beach" and was one of the founders of Congregation Beth Jacob, whose building now houses the Jewish Museum of Florida.

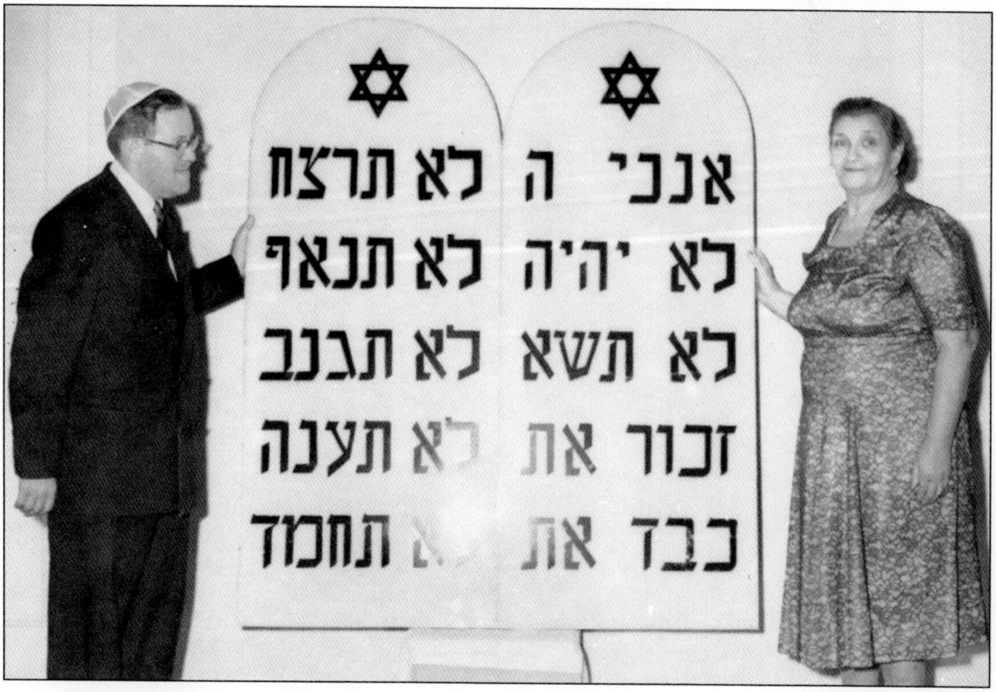

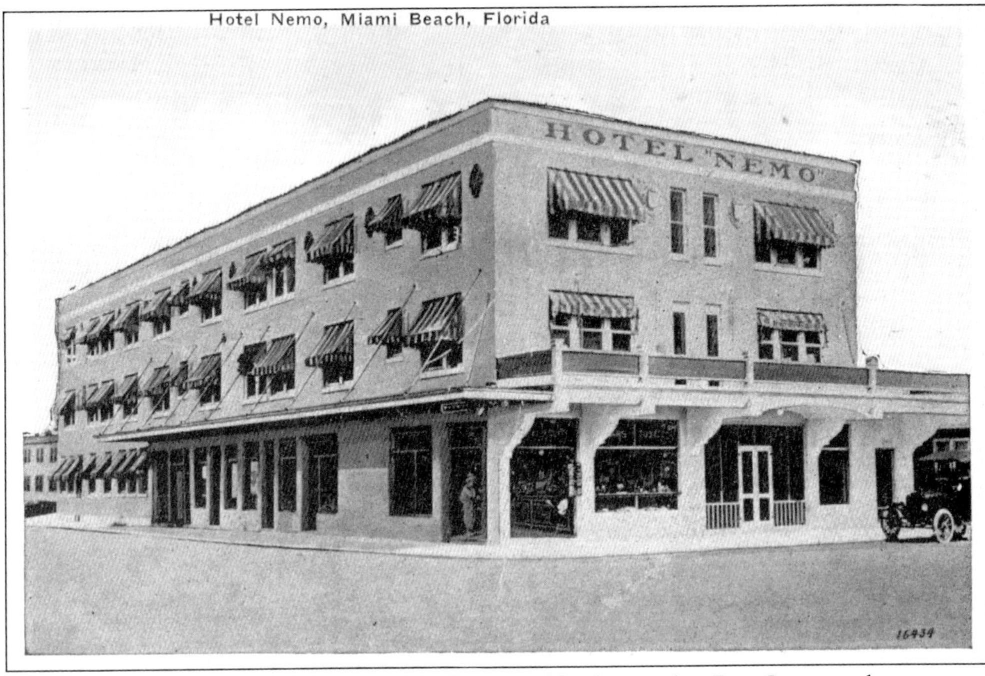

NEMO HOTEL, 1921. Located at First Street and Collins Avenue and built by Joseph Goodkowsky, Harry Goodkowsky, and Samuel M. Magid, this was the first kosher hotel on Miami Beach. The Nemo name was that of Samuel's costume jewelry manufacturing company when he made items for F. W. Woolworth. Today this is the site of a fine restaurant of the same name.

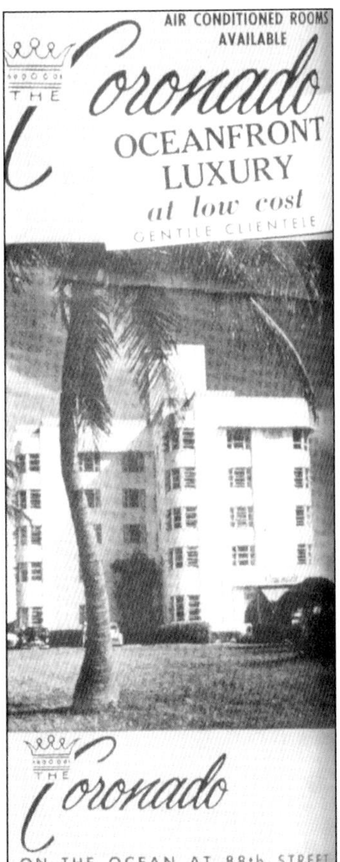

GENTILE CLIENTELE, MIAMI BEACH, 1920S. A form of antisemitism was the exclusion of Jews from hotels. Phrases such as "restricted" or "exclusive clientele" were euphemisms and some even stated, "We have a restricted clientele regarding pets, children under 12 years of age, and the Hebrew religion." As late as 1953, an Anti-Defamation League survey of more than 800 hotels indicated that a sizable percentage still did not want Jews. (Courtesy Seth Bramson.)

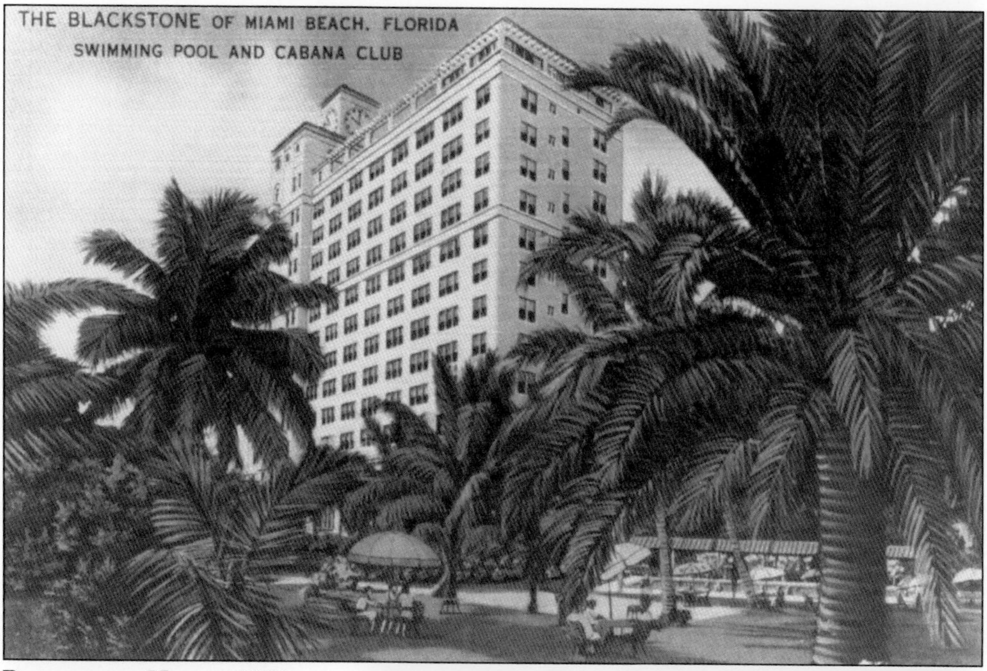

BLACKSTONE HOTEL, 1929. From Odessa to Belgium to New York, where he was a hotel contractor, Nathan Stone finally landed in Miami Beach and built the Blackstone Hotel to accommodate his northern Jewish customers who came to the area and were turned away at other hotels. Assisted by his son Alfred and Alfred's wife, Lily, they opened the largest hotel on South Beach at the time, at Eighth Street and Washington Avenue, less than one year after construction began—the result of round-the-clock building activity. This was the first Miami Beach hotel to welcome blacks, and George Gershwin composed the opera *Porgy and Bess* while reposing in the buff in the rooftop solarium. Blackstone was actually the Anglicized version of Schwartzstein, Nathan's surname. Alfred and Lily (shown right), deeply rooted in the Jewish community and in Israel, were the parents of Florida's U.S. senator Richard Stone.

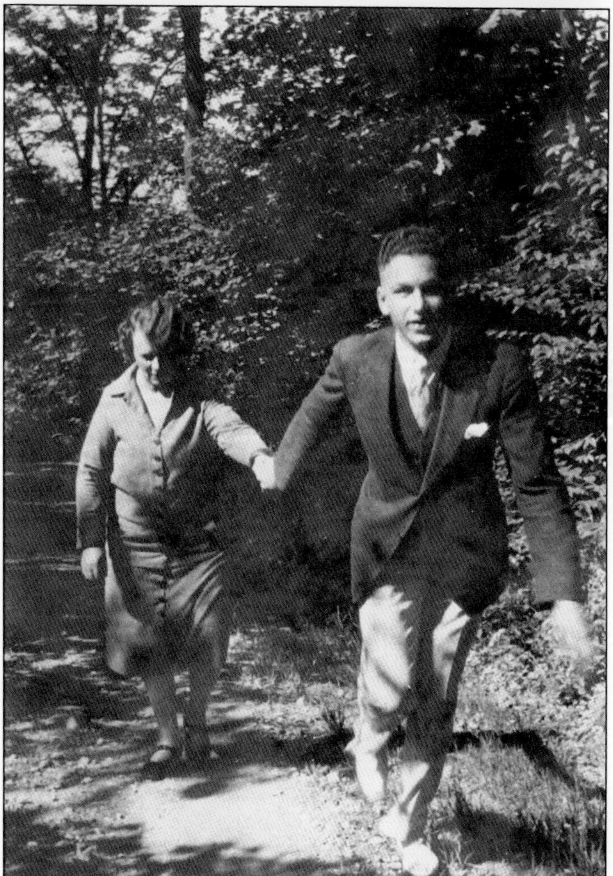

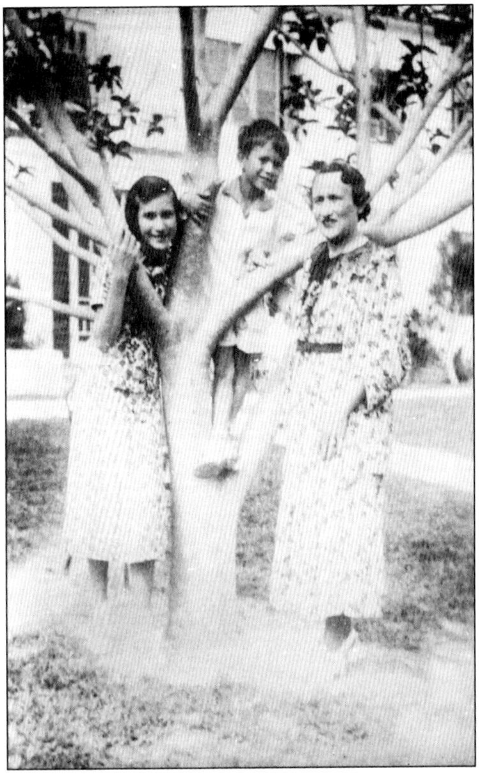

MURIEL, IRWIN, AND EVA SAWITZ, 1936. The Sawitz family traveled to Miami Beach on the Orange Blossom train in 1935 because Irwin had rheumatic fever. They rented an apartment, and Eva had to pay school tuition for the children, as they were not property owners. Eva served the Mount Sinai Hospital information desk for more than 30 years. Muriel, a 1938 graduate of Miami Beach High, volunteered for the opera. Irwin "Say" married JoAnn Weiss, whose parents owned Joe's Stone Crab Restaurant.

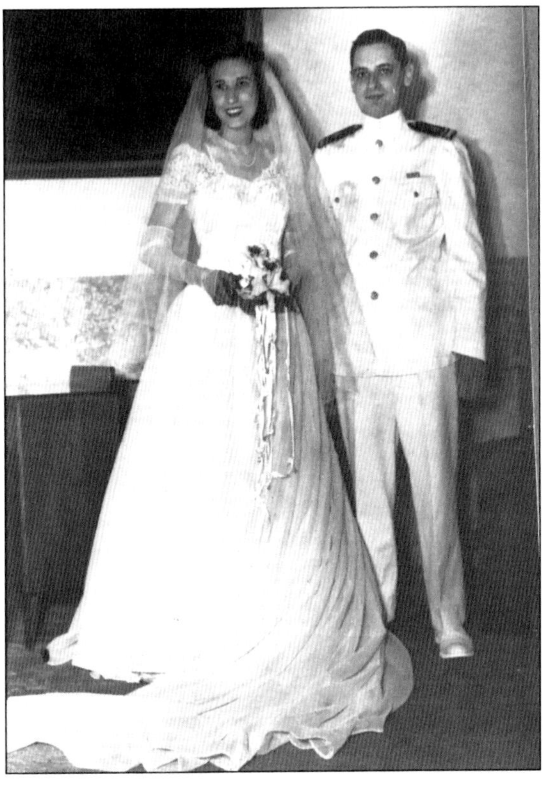

WEDDING OF MURIEL SAWITZ AND ARNOLD ROSEN, 1944. This union of two pioneer families took place at Temple Israel. Rosen's family came to Miami Beach in 1936 to open American Bank and Trust Company. Muriel and Arnold met at a sorority party. Arnold graduated from the University of Florida, served in World War II, and started Lennar Homes. The Rosens have been deeply involved in the arts community, Temple Israel, and the Jewish Museum of Florida.

ARNOLD, FREDA, GODFREY, AND ED NEWMAN, 1937. Middle-class Jewish immigrants from Poland and Germany, Isidor and Freda Newman produced three sons, Godfrey, a lawyer; Arnold, the photographer; and Edward, owner of a funeral home. The family settled in Miami Beach from Atlantic City after losing everything when the banks failed in the Depression. The parents operated hotels and were active in the Jewish community.

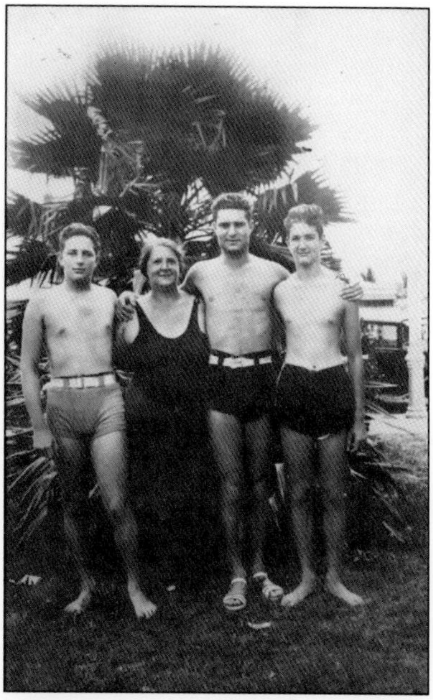

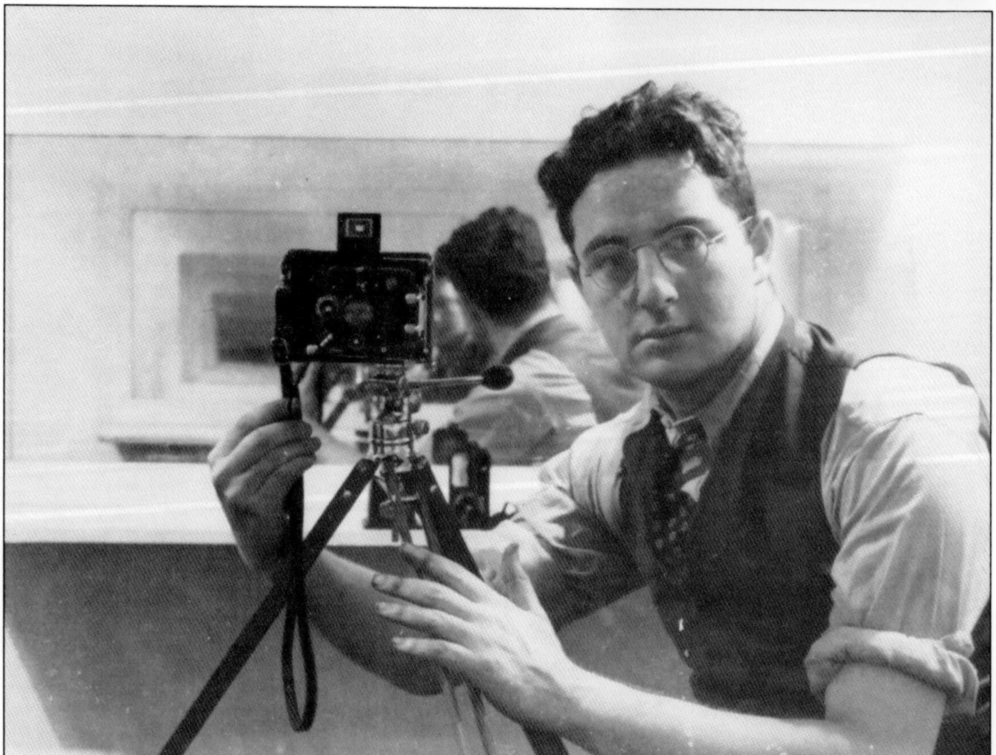

ARNOLD NEWMAN (1918–2006), 1940S. Arnold Newman was a nationally renowned photographer noted for his environmental portraits of artists and politicians. He studied art at the University of Miami and began his career on Miami Beach. He then went to New York in 1941. Newman received many international awards. His work has appeared in *LIFE*, *Look*, and *Harper's Bazaar* and is included in the collections of museums and private collectors worldwide.

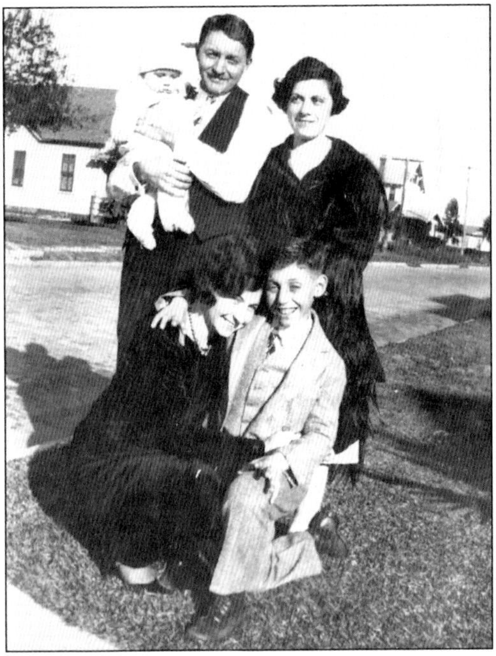

GILLER FAMILY—CHARLES, FATHER MORRIS, AUNT RUTH, MOTHER ESTHER, AND NORMAN, 1929. The Gillers settled in Miami Beach in 1929. Morris became a real estate broker. Esther worked in a dress shop while son Norman delivered newspapers. Norman, who married Frances Schwartz, and Charles grew up to be architects. Norman M. Giller and Associates (renamed Giller and Giller, Incorporated in 1992) has operated from the Beach for 60 years.

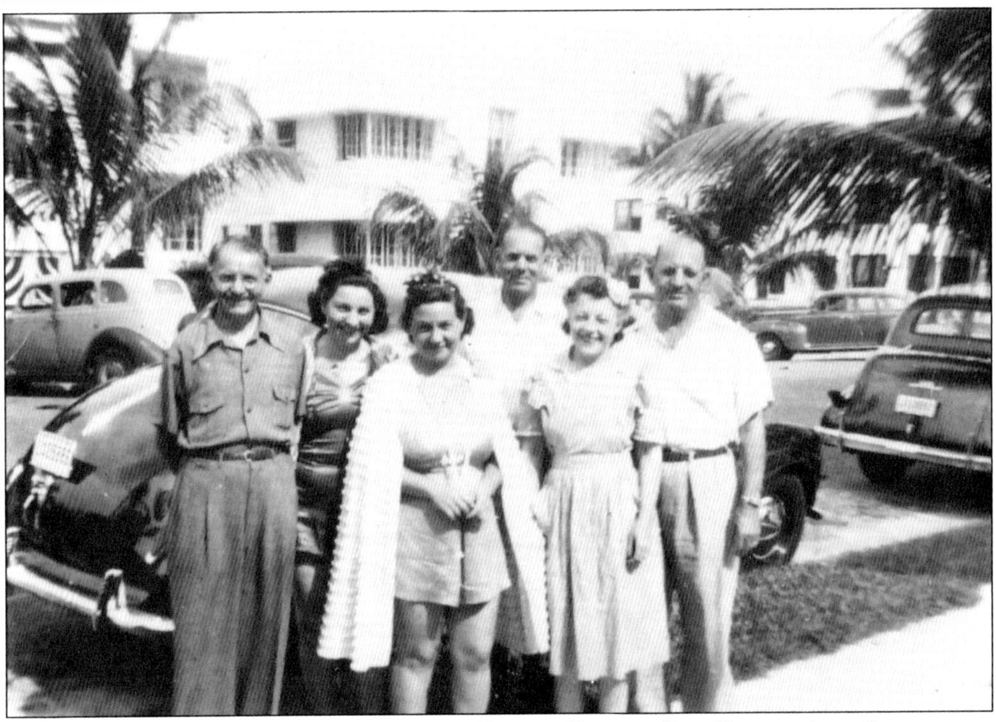

SIBLINGS MORRIS GILLER, RUTH BERNARD, ESTHER POPKIN, SHY GILLER, ANN SILVERMAN, AND BEN GILLER IN FRONT OF ONE OF BEN'S BUILDINGS, 1941. Ben moved to Miami Beach from Jacksonville in 1934, started a concrete-block business, and became a major Florida contractor. He was an early member of Beth Jacob and a bank founder. An avid Zionist and Zionist of America (ZOA) president, Ben raised funds for and sent construction equipment to the new State of Israel.

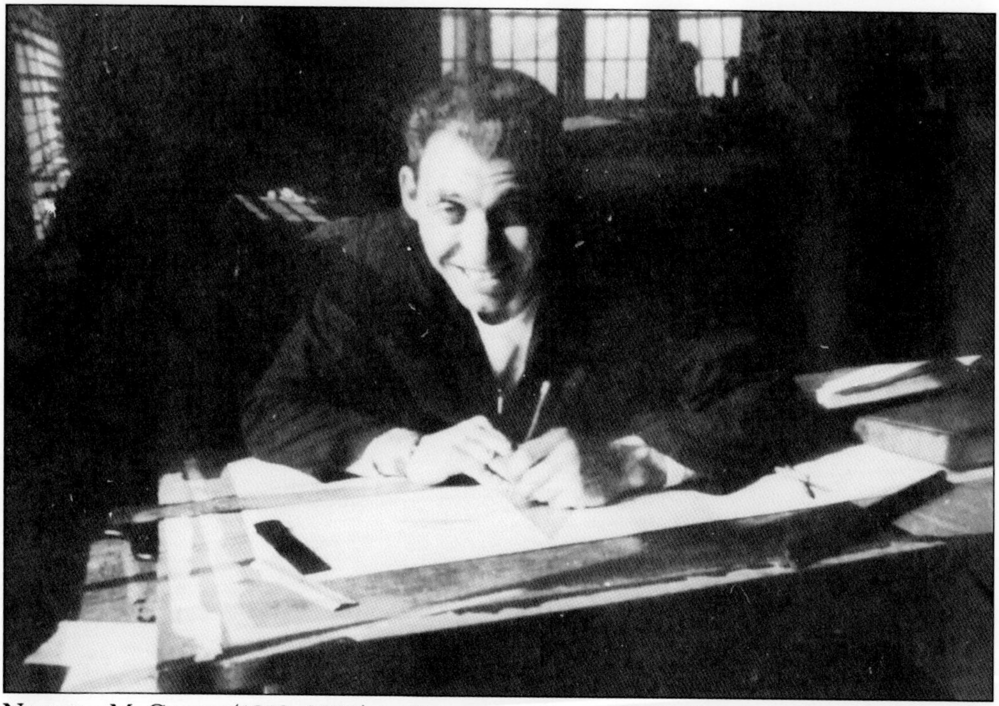

NORMAN M. GILLER (1918–2008) AT DRAFTING TABLE, 1944. Designer of more than 10,000 structures, visionary Giller was a dynamic architect and father of MiMo (Miami Modernism), which represents the postwar era. Norman wore many hats, such as architect, banker, civic leader, World War II veteran, and author. He led the adaptive reuse restoration of the historic Beth Jacob Synagogue to become the Jewish Museum of Florida (1995) and served as its first president.

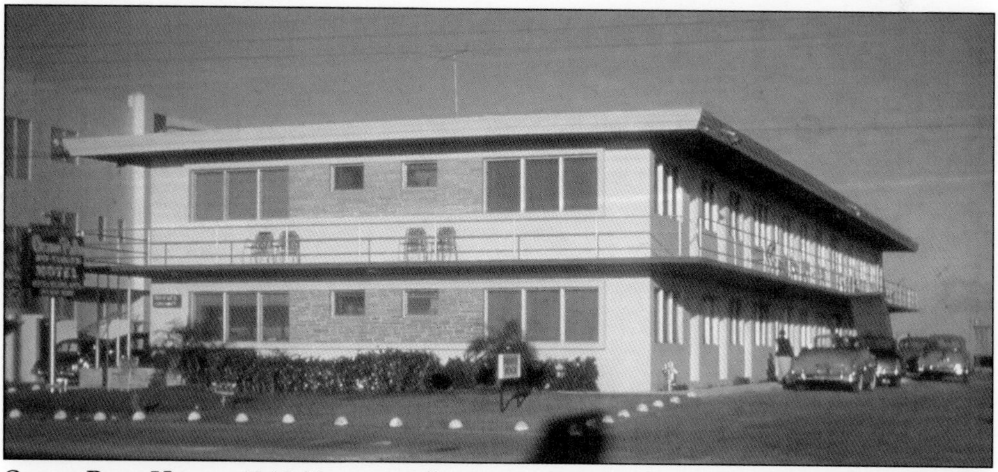

OCEAN PALM HOTEL, 1949. Norman Giller designed the first known two-story motel in Florida. A new concept, the resort motel prompted motel row on the Atlantic Ocean in Sunny Isles. This is the only remaining motel amid towering, multimillion-dollar condos. Giller initiated flat-slab construction with The Carillon (1957), and his most glamorous project was the Diplomat Hotel (1959) in Hollywood, Florida. The Norman M. Giller Bridge, connecting Aventura and Sunny Isles, honors him.

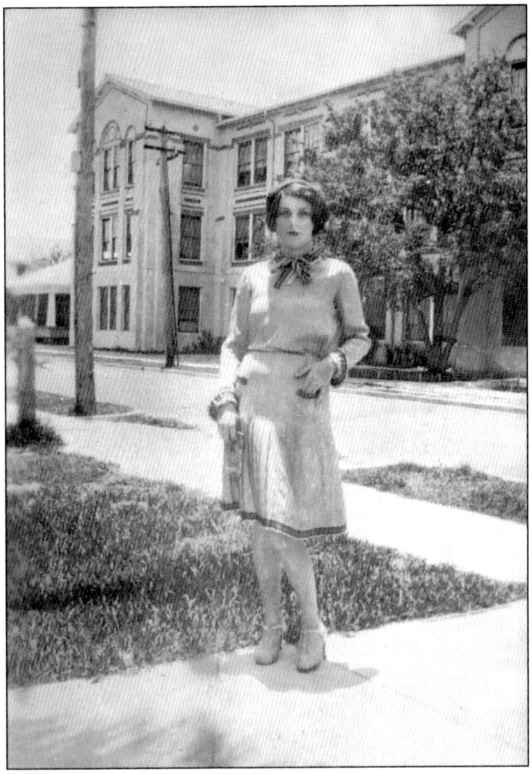

Ruth Kaplan, Miami High, 1927. Ruth came to Miami with her family in the 1920s. She married Max Orovitz, who came to Miami in 1925, and was a founder of Mount Sinai Hospital, where he was the longest-serving chairman of the board. Their three children, Felicia, W. James, and Michael, continue involvement with the hospital. Ruth's sister Mollie married Dan Ruskin.

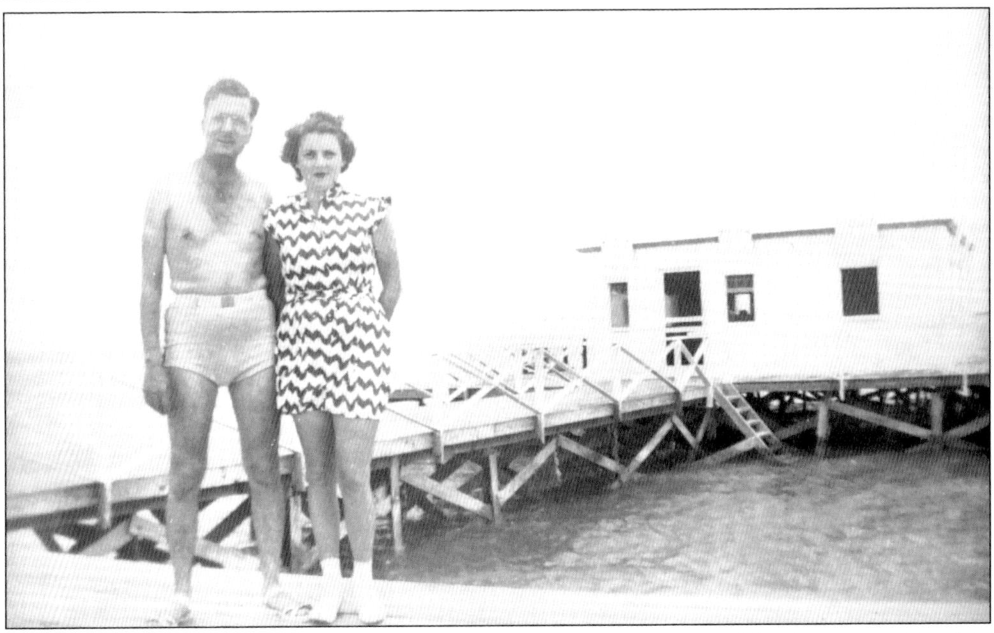

Max Orovitz and Ruth Kaplan Orovitz in Stiltsville, 1938. The Orovitz and Ruskin families spent much of their summers at Stiltsville, away from the crowds in Miami, to avoid polio. These commonly called "shack-like" wooden structures sat on pilings in the shallow water of Biscayne Bay. Reachable only by boat, there were as many as 27; since Hurricane Andrew, only seven remain and may be opened as part of a park.

OROVITZ-BASS-BLUMBERG FAMILIES, 1941. In this fun outing for the cousins are, from left to right, (first row) Susie Bass and W. James (Jim) Orovitz; (second row) Bob Bass, Terry Blumberg, David Blumberg, and Felicia Orovitz; (third row) Miriam Orovitz Bass, Esther Blumberg, Ann Orovitz, and Ruth Kaplan Orovitz.

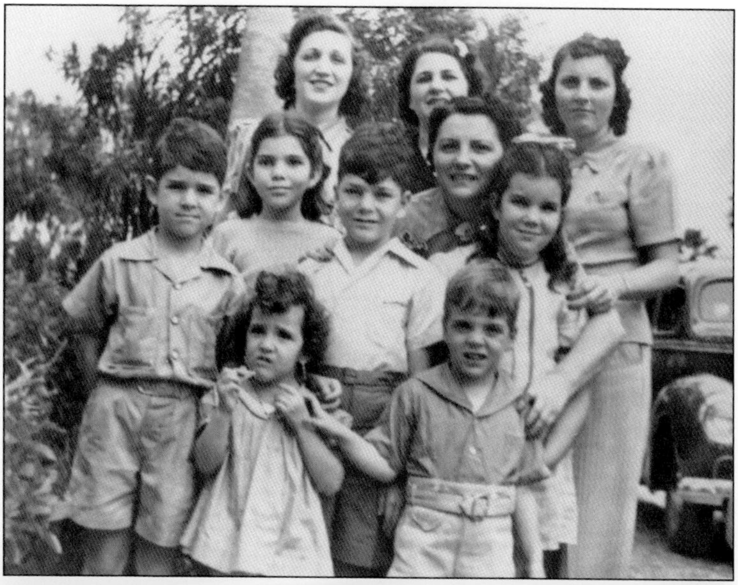

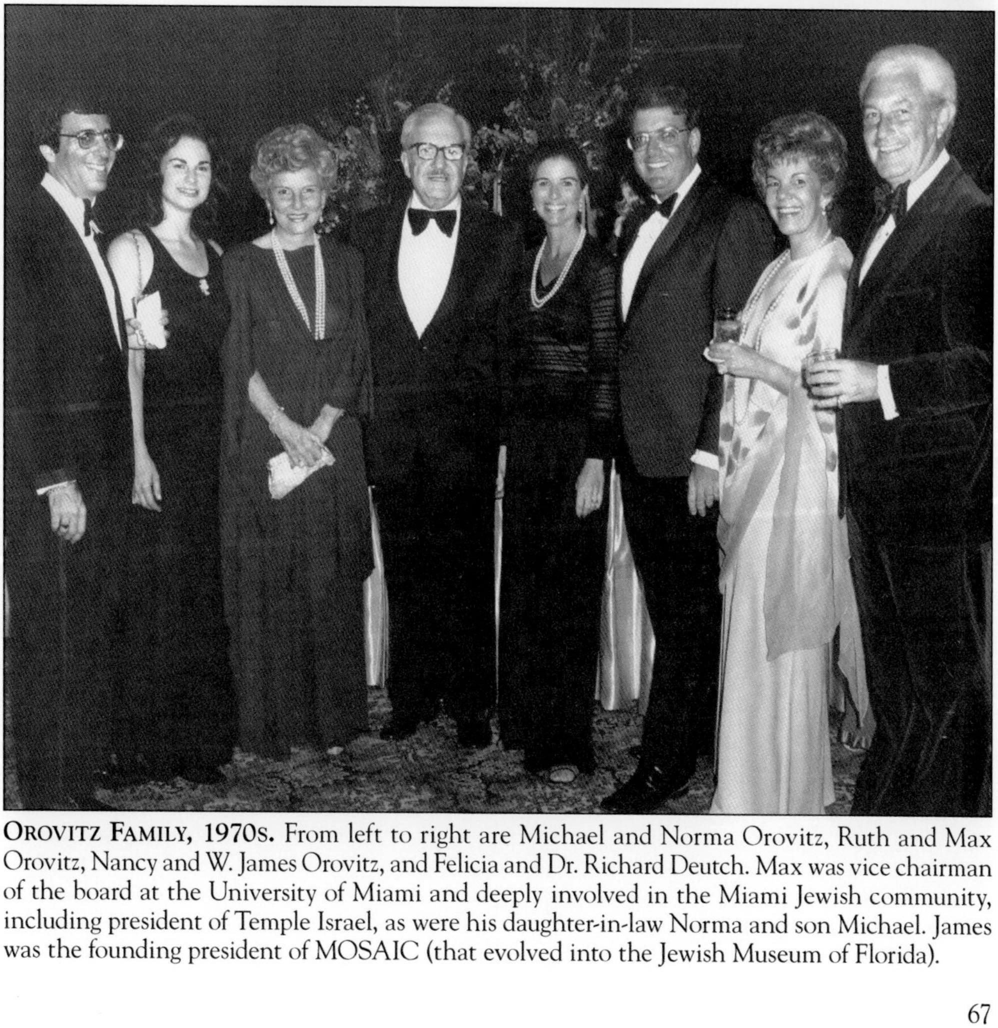

OROVITZ FAMILY, 1970S. From left to right are Michael and Norma Orovitz, Ruth and Max Orovitz, Nancy and W. James Orovitz, and Felicia and Dr. Richard Deutch. Max was vice chairman of the board at the University of Miami and deeply involved in the Miami Jewish community, including president of Temple Israel, as were his daughter-in-law Norma and son Michael. James was the founding president of MOSAIC (that evolved into the Jewish Museum of Florida).

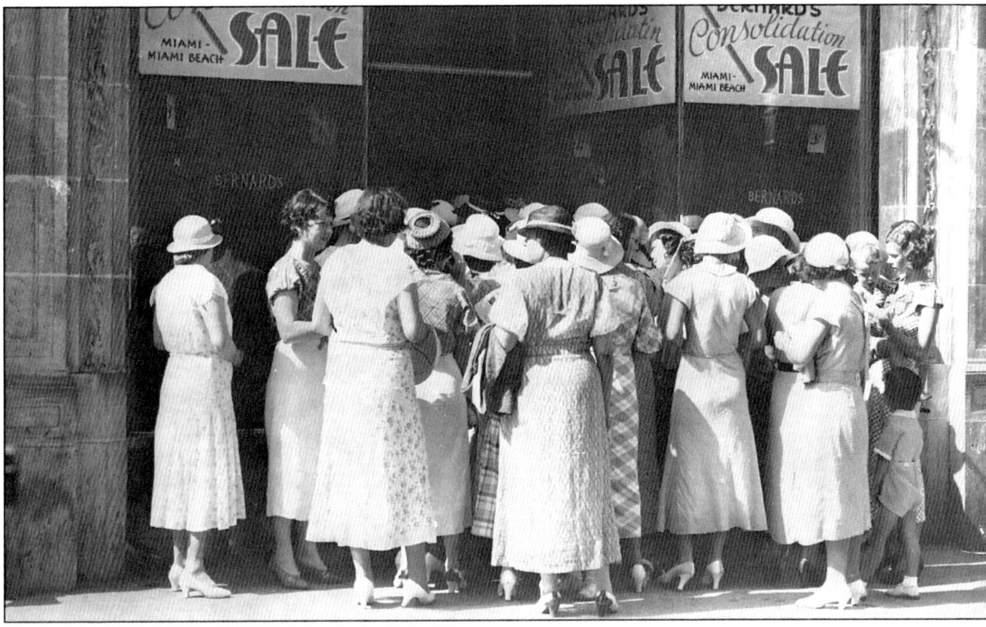

BERNARD'S DRESS SHOP, 1934. Dan Ruskin owned several dress shops and then partnered with brother-in-law Max Orovitz to run Scott-Perry Corporation to build houses (1936–1941). They used non-Jewish names for their company to avoid discrimination. They subsequently owned Public Gas Company and a concrete-making operation, Alfred Destin Company. Dan and Max also owned shares of the Eagle Army Navy stores from 1965 to 1975. Both were Mount Sinai Hospital and Greater Miami Jewish Federation leaders.

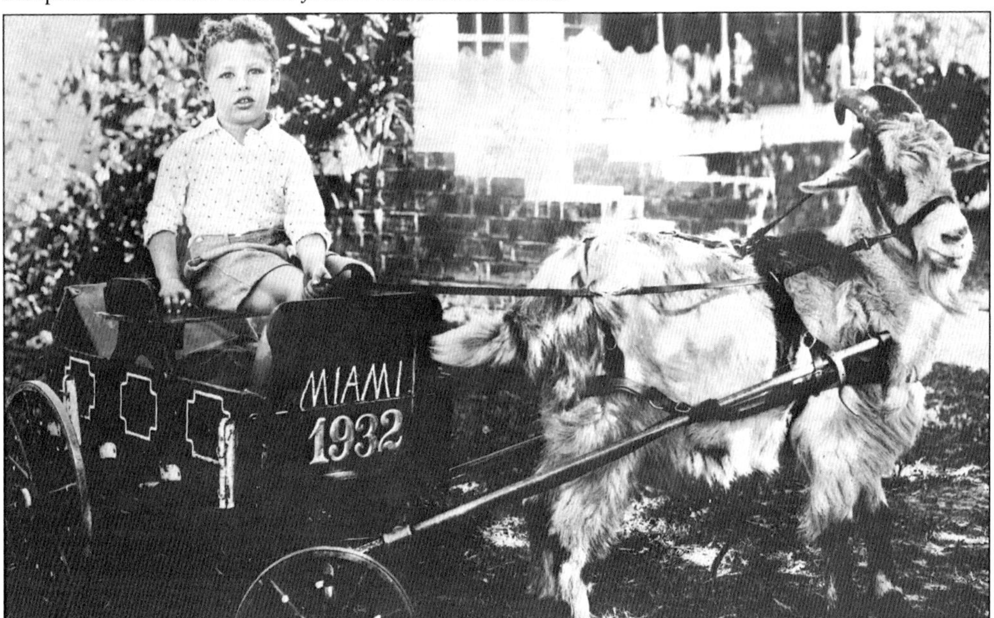

LLOYD RUSKIN, 1932. Son of Mollie and Dan Ruskin, attorney Ruskin has served as vice chairman of the board of Fedco and as first president of the Jewish Vocational Service. He continues his father's involvement with Mount Sinai Hospital. He has two sisters, Charlyne and Andrea.

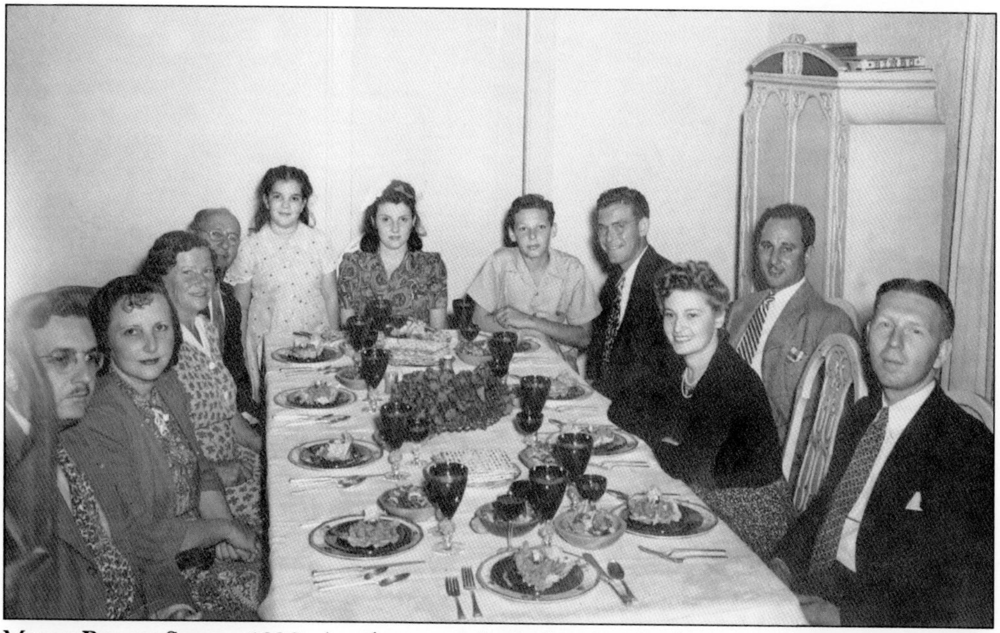

MIAMI BEACH SEDER, 1938. A seder means "order" and is the festive meal and service on the first night of Passover (and also on the second night in the diaspora). It commemorates the exodus of the Jews from Egypt. Celebrating seder are, from left to right, Max Orovitz, Mollie Ruskin, Rosa Kaplan, Sam Kaplan, Felicia Orovitz, Ruth Orovitz, Lloyd Ruskin, ? Koch, Harry Kaplan, Athyle Kaplan, and unidentified.

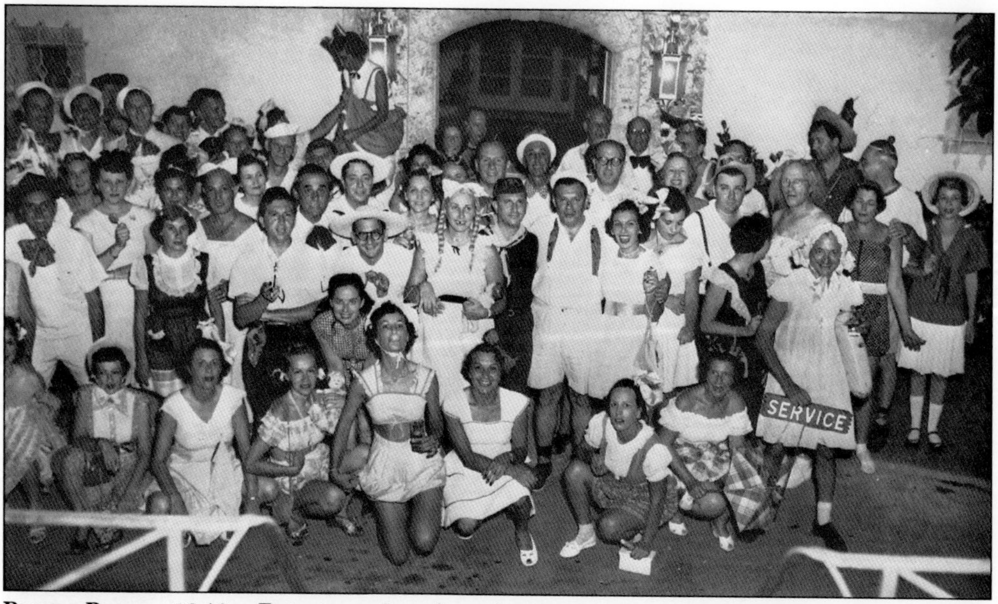

PURIM PARTY, 1940S. Enjoying a Jewish tradition are Leonard and Marjorie Wien, Phyllis Rosenberg, Mollie and Dan Ruskin, Helen and Arthur England, Dr. Louis Capland, Bill Capland, Howard and Eileen Kane, Dr. Leo and Ruth Kupper, Miriam Bass, Charlyne Coolik Meyer, Clarence and Jeanette Feuer, Ed Cornen, Jean Capland, Sylvia Lefcourt, Rose Kramer, Adele Orovitz, Milford Purcell, Maurice Orovitz, Mike Wassel, Sandy Kramer, Barney Spector, Grace Seiden, Sam Coolik, Al Seiden, Joe and Sylvia Postal, Marcella and Aaron Kanner, and Blanche Hart.

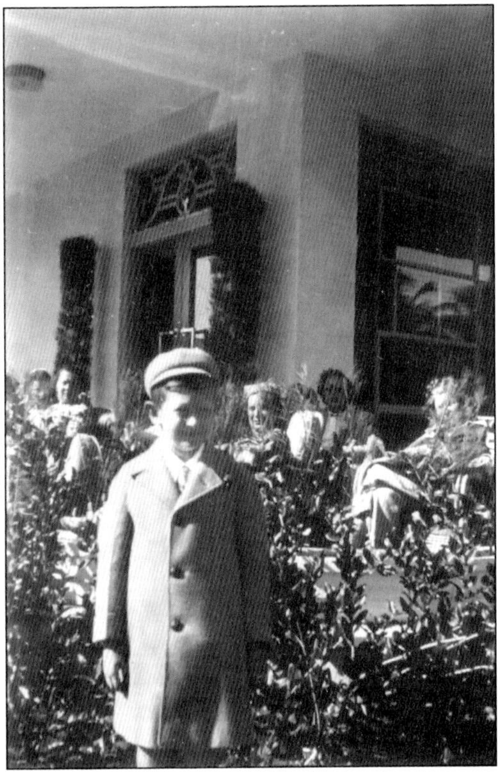

JERROLD GOODMAN, CARDOZO HOTEL, 1939. A totally Jewish project, this art deco jewel was named for U.S. Supreme Court justice Benjamin Cardozo. It was designed by Henry Hohauser and built by Irving Miller, Goodman's stepfather. The Cardozo was the first of the art deco hotels to undergo restoration, after a large portion of South Beach won a place on the National Register of Historic Places as a historical district in 1979.

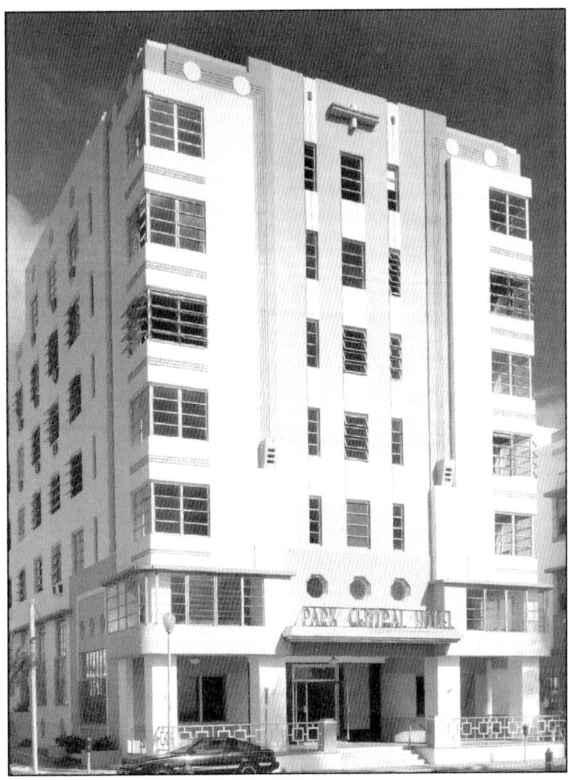

PARK CENTRAL HOTEL, OCEAN DRIVE. Designed by Henry Hohauser, this hotel opened in 1937. Tony Goldman, who bought this hotel in 1985, said, "I got out of my car, saw the Park Central and felt like I had fallen upon King Solomon's mines." This deco jewel was among the earliest hotels to be restored in the historic district and to lure the nightlife set and fashion photographers.

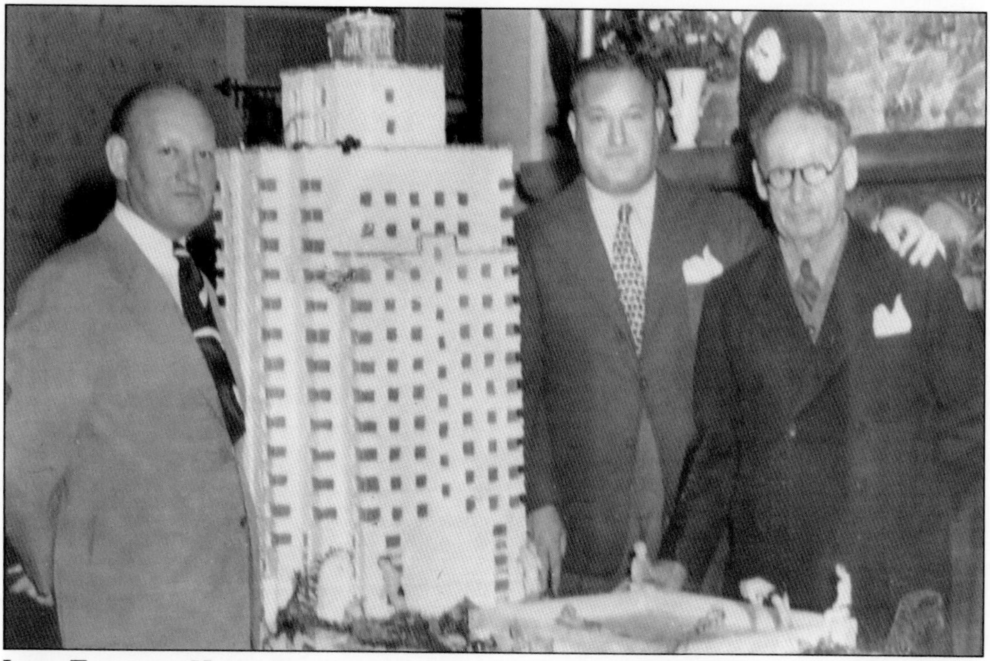

LORD TARLETON HOTEL DEDICATION, 1940. Arriving in 1924 and at first operating a grocery store, Samuel "Pop" and Rose Jacobs and their family were Miami Beach hoteliers for 65 years. The first of many hotels was the Biscayne Collins, and then they built the Alamac. Here Al Jacobs (left), Walter Jacobs, and Samuel Jacobs (right) dedicated the Beach's first skyscraper, the 18-story, kosher Lord Tarleton Hotel, which cost $600,000 to build.

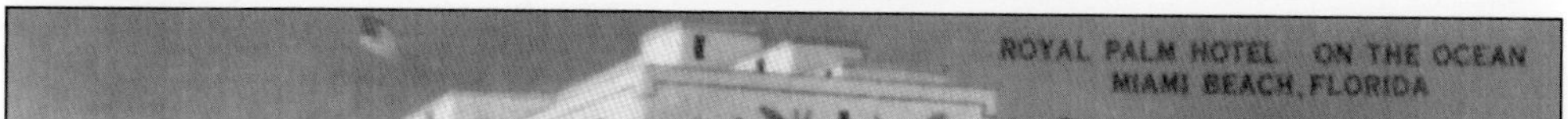

ROYAL PALM HOTEL, 1939. Russian immigrant Joseph Rose came to Florida with his wife, Sylvia, in 1924 for health reasons. He soon was building apartments in South Beach. Joe's noted accomplishment was the art deco–styled Royal Palm Hotel on Collins Avenue, which stayed in the family until 1995. Rose was active in Democratic party politics, synagogues, and many Jewish organizations, including B'nai B'rith.

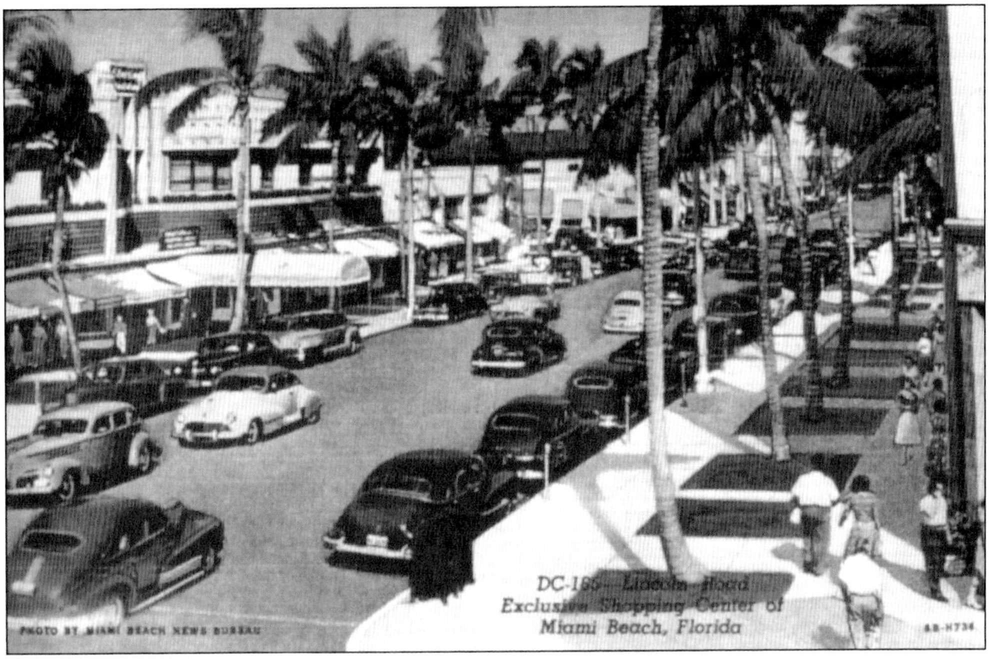

LINCOLN ROAD, 1935. This was envisioned to be the great fashion street and it was, boasting real estate offices, posh automobile dealerships, ladies' and men's shops, restaurants, and Saks Fifth Avenue.

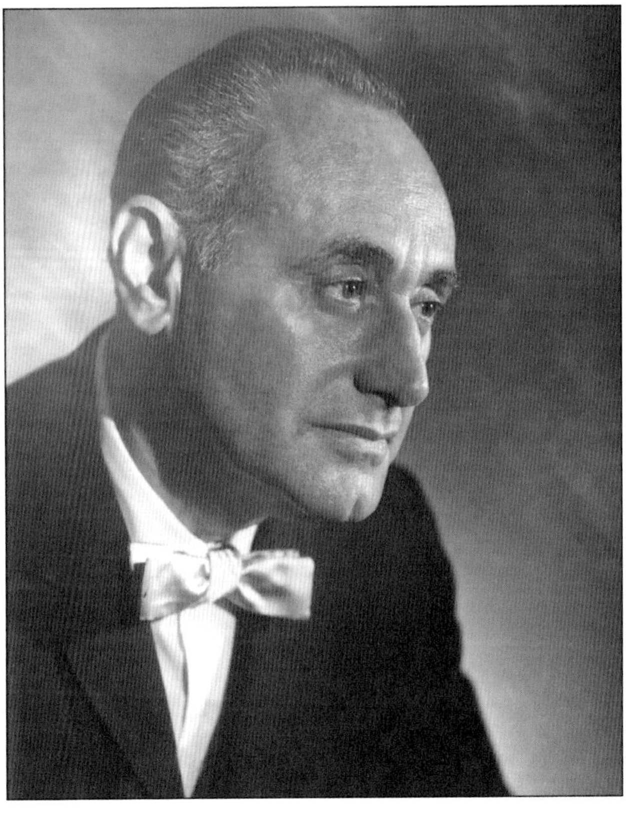

ARCHITECT MORRIS LAPIDUS. As new shopping centers opened in the 1960s, Lincoln Road had a downturn. Lapidus was asked how it could be saved. He designed an artistic open-air mall, closed to vehicles, one of the first in the United States. His plans were controversial and radical. With the attitude that "too much is never enough," Lapidus propelled his success and designed hotels, synagogues, apartments, schools, and hospitals in Greater Miami, elsewhere in Florida, the United States, and the world.

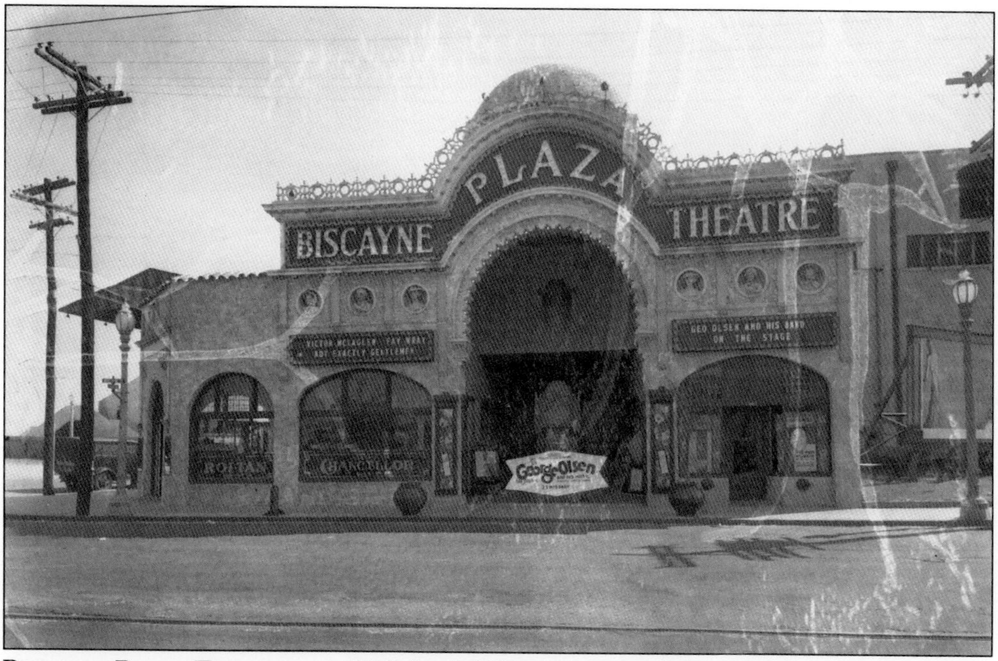

BISCAYNE PLAZA THEATRE, C. 1930. Jacob Schacter managed the area's first Yiddish theater. Some of the stars he brought to the theater were Jenny Goldstein, Moische Oischer, and Mollie Picon, who performed in Yiddish. Some said, "It was like taking the Catskills mountains . . . and bringing it down to the South." Schacter then had a radio show *Yiddish Program*, and the broadcasts originated from a studio atop the Blackstone Hotel on Miami Beach.

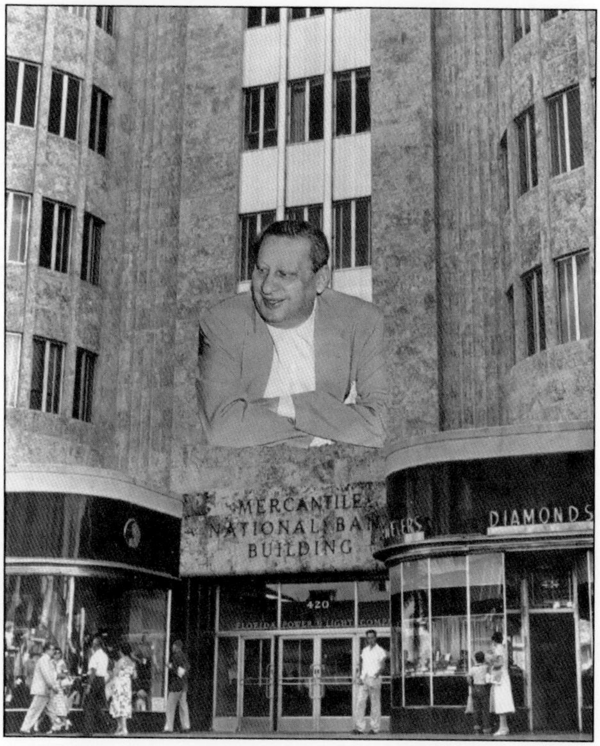

MERCANTILE NATIONAL BANK. In 1930, Philip Liberman organized the first commercial bank for Miami Beach. In 1937, Marcie Liberman (inset) took over his father's bank. Shepard Broad bought the bank, which eventually became part of Barnett Bank through acquisition. Marcie was the mayor of Miami Beach from 1947 to 1949.

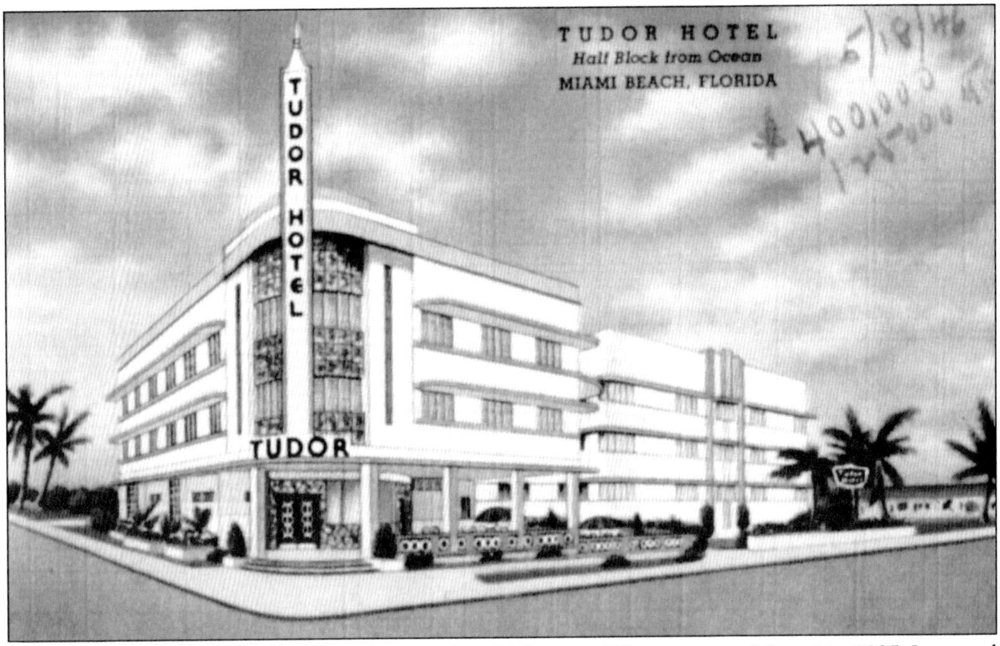

LEONARD WIEN'S HOTELS, 1930S. Leonard and Marjorie Wien came to Miami in 1935. Leonard started with Dade Millwork and Lumber Company and then, with his brothers, he began building hotels on South Beach. The 1100 block of Collins Avenue includes three of his hotels—the Tudor, Palmer House, and Kent, all examples of the streamline moderne or art deco styles of architecture.

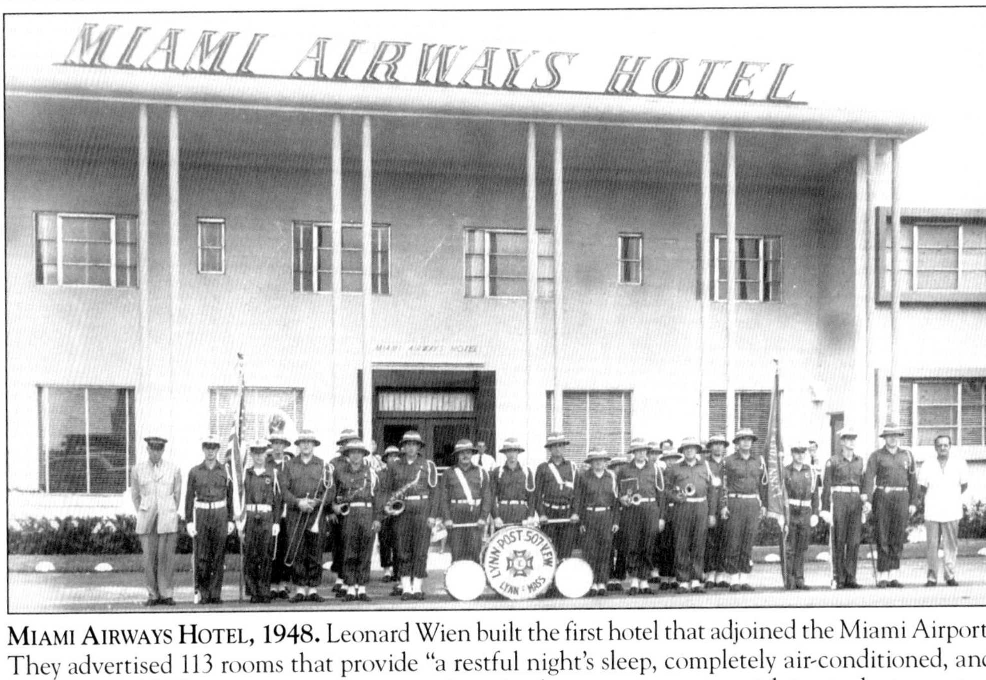

MIAMI AIRWAYS HOTEL, 1948. Leonard Wien built the first hotel that adjoined the Miami Airport. They advertised 113 rooms that provide "a restful night's sleep, completely air-conditioned, and soundproofed." The most expensive menu item in the restaurant was a sirloin steak at a cost of $4.50. In addition to hotels, Leonard Wien built about 1,000 homes in Westchester with Neil Schiff and owned property in Kendall, Miami Beach, and at a location near the Miami Airport.

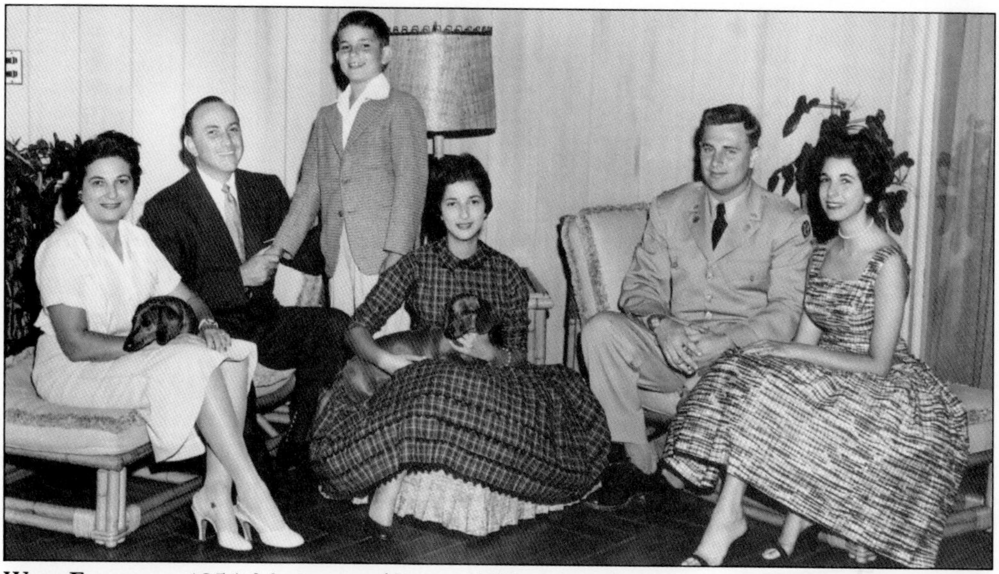

WIEN FAMILY, C. 1954. Marjorie and Leonard Wien were founders of Mount Sinai Hospital and major leaders in both the Jewish and civic communities. From left to right are Marjorie, Leonard Sr., Leonard Jr., Josie, Larry Porter, and Carole. During this decade, Leonard purchased 1,000 acres in the Kendall area for $500–$750 per acre, and the selling price on the last piece in 2005 was roughly $80,000 per acre. Leonard Jr. is currently president of the Jewish Museum of Florida.

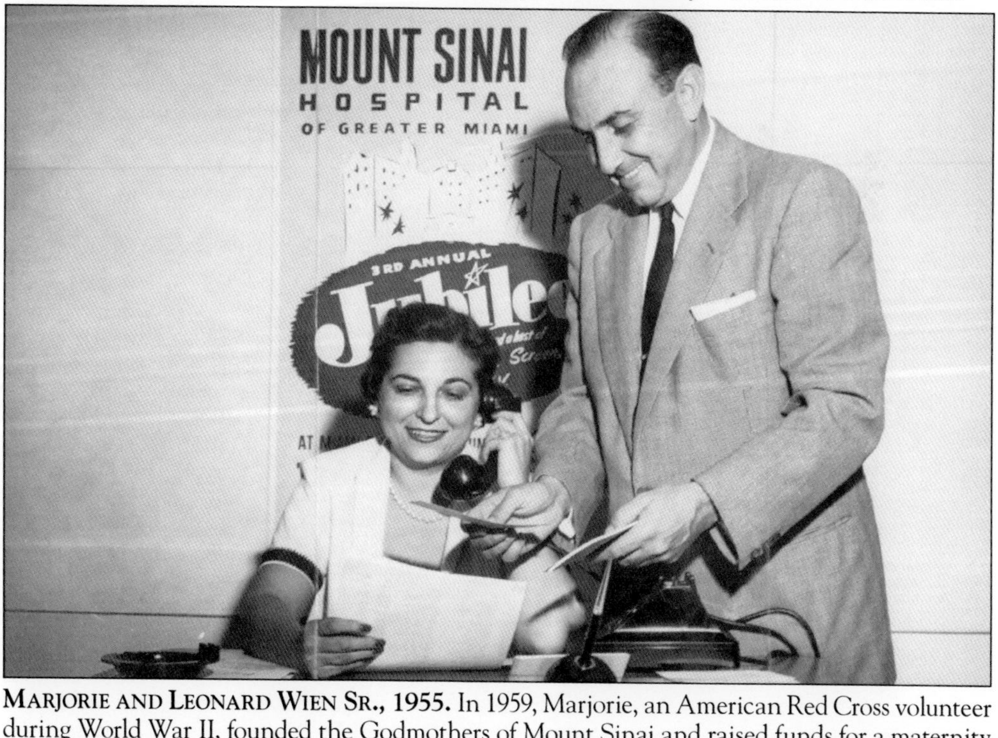

MARJORIE AND LEONARD WIEN SR., 1955. In 1959, Marjorie, an American Red Cross volunteer during World War II, founded the Godmothers of Mount Sinai and raised funds for a maternity wing. In 1986, the hospital honored the Wiens, naming the Wien Center for Alzheimer's Disease and Memory Disorders. They were early supporters of the Jewish Museum of Florida and many other organizations, and Leonard was a founder of Community Chest, the forerunner of United Way.

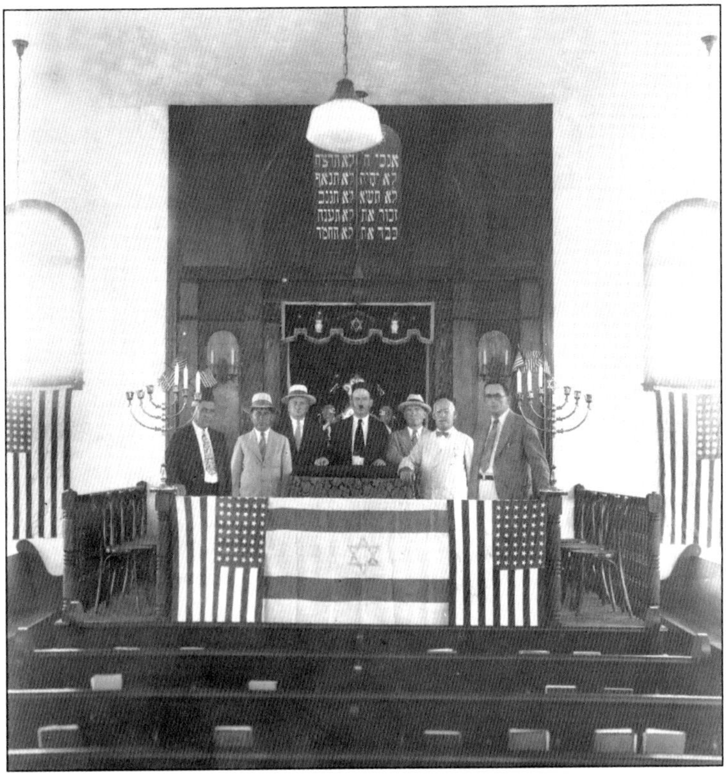

FOUNDERS OF MIAMI BEACH'S FIRST CONGREGATION, BETH JACOB. Founded in 1927, the leadership met in their new shul, built for $25,000 in 1928–1929 at 311 Washington Avenue. From left to right are Joseph Tilzer, Benjamin Kaplan, Harry Levitt, Harry Wasserman, Lazarus Abromowitz, Louis Topkis, and Max Feit. The location of the synagogue was dictated by property deeds that restricted Jews to live and do business south of Fifth Street.

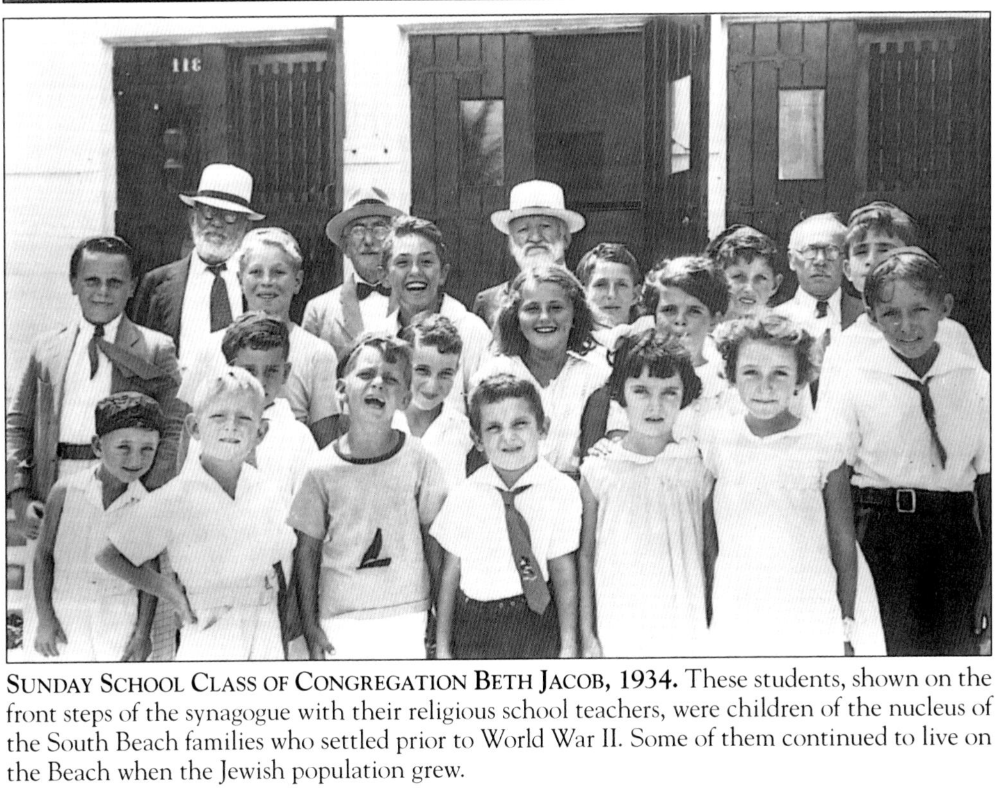

SUNDAY SCHOOL CLASS OF CONGREGATION BETH JACOB, 1934. These students, shown on the front steps of the synagogue with their religious school teachers, were children of the nucleus of the South Beach families who settled prior to World War II. Some of them continued to live on the Beach when the Jewish population grew.

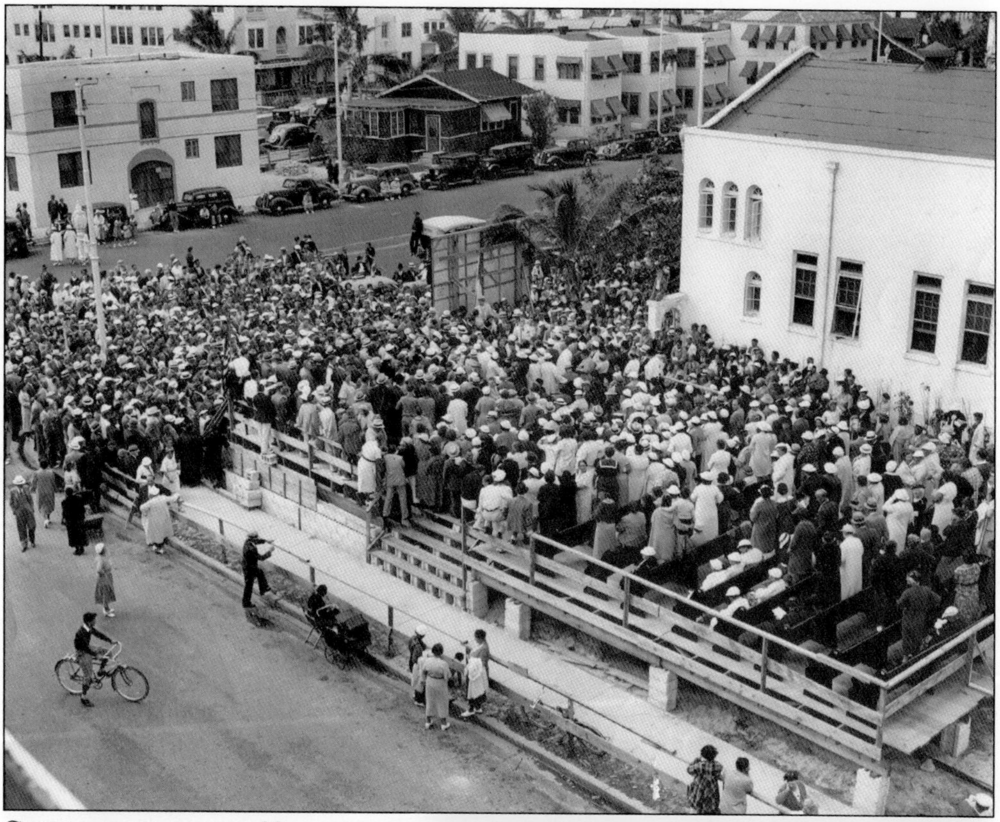

GROUNDBREAKING FOR NEW SYNAGOGUE FOR CONGREGATION BETH JACOB, 1935. The original building did not have sufficient space to accommodate the winter visitors during what they call the "season." The congregation purchased the lot next door and hired a new congregant, Henry Hohauser, to design their new synagogue, which was built for $40,000.

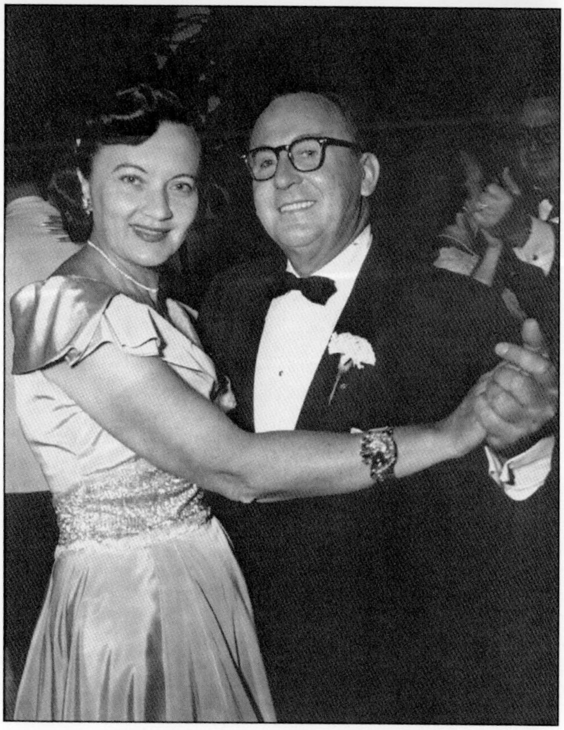

HENRY HOHAUSER AND HIS WIFE, GRACE, 1940S. After training and practicing as an architect in New York, Hohauser moved to the Beach and began to build a reputation for his streamline moderne designs. Over five years, Hohauser created more than 100 hotels and apartments on Miami Beach, including many in the Art Deco District.

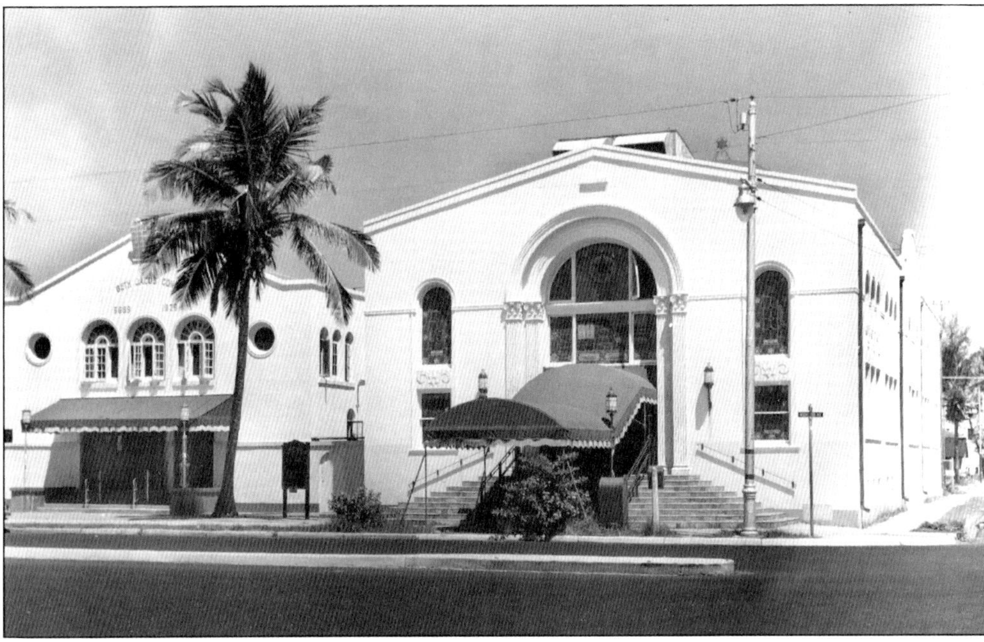

CONGREGATION BETH JACOB, c. 1938. The original shul, on the left, served as the social hall when the new synagogue opened in 1936. In 1946, a two-story addition was added to the eastern side of the original shul for religious school classrooms. The Jewish Museum of Florida leased the 1936 building in 1992 and purchased these two buildings and the adjacent parking lot for their expansion in 2005.

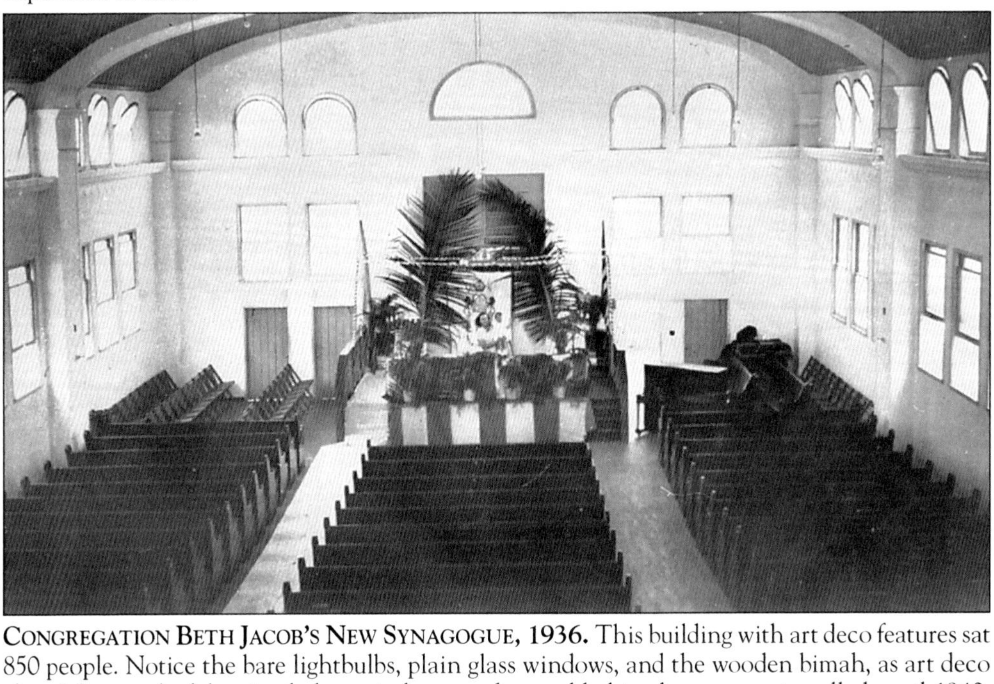

CONGREGATION BETH JACOB'S NEW SYNAGOGUE, 1936. This building with art deco features sat 850 people. Notice the bare lightbulbs, plain glass windows, and the wooden bimah, as art deco chandeliers, colorful stained-glass windows, and a marble bimah were not installed until 1940. Also, here they used fans, as this was before air-conditioning. Being an Orthodox congregation, the women sat upstairs in the balcony.

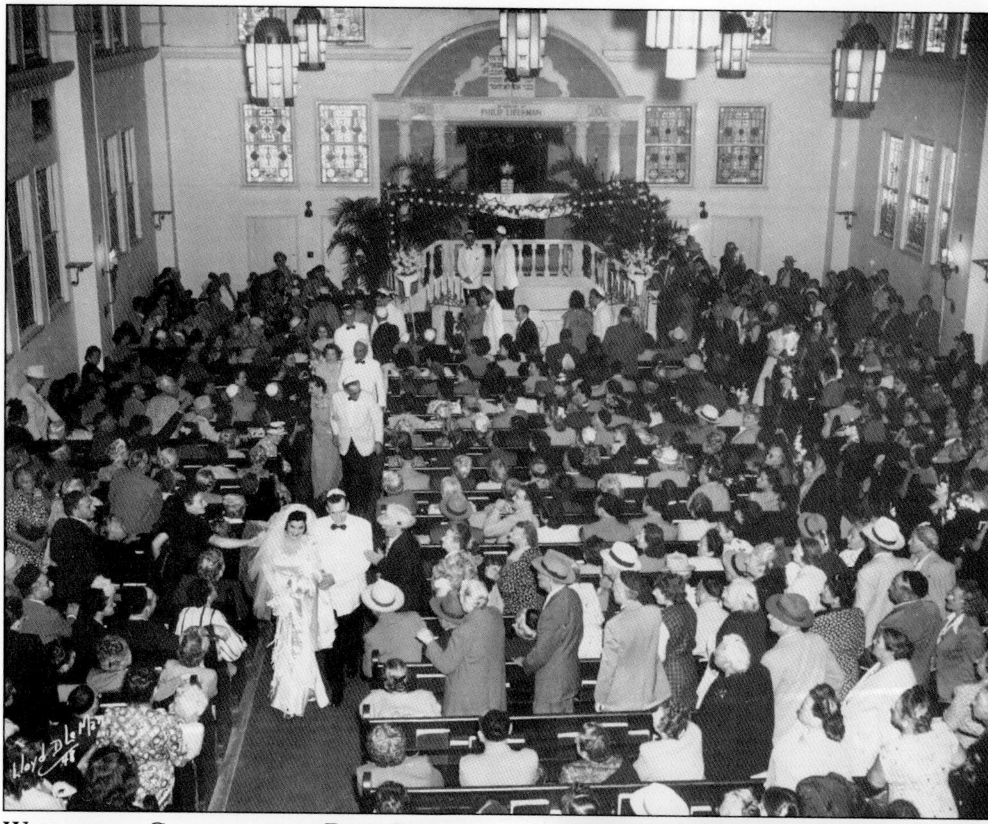

WEDDING IN CONGREGATION BETH JACOB, 1948. The ceremony has ended in the updated sanctuary, and Miriam Feit and Saul Rose walk down the aisle as a couple, welcomed by the jubilant members of the congregation. This is not a religious service, so the women and men are sitting together, without a *mehitsa* (divider to separate men and women during prayer in an Orthodox synagogue).

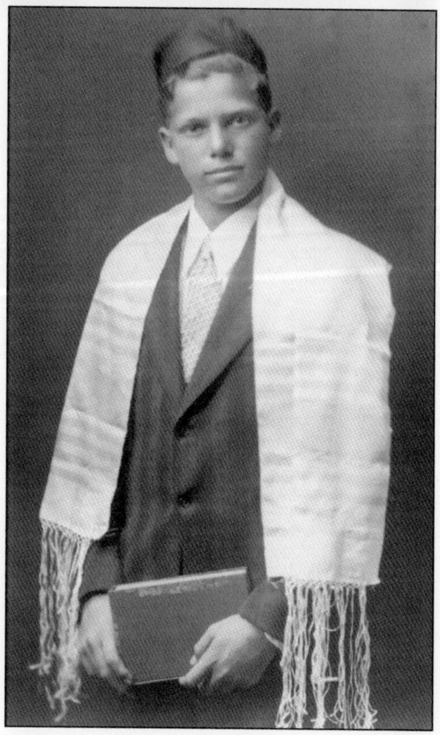

BAR MITZVAH IN BETH JACOB, 1930. In his youth, Milton Gaynor delivered the *Miami Herald* to help support his family. He was a fine athlete, an officer in the U.S. Army Air Corps in World War II, and, afterwards, achieved success in the public and private sectors.

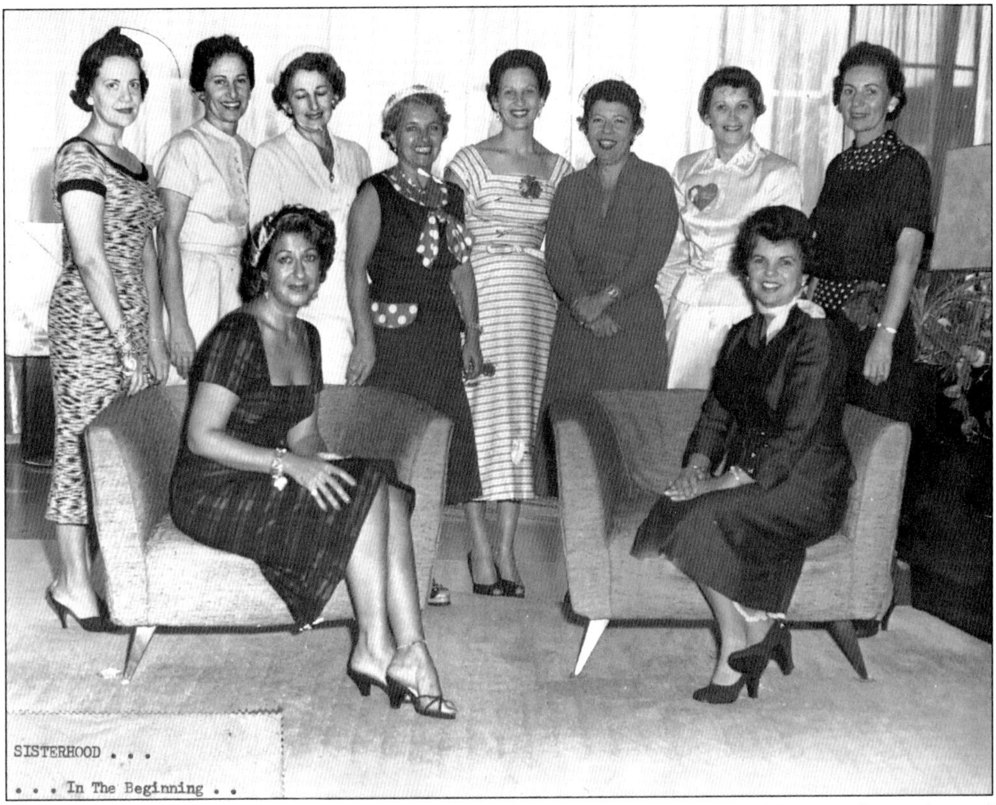

FIRST SISTERHOOD OF WHAT BECAME TEMPLE EMANU-EL, 1940. In 1938, several members of Beth Jacob organized a new congregation, Jacob Joseph. They changed the name in 1941 to the Miami Beach Jewish Community Center and then, in 1954, to Temple Emanu-El.

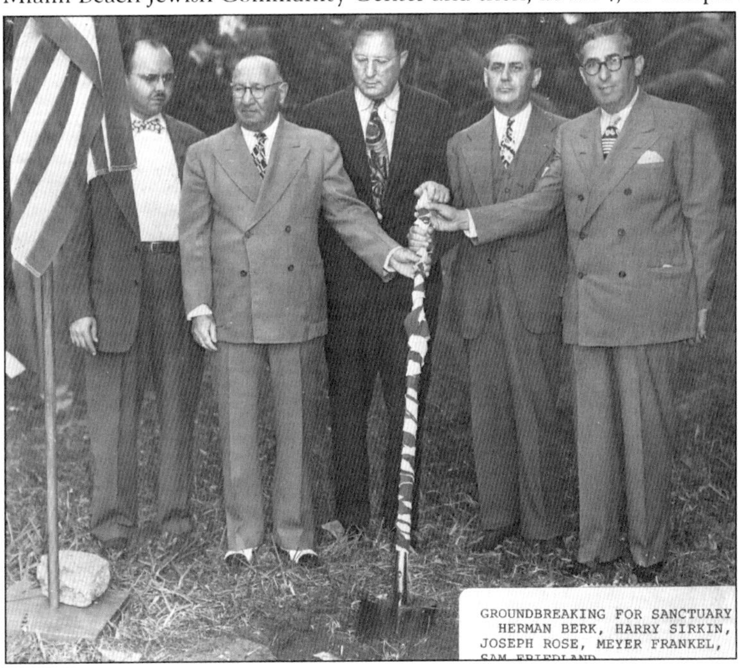

GROUNDBREAKING FOR MIAMI BEACH JEWISH CENTER, EUCLID AVENUE 1941. The congregation grew quickly as the Jewish population on Miami Beach mushroomed. From left to right are Herman Berk, Harry Sirkin, Joseph Rose, Meyer Frankel, and Samuel Friedland.

Bulletin Cover for Temple Emanu-El, "May God Be with Us," c. 1960. By 1944, the congregation again needed more space. They bought two lots on Washington Avenue and planned for the building to seat 1,800 worshippers. Architect Charles Greco of Boston designed the structure with a Byzantine copper dome after a similar building in Palestine. The congregation moved in 1948.

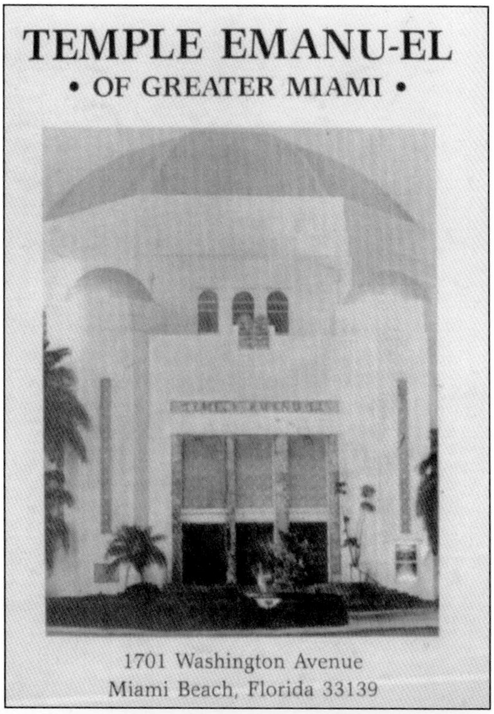

Installation Dinner for Rabbi Irving Lehrman, Miami Beach Jewish Community Center, 1943. The dinner was held in the London Arms Hotel on Miami Beach. Rabbi Lehrman's father, Rabbi Abraham Lehrman, delivered the installation address. Renamed Temple Emanu-El in 1954, Rabbi Lehrman's compelling sermons and leadership sparked this congregation to become the largest Conservative congregation in the southern United States.

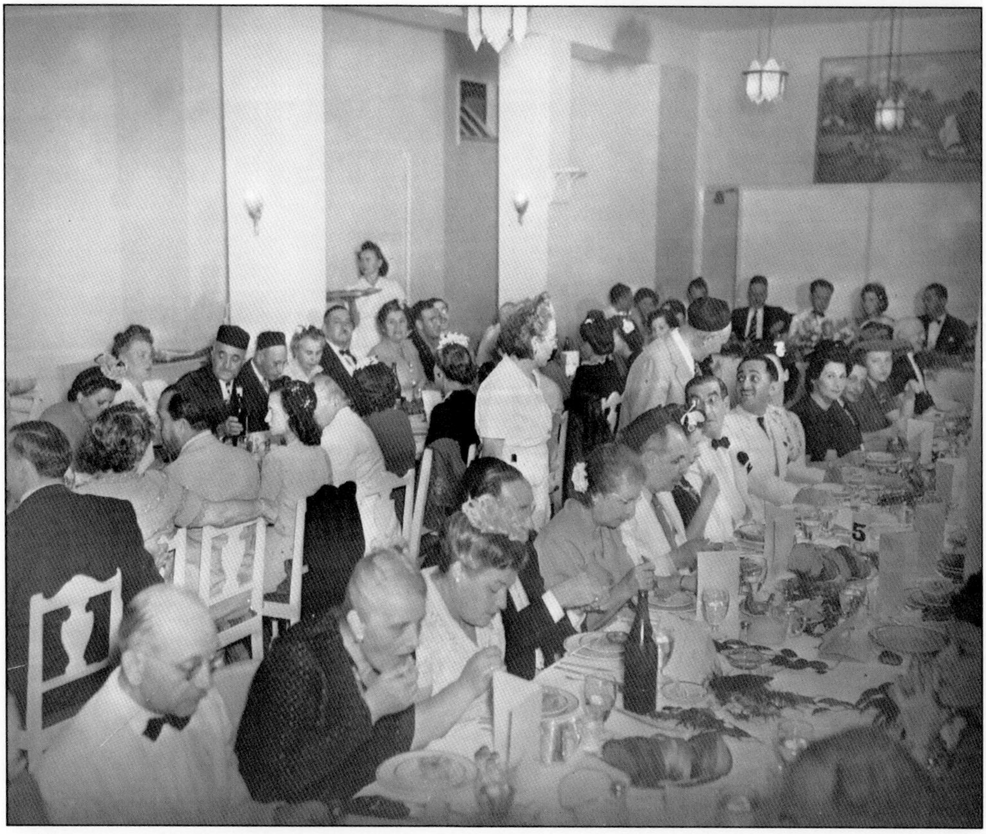

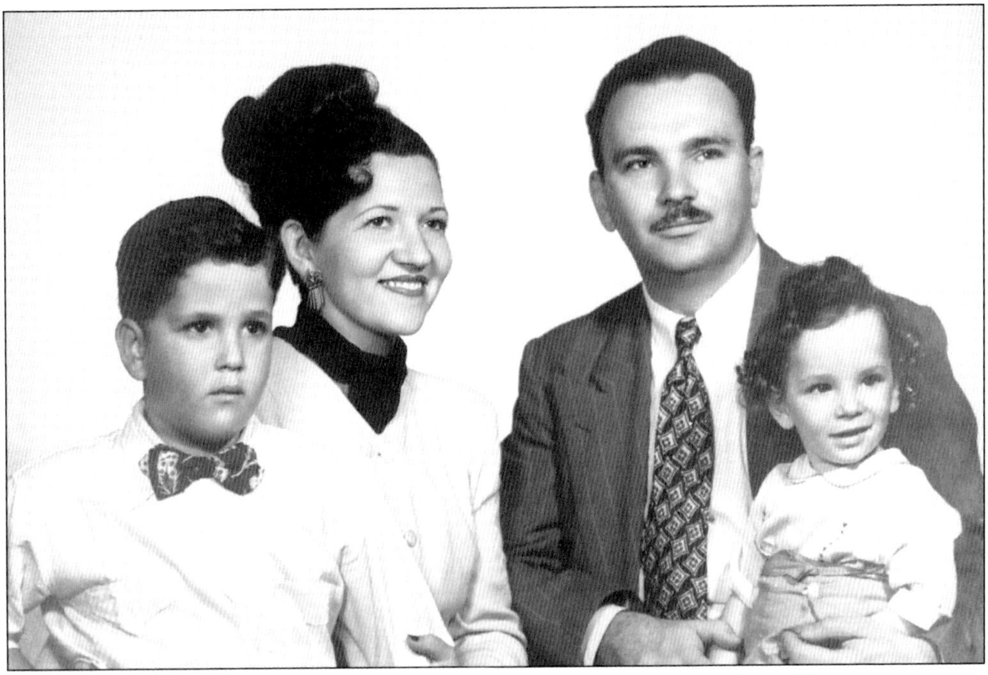

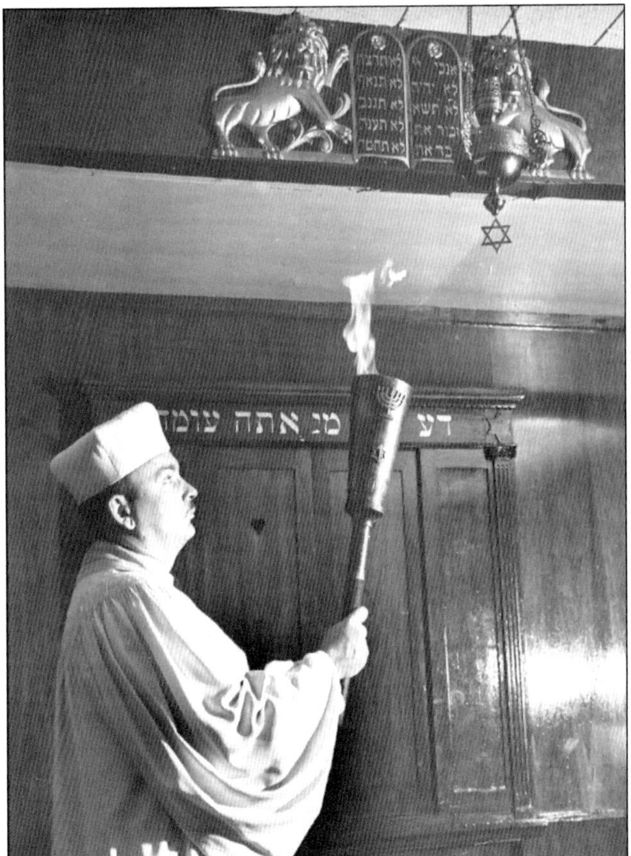

RABBI LEON KRONISH AND FAMILY, 1944. Dr. Stephen Wise ordained Rabbi Leon Kronish in 1942, the same year that Beth Sholom was founded with 20 Miami Beach families. Then two years later, Kronish was invited to serve Beth Sholom Jewish Center. Rabbi Kronish joined Rabbi Lehrman on Miami Beach, and both served their respective congregations for 50 years as powerful and charismatic leaders in both the Jewish and civic communities.

RABBI LEON KRONISH LIGHTING THE ETERNAL FLAME, C. 1947. The center was renamed Temple Beth Sholom in 1945, when the congregation moved to a two-story house at 4141 Chase Avenue.

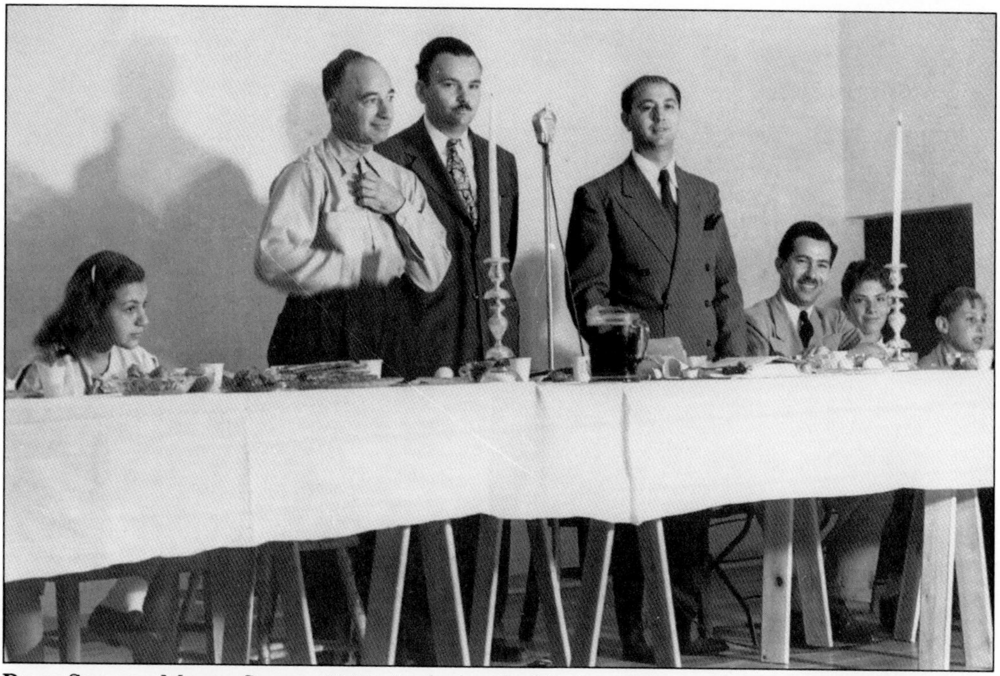

BETH SHOLOM MODEL SEDER, 1944. At the head table, from left to right, are Ann Broad (Bussel); future Israeli leader Shimon Peres; 27-year-old Rabbi Leon Kronish; Cantor Kelemer; founder of the Bureau of Jewish Education, Dr. Abe Gannes; Dr. Gratz; and unidentified.

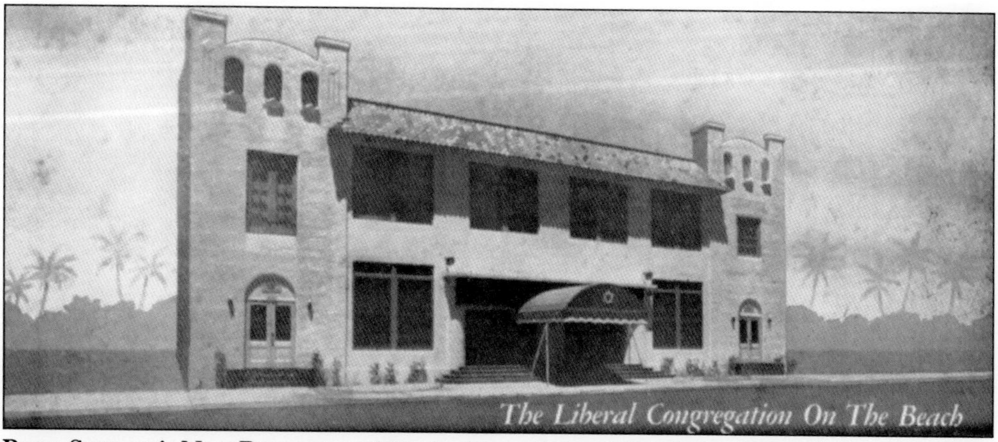

BETH SHOLOM'S NEW BUILDING, 1956. Architect Percival Goodman designed a new sanctuary on the same location, and in 1961, the congregation expanded with the addition of a school. Since that time, many renovations and expansions have been executed at this site.

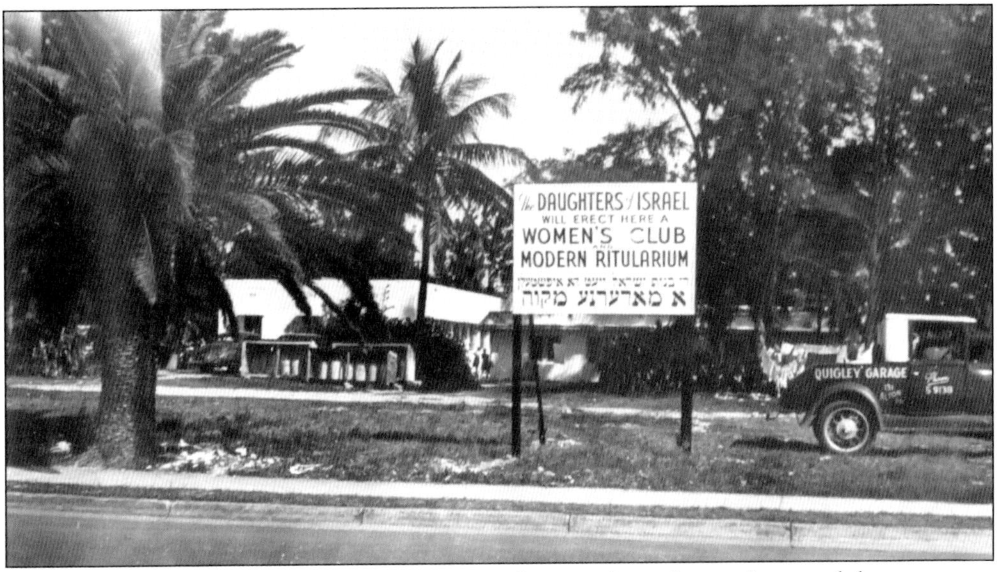

First *Mikvah* in Miami-Dade County, 1944. Prior to this, religious Jews used the ocean as a *mikvah*. Rabbi Moses Mescheloff, with his wife, Magda, led the effort to build this $35,000 *mikvah* and almost went to jail in the process, as it was during the war and building materials were scarce. By 1970, the building was deteriorating, so another was built at the same site.

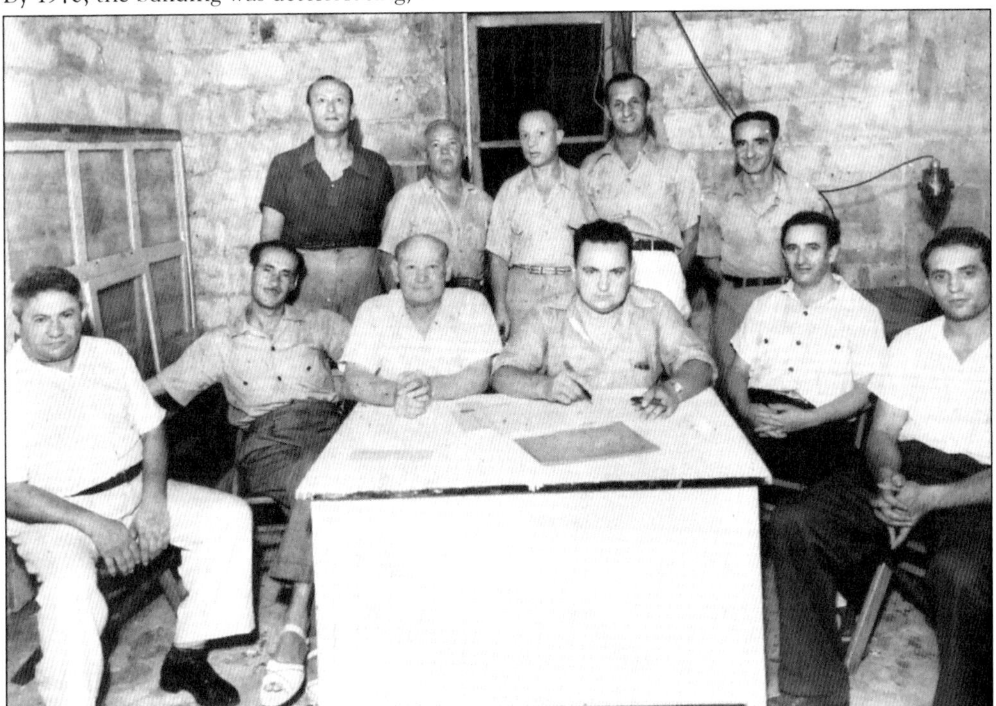

Kosher Butchers Guild, 1930s. There were dozens of kosher markets in the South Beach neighborhood to accommodate the Jewish community. Those identified in the photograph are David Whitman, Sam Sussman, Sam Bresslove, Frank Cats, Saul Kenholz, Leo Schuger, Joe Reissman, Phil Romer, and Milton Breger. Kosher butchers must slaughter animals to prevent undue suffering and the meat must be devoid of disease. Kosher meat is drained of any vestiges of blood.

SOL KAHLENBERG, KOSHER BUTCHER, 1940. Kahlenberg came to Miami Beach in 1939 and was first employed at Malters Market, at Collins Avenue and Fourth Street. He opened his own kosher meat department within the market at 618 Collins Avenue in 1944.

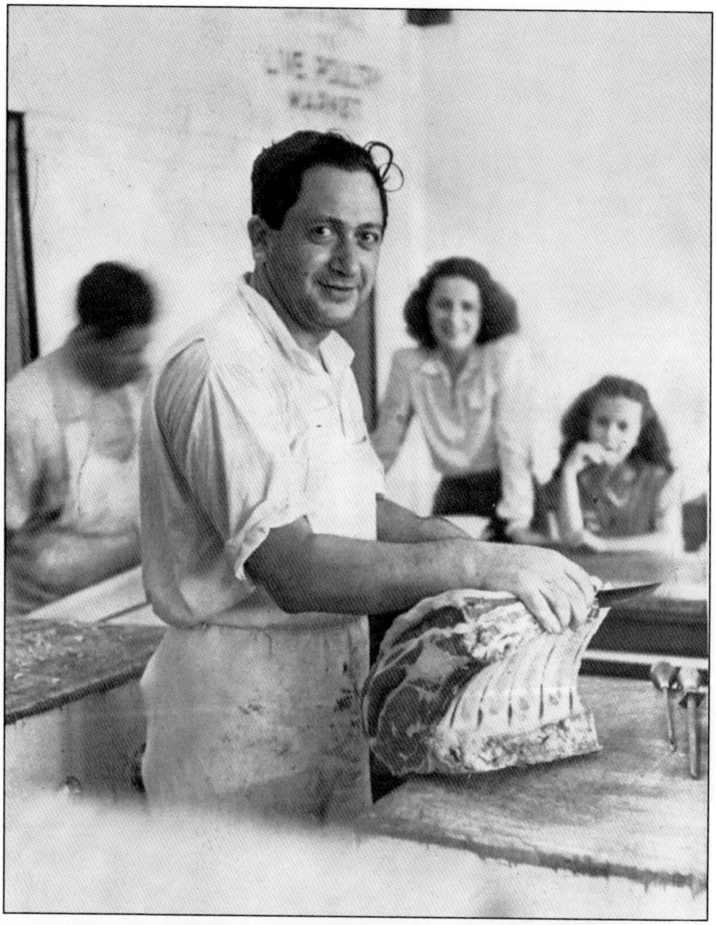

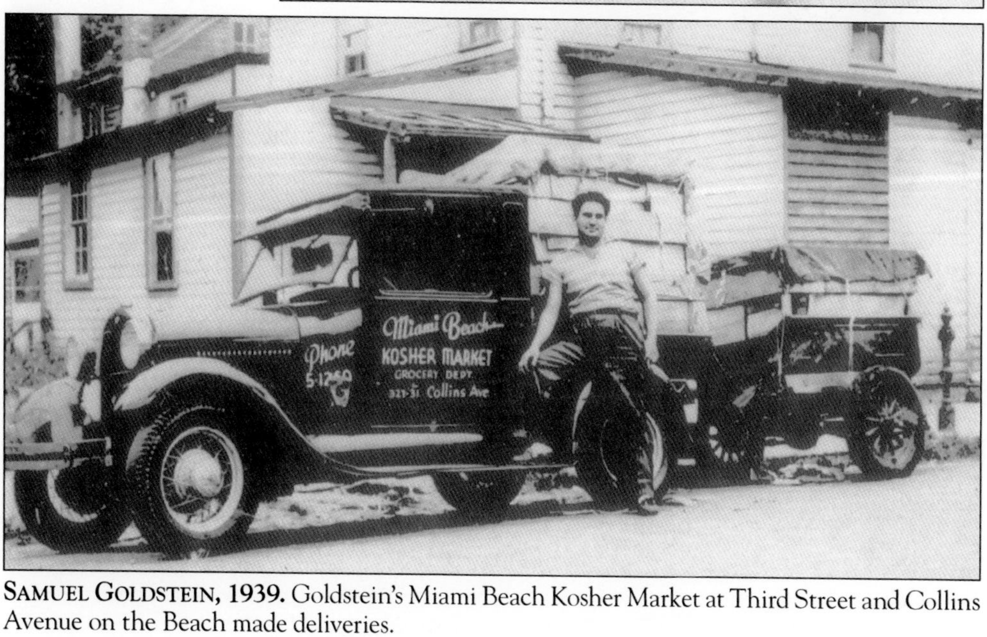

SAMUEL GOLDSTEIN, 1939. Goldstein's Miami Beach Kosher Market at Third Street and Collins Avenue on the Beach made deliveries.

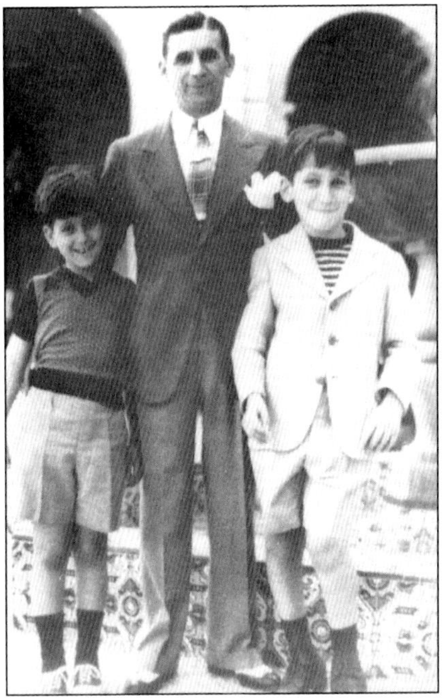

MEYER LANSKY WITH SONS, 1940. Born in Russia around 1900, Lansky came with his family to New York about 1910. His career in crime began with the nickel his mother gave him to take the Sabbath *cholent* to the bakery. He used the nickel for a crap game. This expanded to bootlegging and then gambling, and Lansky established a strong South Florida presence that included Miami Beach in the 1930s. He died there in 1983.

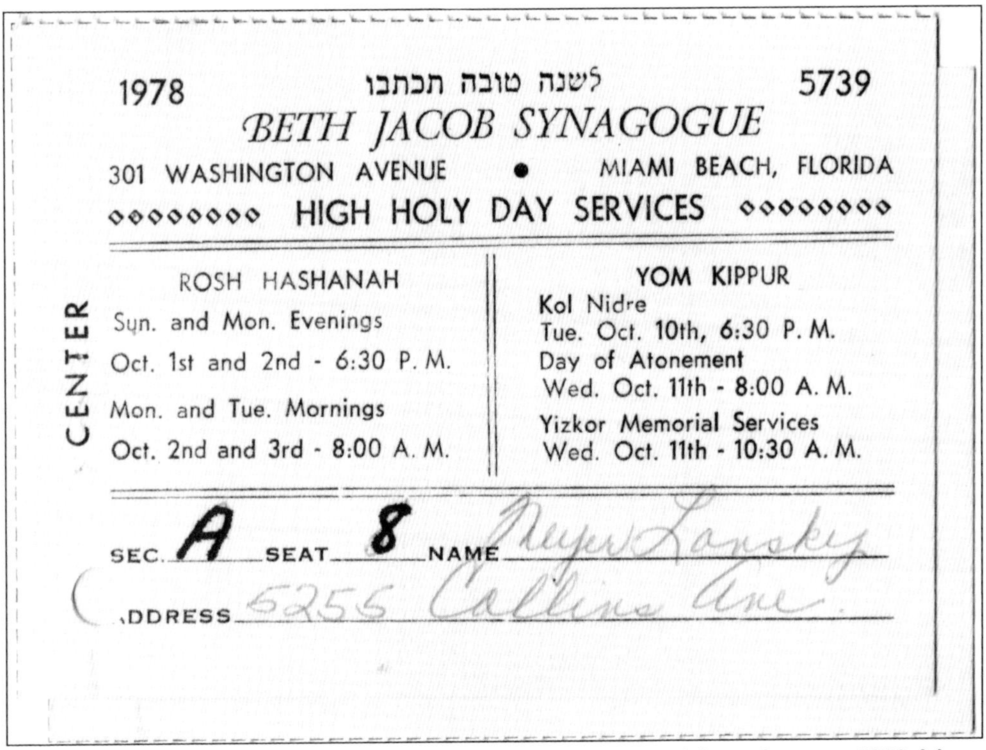

1978 לשנה טובה תכתבו 5739

BETH JACOB SYNAGOGUE

301 WASHINGTON AVENUE • MIAMI BEACH, FLORIDA

HIGH HOLY DAY SERVICES

CENTER

ROSH HASHANAH	YOM KIPPUR
Sun. and Mon. Evenings Oct. 1st and 2nd - 6:30 P. M. Mon. and Tue. Mornings Oct. 2nd and 3rd - 8:00 A. M.	Kol Nidre Tue. Oct. 10th, 6:30 P. M. Day of Atonement Wed. Oct. 11th - 8:00 A. M. Yizkor Memorial Services Wed. Oct. 11th - 10:30 A. M.

SEC. A SEAT 8 NAME Meyer Lansky

DDRESS 5255 Collins Ave.

CONGREGATION BETH JACOB HIGH HOLIDAY TICKETS ISSUED TO MEYER LANSKY, 1978. Meyer Lansky and his second wife, Teddy, were members of Congregation Beth Jacob and contributors to Israel. They also rescued Jews from the Nazis and transported them to Cuba. He used his business acumen to set up casinos in Cuba and then in Las Vegas. Estes Kefauver's Senate Crime Committee named Lansky as one of the "leaders of organized crime" in America.

Four

World at War and the Boom that Follows

Economic Opportunity

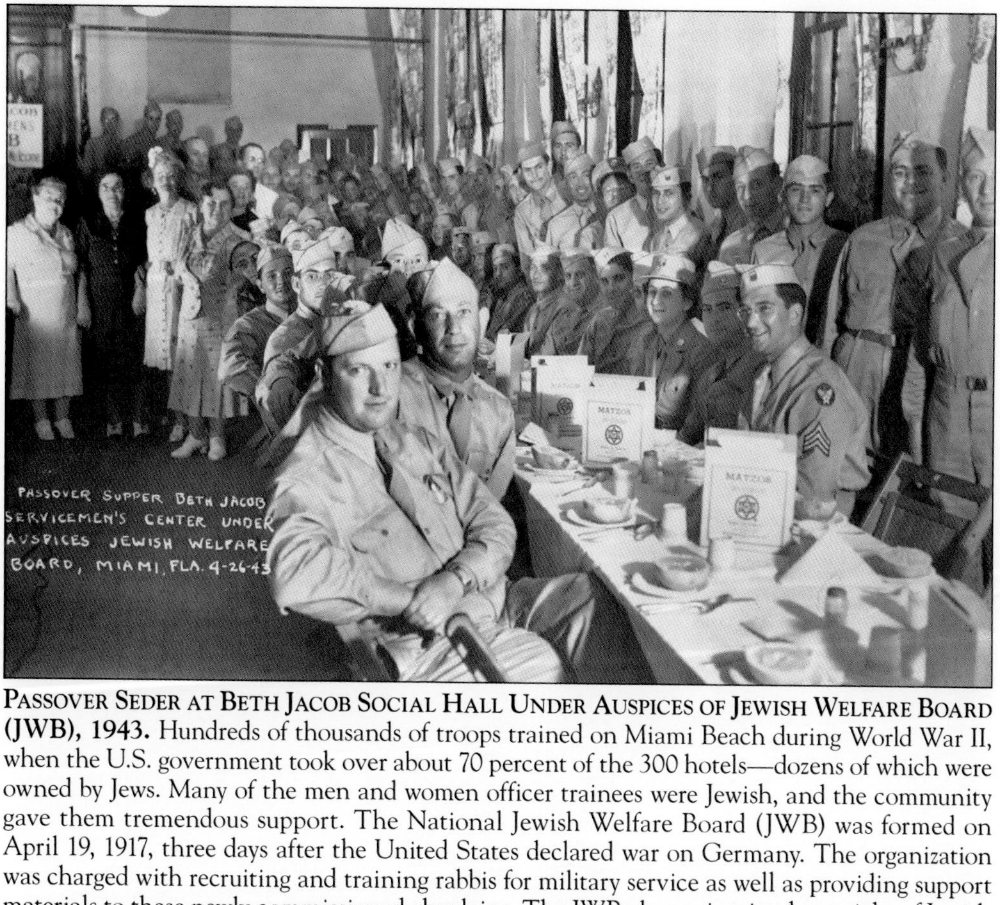

Passover Seder at Beth Jacob Social Hall Under Auspices of Jewish Welfare Board (JWB), 1943. Hundreds of thousands of troops trained on Miami Beach during World War II, when the U.S. government took over about 70 percent of the 300 hotels—dozens of which were owned by Jews. Many of the men and women officer trainees were Jewish, and the community gave them tremendous support. The National Jewish Welfare Board (JWB) was formed on April 19, 1917, three days after the United States declared war on Germany. The organization was charged with recruiting and training rabbis for military service as well as providing support materials to these newly commissioned chaplains. The JWB also maintained oversight of Jewish chapel facilities at military installations. In 1941, in a response to a mandate from Pres. Franklin D. Roosevelt, six private organizations—the YMCA, YWCA, NCSS, National Jewish Welfare Board, the Traveler's Aid Association, and the Salvation Army—were challenged to handle the on-leave morale and recreational needs for members of the armed forces. The six organizations pooled their resources and the United Service Organizations, which quickly became known as the USO, was incorporated in New York on February 4, 1941.

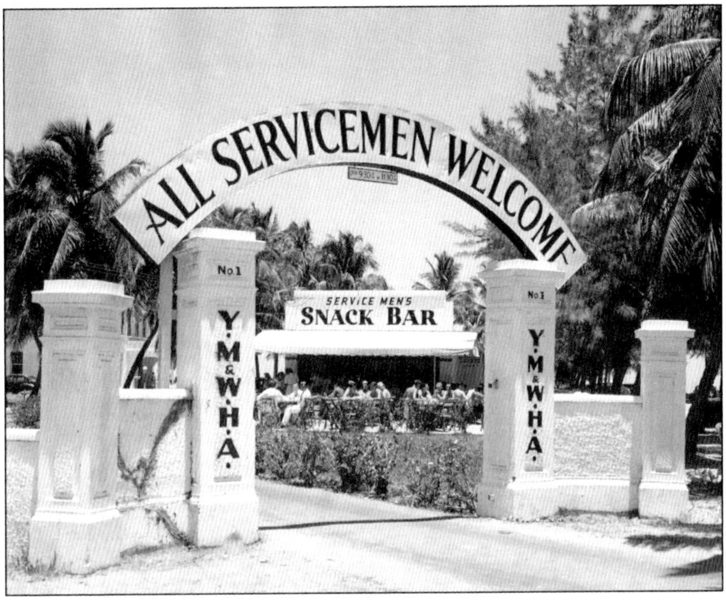

YMHA AND YWHA SERVICEMEN'S CENTER, 1944. Members of the local Jewish community served as volunteers at the Young Men and Women's Hebrew Association facility, providing rest and relaxation, food, and entertainment for Jewish men and women serving in the armed forces. Lured by the weather, lifestyle, and hospitality, many returned to settle in the Miami area after the war.

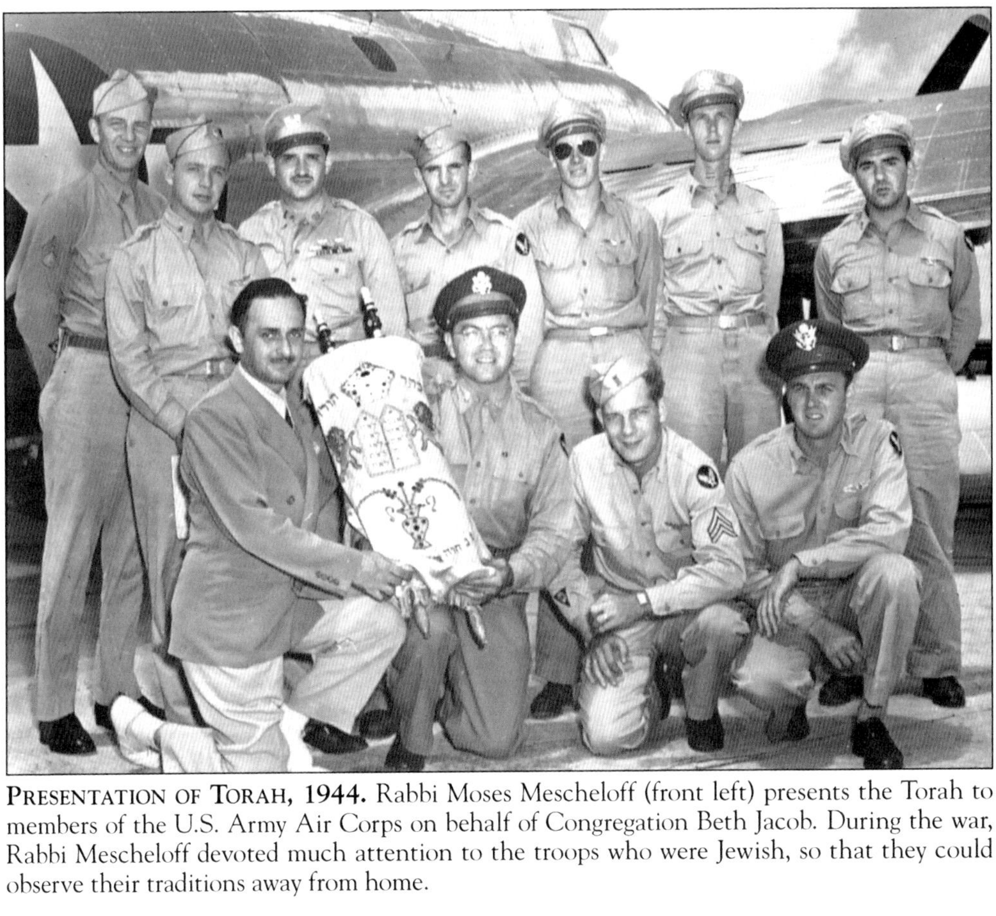

PRESENTATION OF TORAH, 1944. Rabbi Moses Mescheloff (front left) presents the Torah to members of the U.S. Army Air Corps on behalf of Congregation Beth Jacob. During the war, Rabbi Mescheloff devoted much attention to the troops who were Jewish, so that they could observe their traditions away from home.

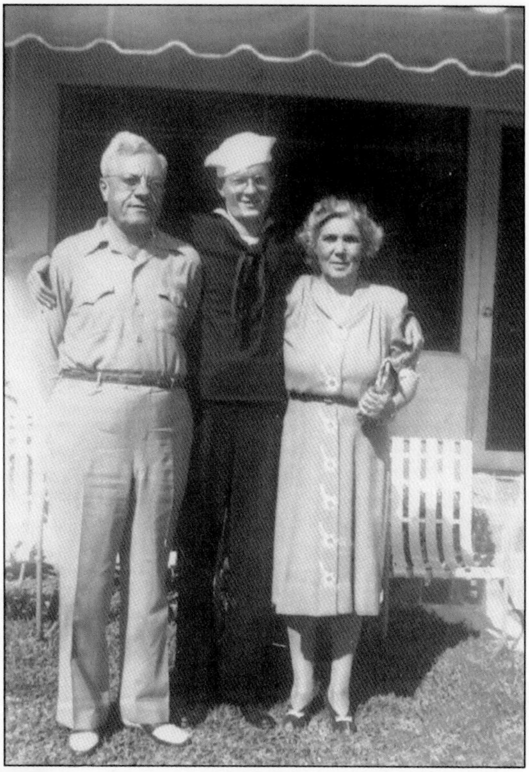

U.S. Navy Seabee David Catsman Saying Goodbye to His Parents, 1942. Like so many Jewish parents, Philip and Anna Catsman were proud of their son's participation to defend democracy as Hitler stormed across Europe. Catsman returned to play a major role in breaking the discrimination policies on Miami Beach. He and fellow veteran Burnett Roth visited every hotel and apartment owner to persuade them to eliminate their restrictive covenants.

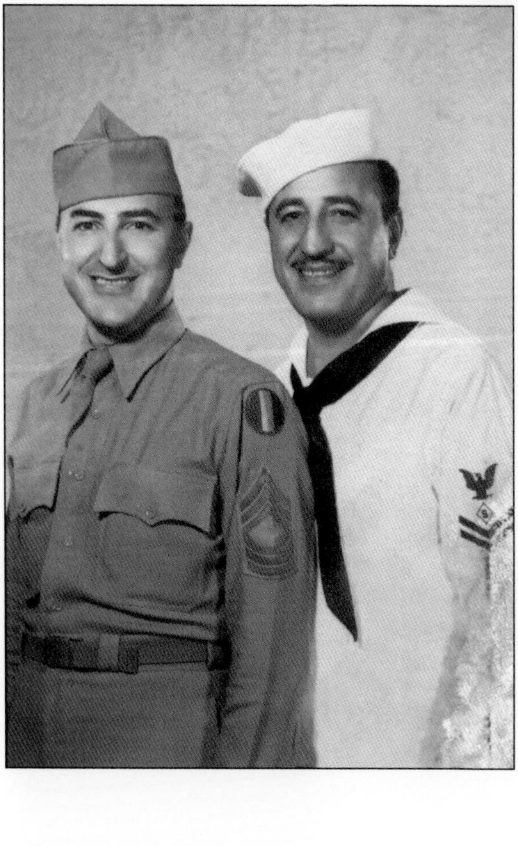

Burnett (1912–2008) and Dan Roth, World War II, 1944. Burnett (left) fought for human rights his entire life. In 1935, he helped establish the Anti-Defamation League (ADL) in Dade County and served nationally for 40 years. He was deeply involved in integrating public schools and took on employment, "Gentile clientele," and "whites only" policies. Dan was president of Beth Jacob for 15 years and Exalted Ruler of the Elks of Miami Beach, among other activities.

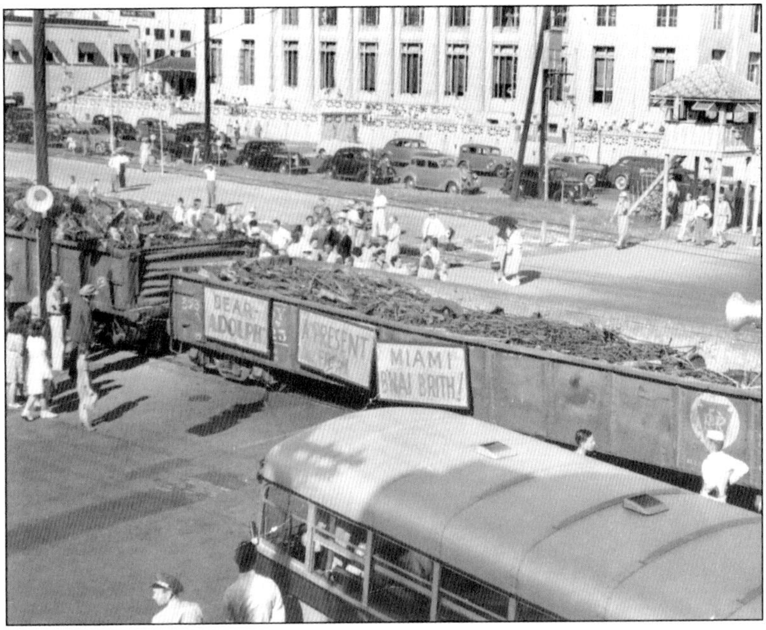

B'NAI B'RITH SCRAP-METAL DRIVE, 1942. All of the Jewish organizations got involved in the war effort. The members came up with creative ideas to support their nation and democracy. During World War II, recyclable materials were collected to support military production.

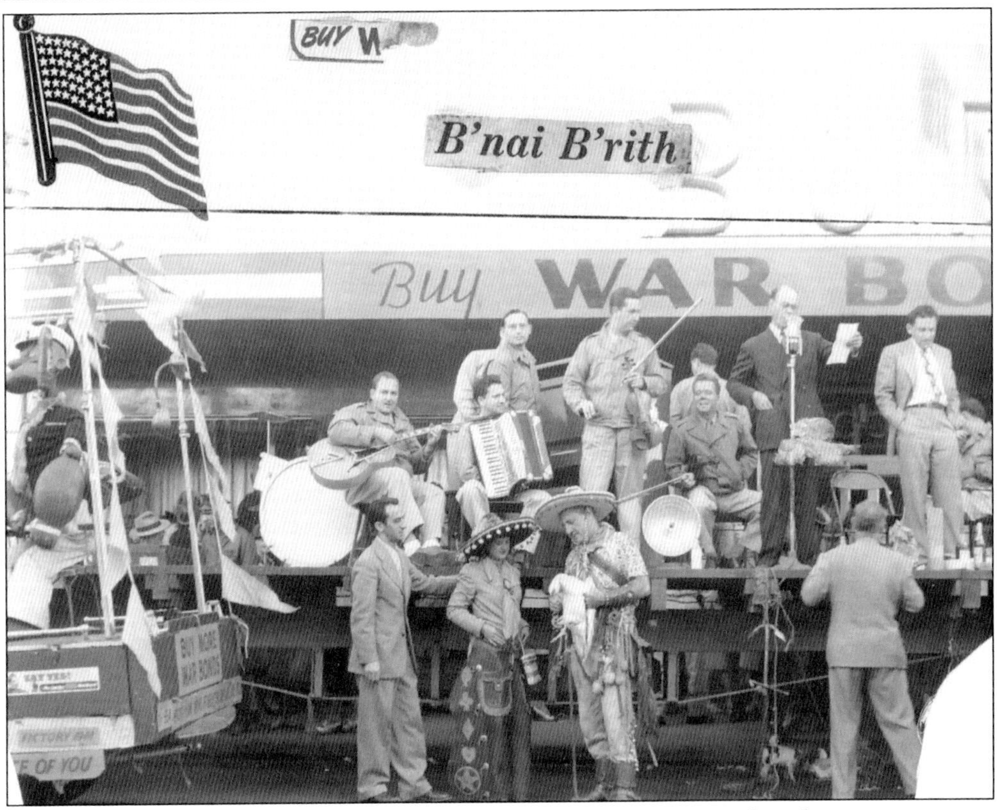

B'NAI B'RITH SELLING WAR BONDS, 1942. To express their patriotism, Jewish organizations, as well as individual Jews, helped raise money for the war. During World War II was the last time the United States issued war bonds, which were a way to reduce inflation. Half the population purchased bonds.

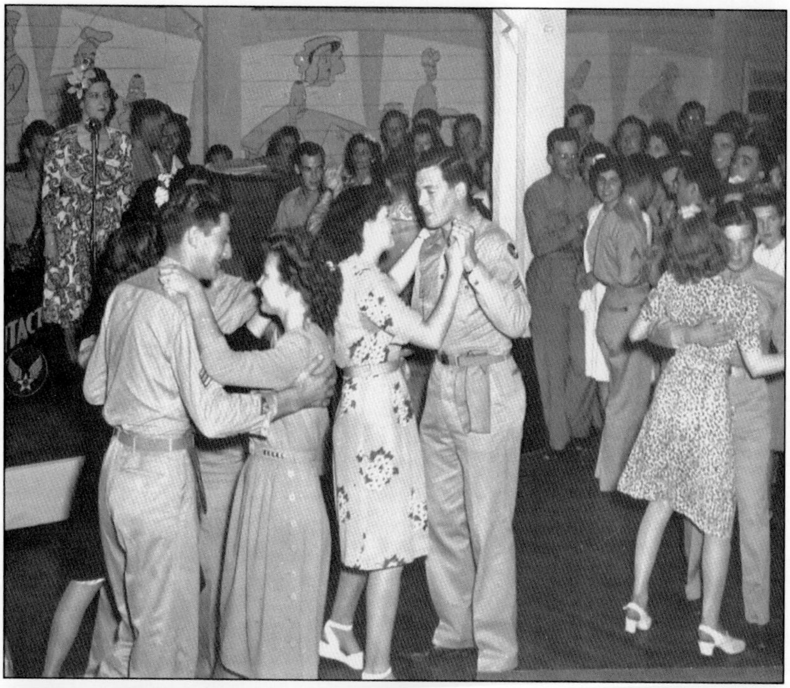

SOLDIERS AND LOCAL MIAMI GIRLS, ENGLERETTES, "CUT A RUG," 1945. Ida Engler and her two daughters (the Englerettes) organized 1,000 volunteer hostesses to entertain servicemen from Homestead to Boca Raton during the war years. This dance is at Homestead Air Force Base. Ida Engler is singing at the mike.

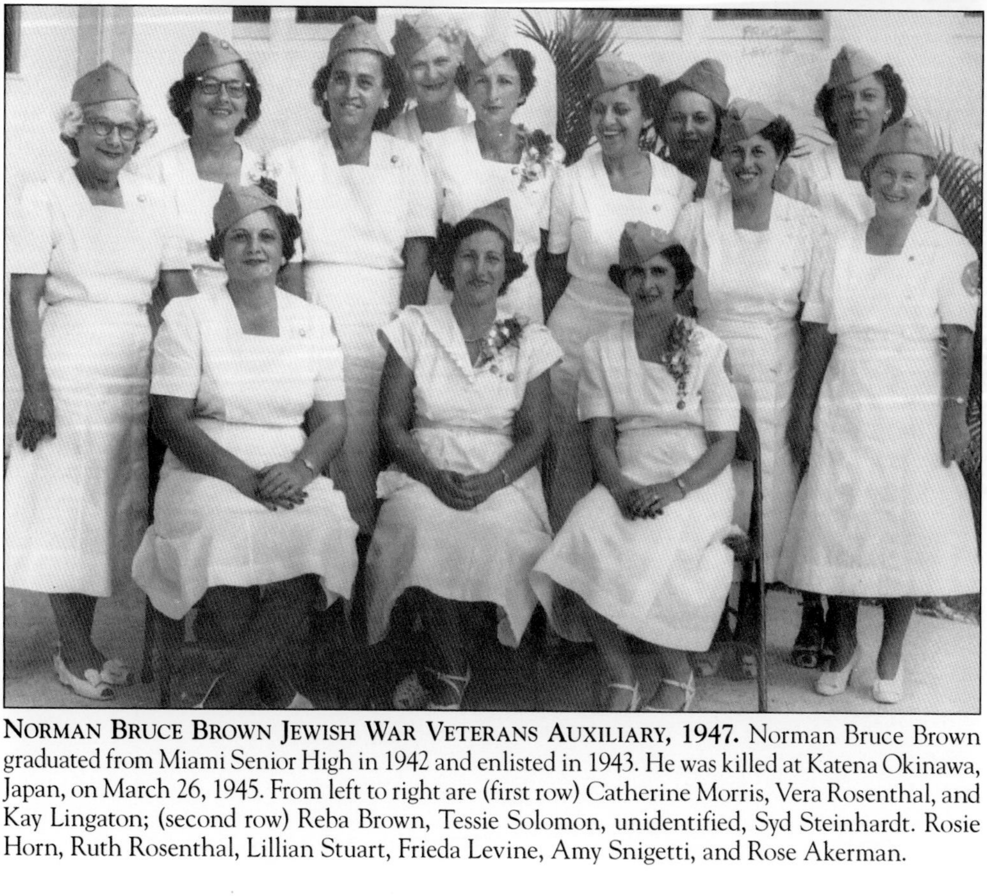

NORMAN BRUCE BROWN JEWISH WAR VETERANS AUXILIARY, 1947. Norman Bruce Brown graduated from Miami Senior High in 1942 and enlisted in 1943. He was killed at Katena Okinawa, Japan, on March 26, 1945. From left to right are (first row) Catherine Morris, Vera Rosenthal, and Kay Lingaton; (second row) Reba Brown, Tessie Solomon, unidentified, Syd Steinhardt. Rosie Horn, Ruth Rosenthal, Lillian Stuart, Frieda Levine, Amy Snigetti, and Rose Akerman.

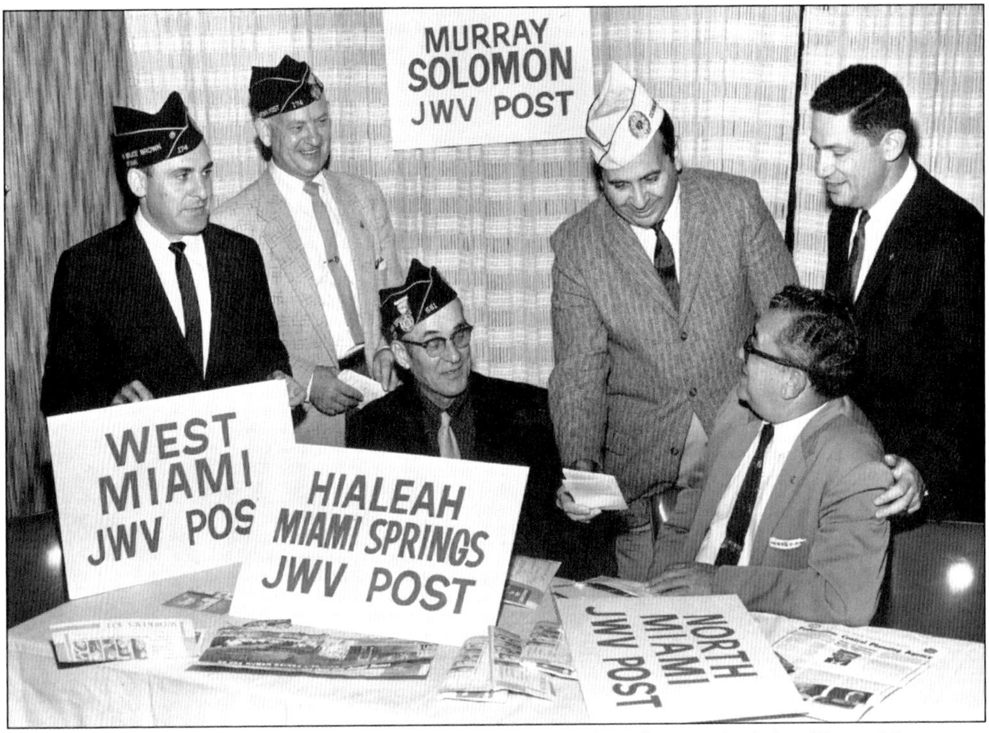

JEWISH WAR VETERANS FROM MIAMI POSTS, 1959. Standing first on the left is Henry Norton, at right is judge Milton Friedman, sitting at right is Ralph Grossman, and the others are unidentified. Friedman was a leader in most early Jewish organizations, especially B'nai B'rith. Even facing antisemitism, he was elected a U.S. Circuit Court judge (1968–1985). In 2001, the Miami City Commission designated a street to be named Judge Milton A. Friedman Way to "honor the judge who ordered desegregation of the Miami courts."

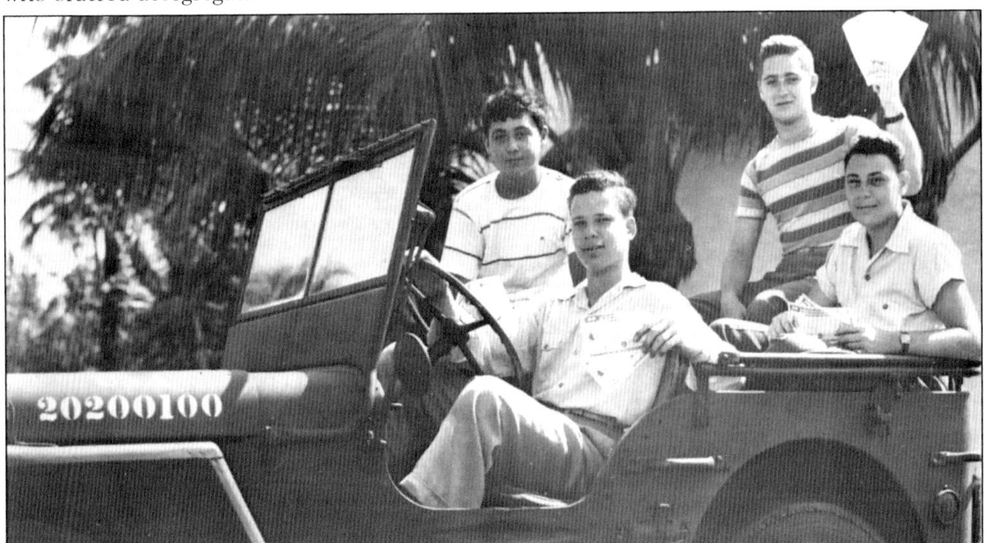

AZA, 1945. Aleph Zadik Aleph is a Zionist youth organization of B'nai B'rith. The Royal Palm chapter raised $14,400 in the War Bond Campaign to buy 12 jeeps. From left to right are Norton Segal, Mel Frumkes, Jack Platte, and Richard Cohen.

MILTON WEISS. When the Greater Miami Jewish Federation offices were erected in 1970, Milton (left) was the president. Here he is joined by Robert Miller. Milton, son of pioneer Rosie Weiss, was the first Jewish Dade County School Board member (1941–1953). Other Jewish members who have served on the board are Anna Brenner Meyers (1953–1972), Jack Gordon (1961–1969), William Lehman (1967–1972), Phyllis Miller (1972–1980), Michael Krop (1980–1992), Betsy Kaplan (1988–2004), and Martin Karp (2004–present).

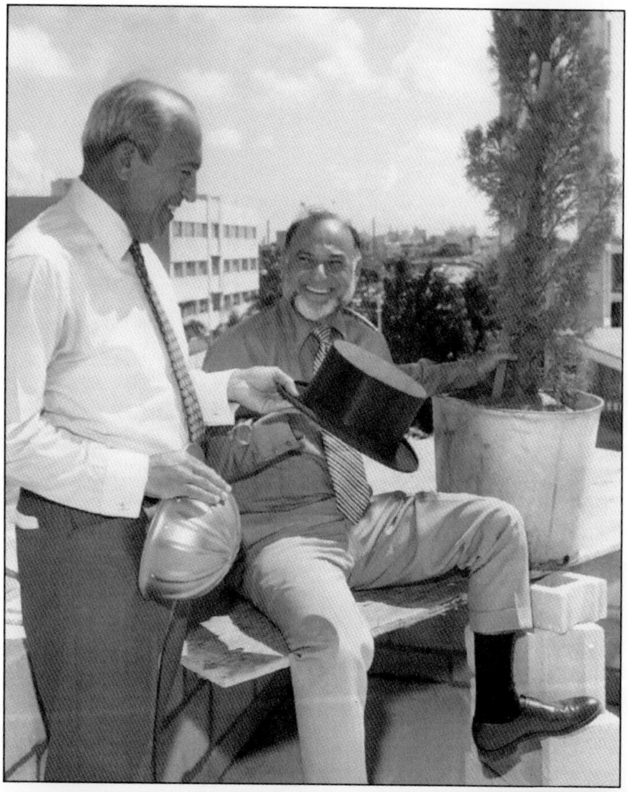

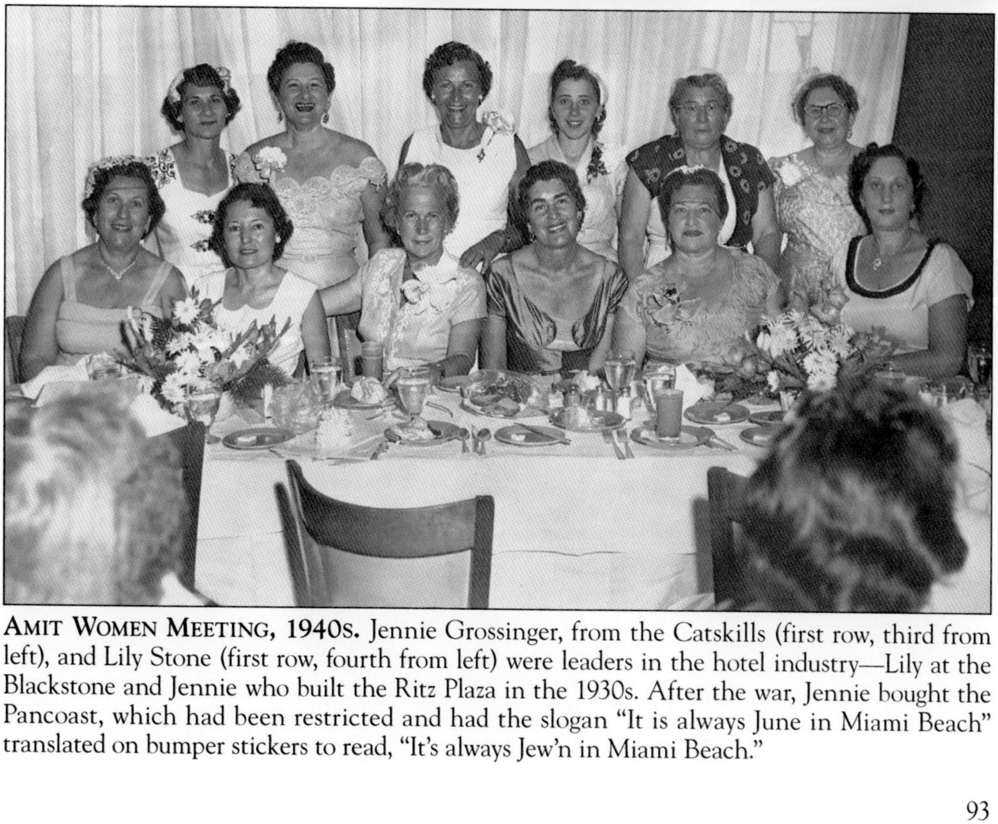

AMIT WOMEN MEETING, 1940S. Jennie Grossinger, from the Catskills (first row, third from left), and Lily Stone (first row, fourth from left) were leaders in the hotel industry—Lily at the Blackstone and Jennie who built the Ritz Plaza in the 1930s. After the war, Jennie bought the Pancoast, which had been restricted and had the slogan "It is always June in Miami Beach" translated on bumper stickers to read, "It's always Jew'n in Miami Beach."

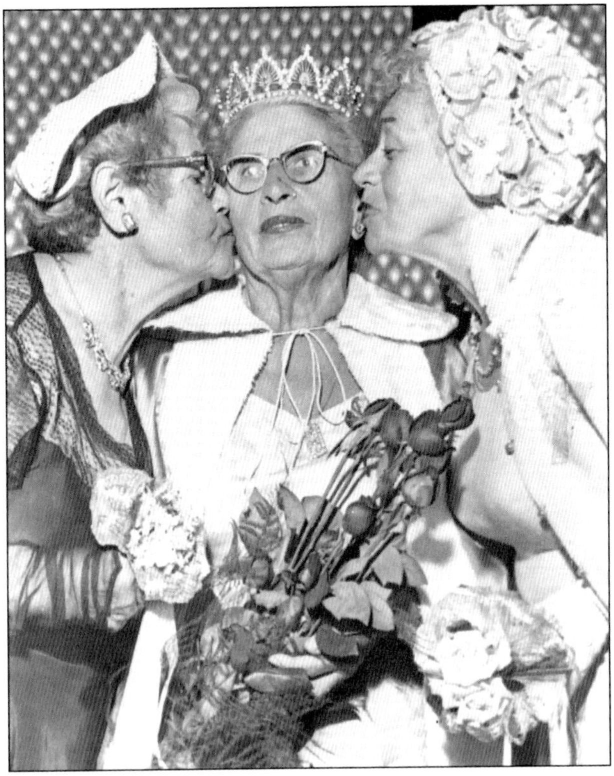

IDA COHEN, 1959. The Women's Auxiliary for the Miami Jewish Home and Hospital of the Aged (MJHH) honored their founder. Kissing Ida are Celia Wohl and Minnie Levine. In 1940, a non-Jew, Adam Reis, left Ida $10,000 for a "worthy Jewish cause," as he stated. She called a meeting and proposed they create a home for indigent Jews. Today MJHH Douglas Gardens' 20-acre campus has expanded beyond the county line and is considered by those in the field the most comprehensive geriatric care center in the Southeast.

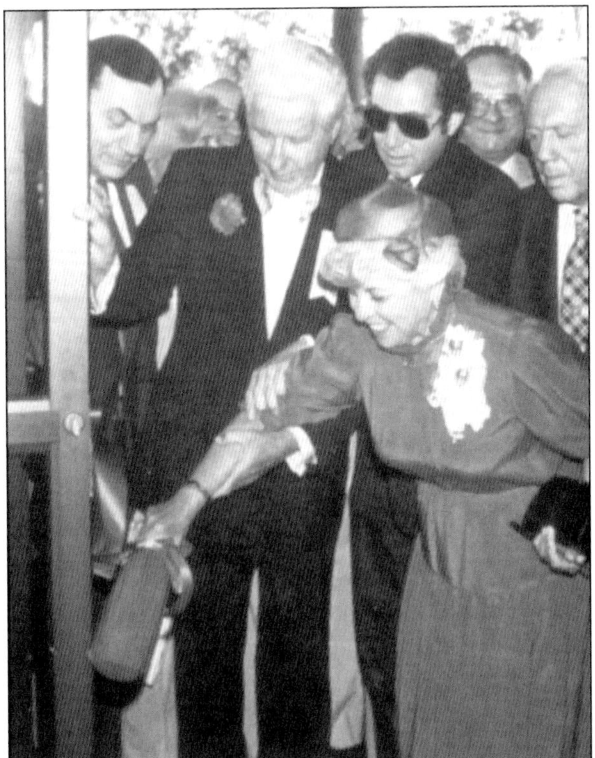

IRVING AND HAZEL CYPEN. Judge Irving Cypen (center) has served on the board of the Miami Jewish Home and Hospital for the Aged Douglas Gardens for more than 50 years, and with his wife, Hazel (front), remains in top leadership. Irving Cypen served as municipal judge for the City of Miami Beach and then as judge in the 11th Judicial Circuit Court of Florida from 1958 to 1963.

ISADORE AND FLORENCE HECHT, 1940S. Isadore Hecht settled on Miami Beach in 1929. Ten years later, he brought his bride, Florence, to join him. The Hechts have played important roles in the Jewish, business, civic, and philanthropic communities. They have been major donors to Florida State University and the University of Miami, where the first residential college is dedicated to Florence.

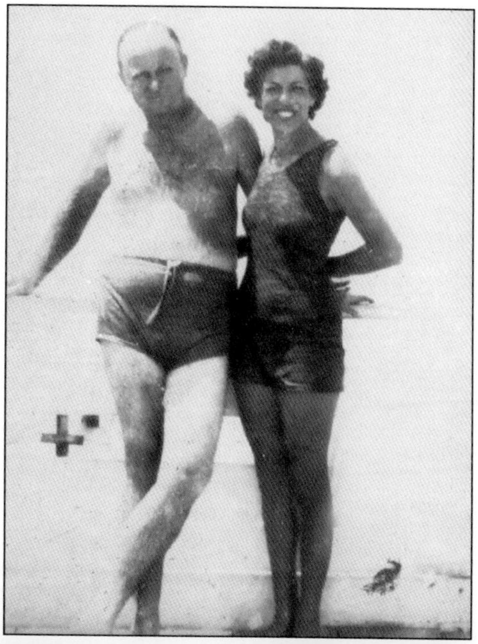

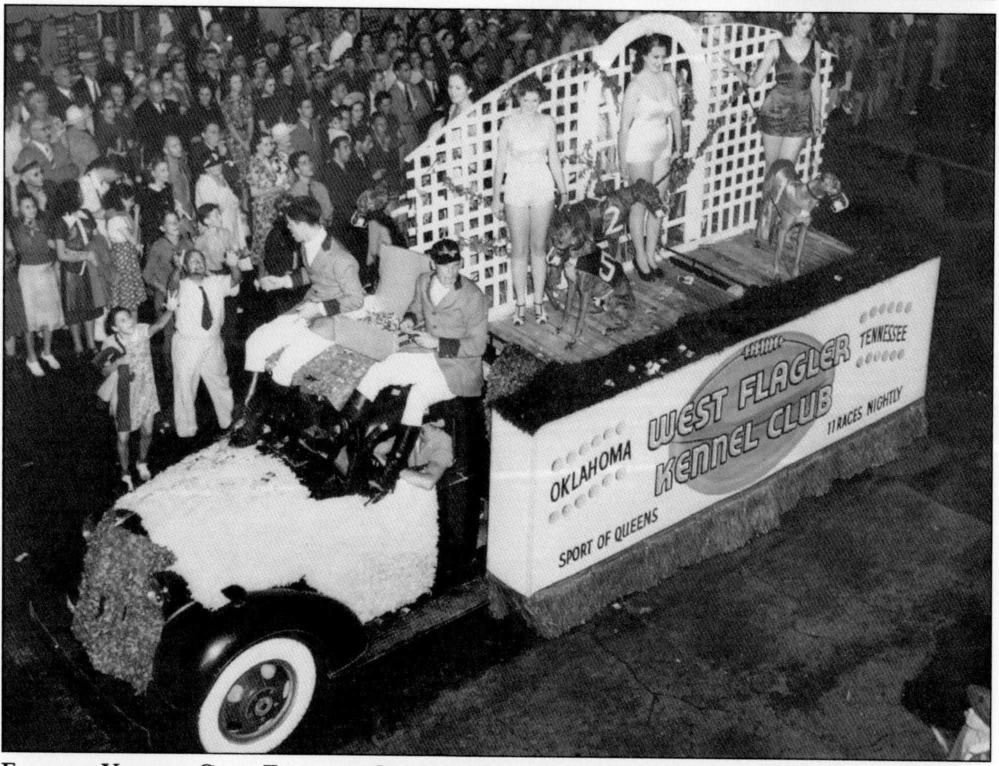

FLAGLER KENNEL CLUB FLOAT IN ORANGE BOWL PARADE IN MIAMI, 1950S. In 1953, Isadore Hecht purchased the Kennel Club of Miami, which became the largest greyhound facility in America. The family still owns and manages the club as Flagler Dog Track. Hecht began his climb to success by unloading produce at his father's market in Jacksonville and founded the West Indies Fruit Company, which was later acquired by Del Monte Corporation.

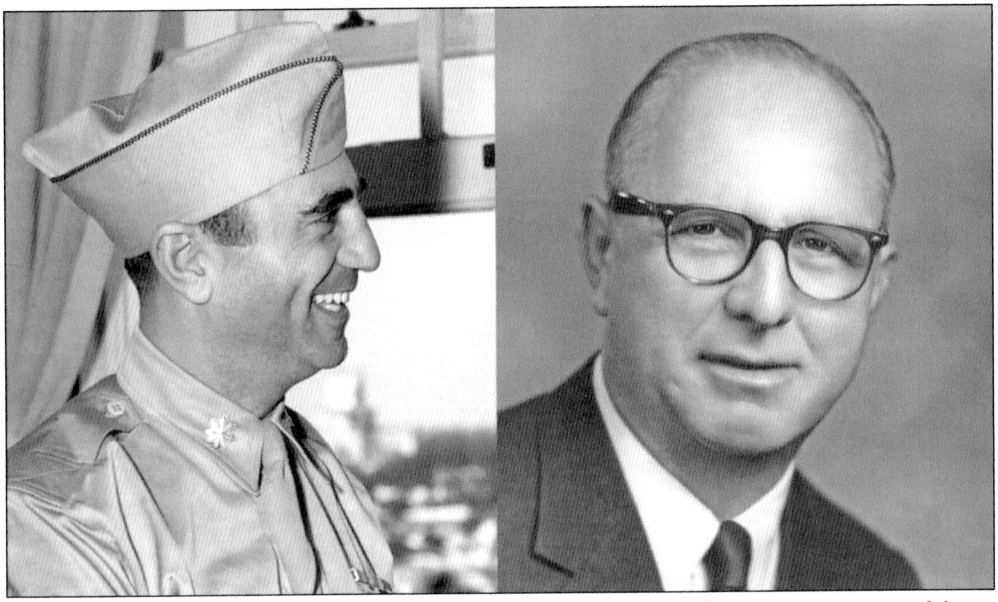

Baron De Hirsch Meyer (Left) and Leonard Abess, 1940s. They met at a party on Miami Beach in 1926, discussed some investments, agreed, shook hands, and these "Gold Dust Twins" started a 48-year business partnership and friendship that included building homes, hotels, and banks. Both were deeply involved in the Jewish and civic communities, including their position as leaders of Mount Sinai Medical Center from the time of its creation to the end of their lives.

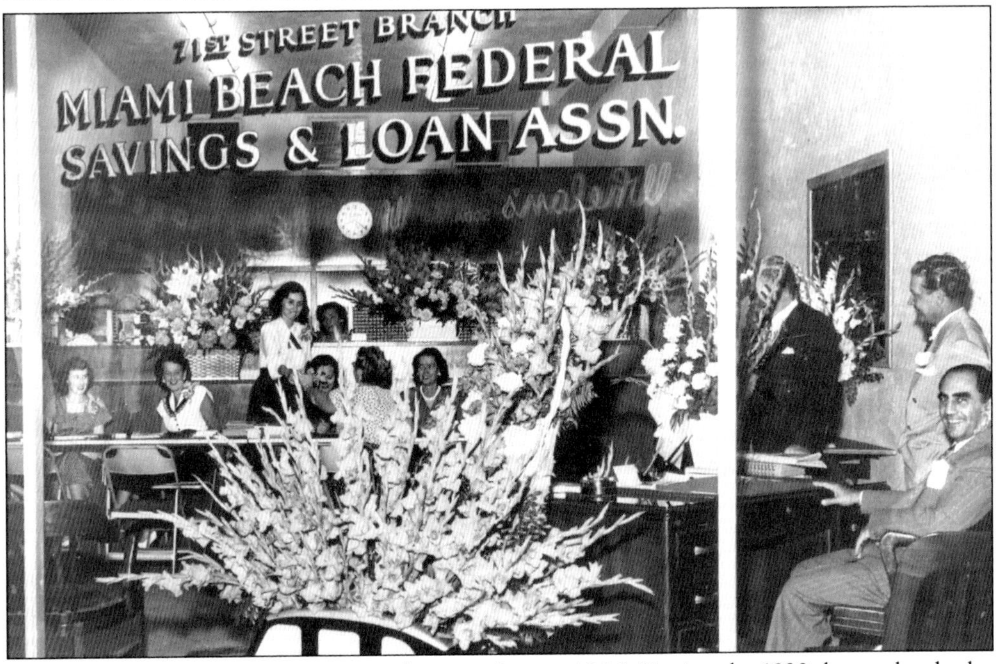

Opening of Miami Beach Federal Savings Loan, 1936. During the 1920s boom, land sales were soaring. Some Jews became involved in construction, others in land sales. These required financing and soon charters for federal savings and loan associations were granted. Baron de Hirsch Meyer (far right) and Leonard Abess were granted the second charter in the United States in 1933.

EVOLUTION OF CITY NATIONAL BANK. In the 1940s, Shepard Broad organized North Shore Bank. Leonard Abess and Baron deHirsch Meyer were stockholders. Broad left and Abess and deHirsch Meyer continued with the bank that evolved into City National Bank. There was a rocky period, and the Abess family was forced out. In 1983, Leonard Abess Jr. became the new CEO, reversed the fate, and headed the expanding family business until a sale in 2008.

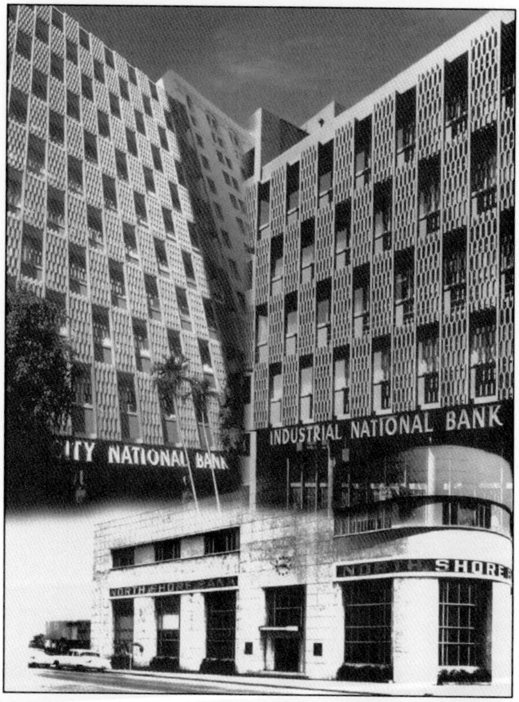

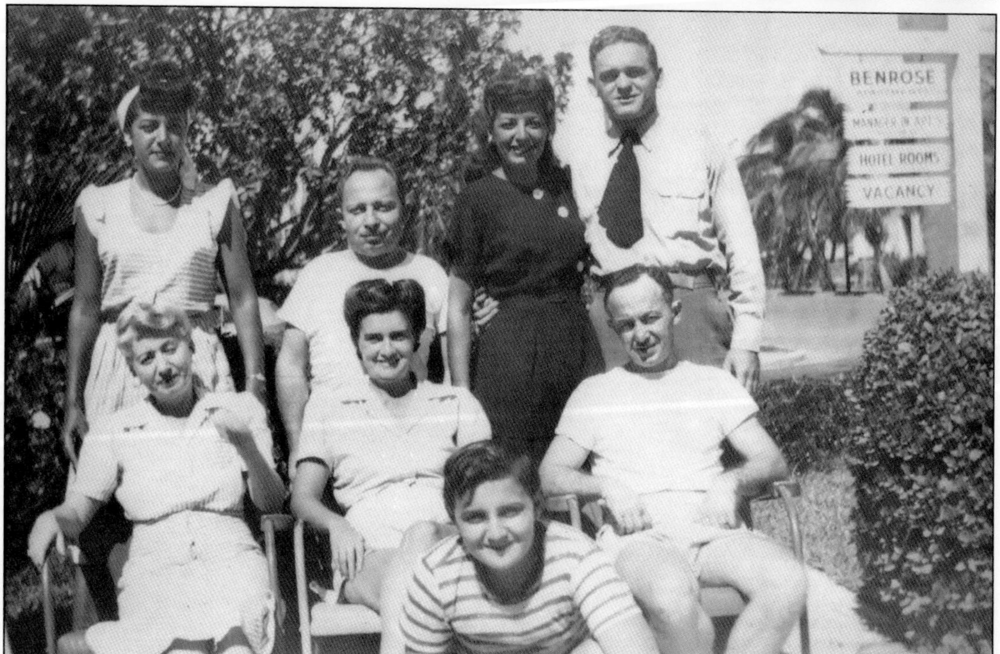

SAMUEL AND SHIRLEY GOLDBERG FAMILY, 1943. Samuel (seated, right) owned Beach Hardware and Paint. His son Bart Goldberg (front center) grew up to be an attorney who joined Jefferson Bank in 1964 and has worked through civic organizations to upgrade and redevelop Miami Beach. Bart is chairman for the South Florida Region of Colonial Bank, which purchased Jefferson in 1997. This photograph includes Shirley Hoffman, Harry Goldberg, and Shirley Kleper Goldberg (seated center).

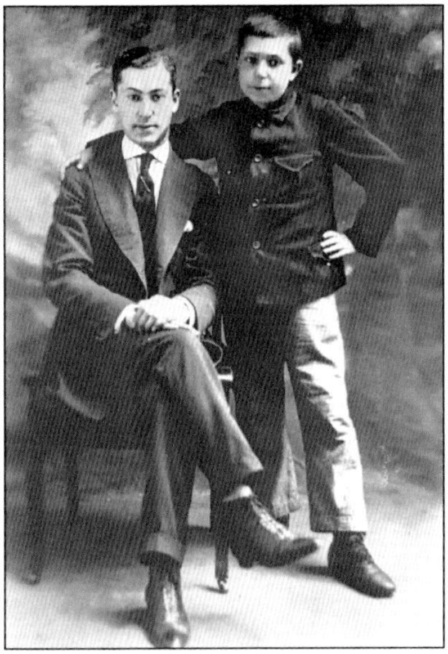

SHEPARD BROAD, 1920. Orphaned, Broad (right) left Russia at age 14 and was sent to Canada by HIAS (Hebrew Immigrant Aid Society). Adolph Stark (left) rescued him from the ship. He was sent to New York to meet a relative, and he later went to law school and began practicing there. A fishing trip with clients to Florida set the life stage for Broad, who became a giant personality in Greater Miami.

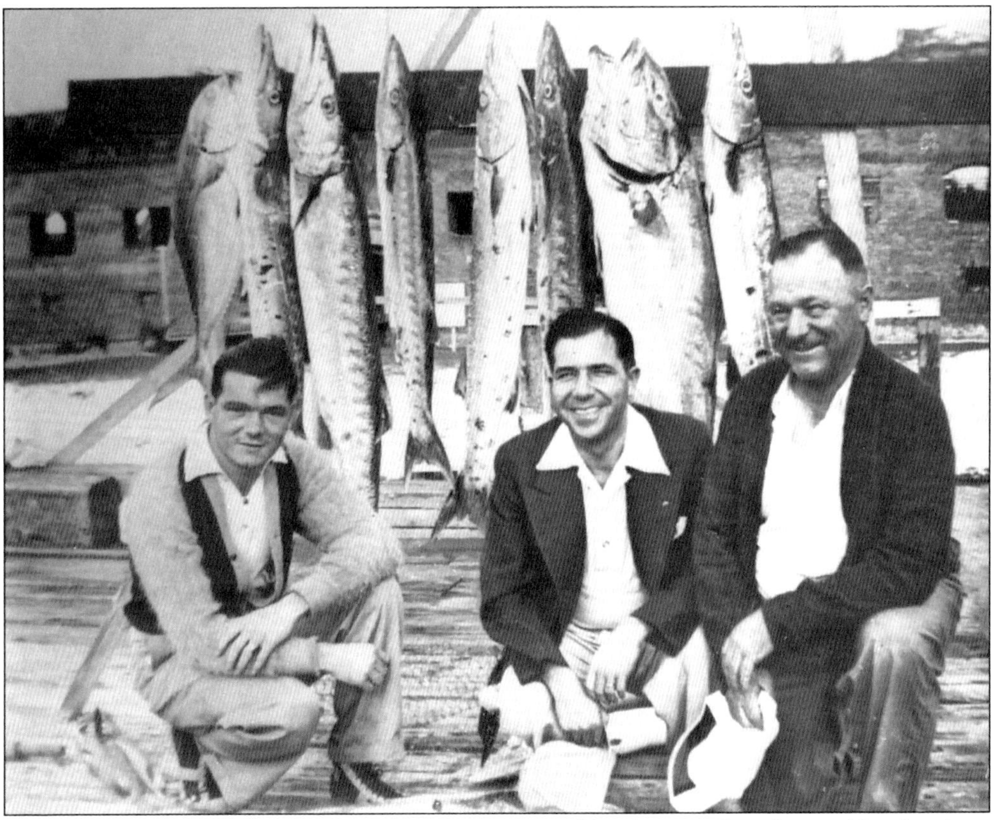

SHEPARD BROAD (CENTER), KEY WEST, 1939. Inspired by this trip, Broad moved his family to Miami Beach. He became a key person for Aliyah Bet, the clandestine movement that illegally brought Holocaust survivors to Palestine by sea. He organized the local effort to purchase and refit three ships (*Hatikva, Geula,* and *The Jewish State*) on the Miami River then stocked them for the journey from Miami to Europe to rescue 70,000 stranded Jews.

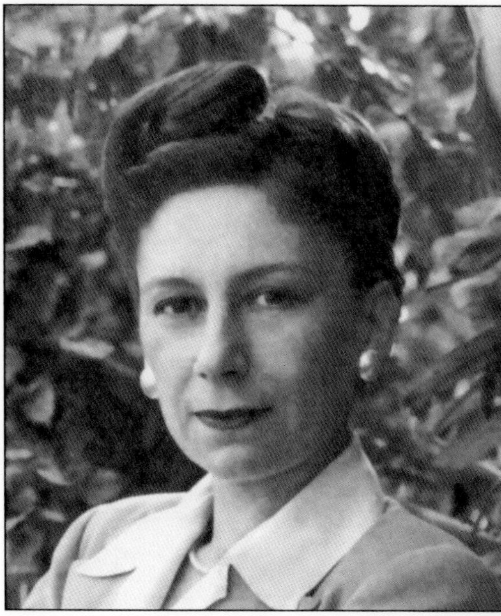

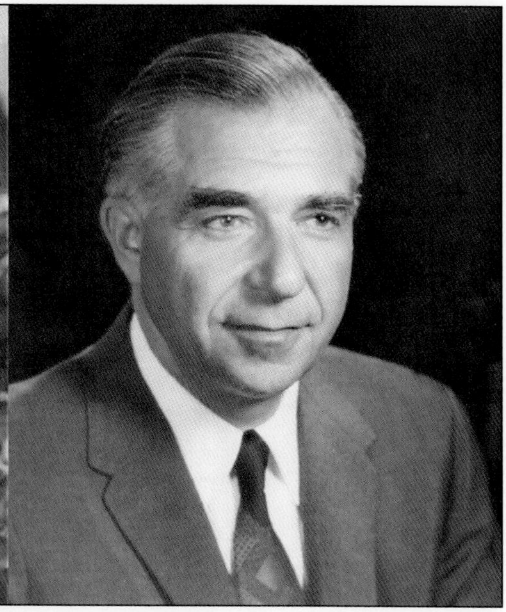

RUTH K. AND SHEPARD BROAD, 1940S. Ruth was a decision-making partner to Shepard. In 1945, they acquired mangrove swamp between the beach barrier island and mainland of North Miami. They dredged it to create their town, Bay Harbor Islands (BHI), by 1947. Island waterfront lots were delivered bulkhead (with seawalls) to the purchasers, which was a first for this area. Shepard Broad was elected the first mayor of BHI and served for 26 consecutive years.

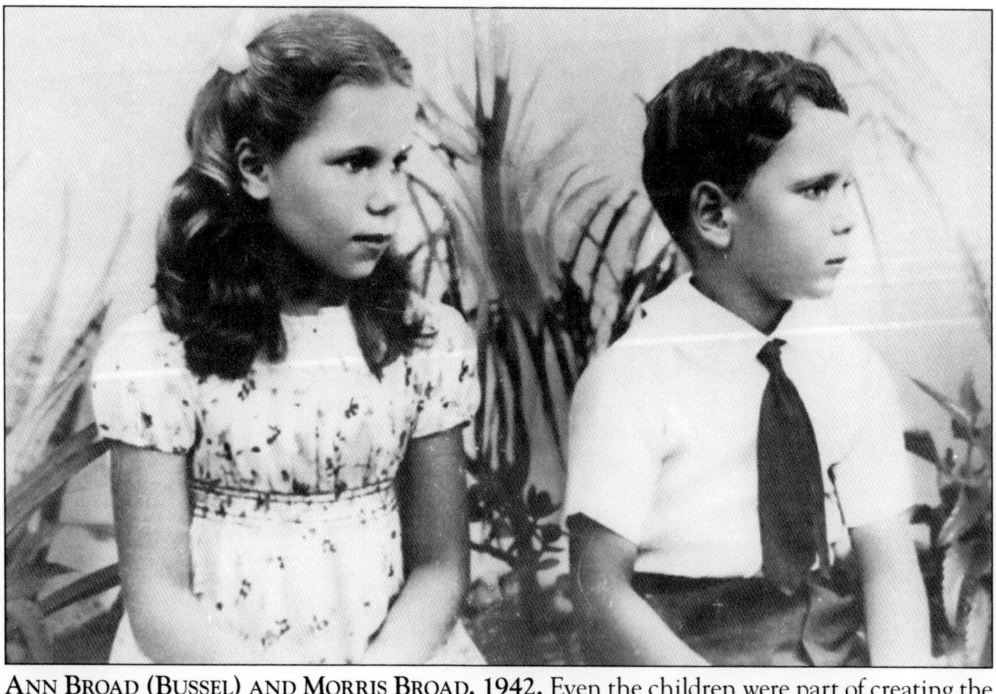

ANN BROAD (BUSSEL) AND MORRIS BROAD, 1942. Even the children were part of creating the town, by running errands and providing construction oversight. They grew up in a Zionist home, visited by many personalities from the State of Israel. In Miami, Shepard was a founder of American Savings and Loan Association and other banks, and the law firm of Broad and Cassel.

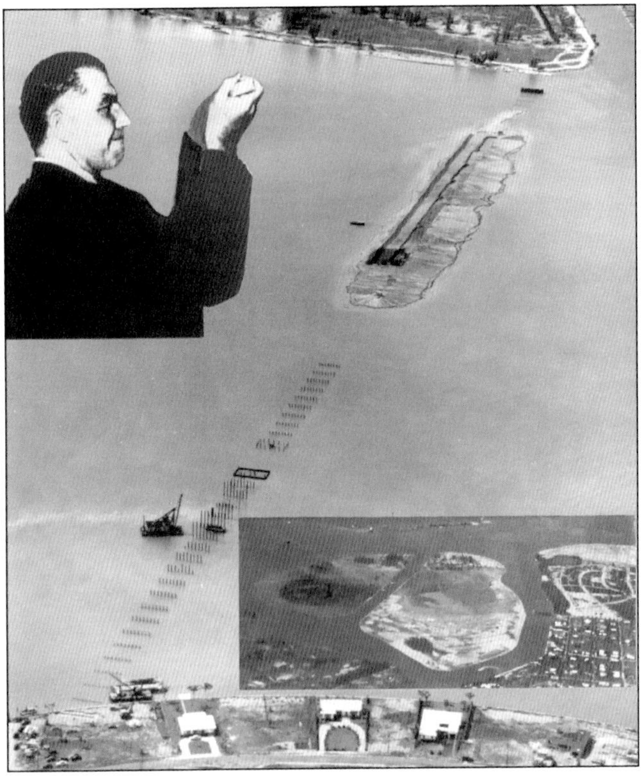

BROAD CAUSEWAY, 1951. Bay Harbor Islands lots (lower right) sold well, but the Broads knew they needed to provide a shorter route between the mainland and the Beach to keep pace with the increased traffic. By 1951, the $2,150,000 causeway opened (shown under construction here); it is used by millions of motorists each year. Shepard Broad (shown pulling the dredge switch) died in 2001 at the age of 95 in his Bay Harbor Islands home.

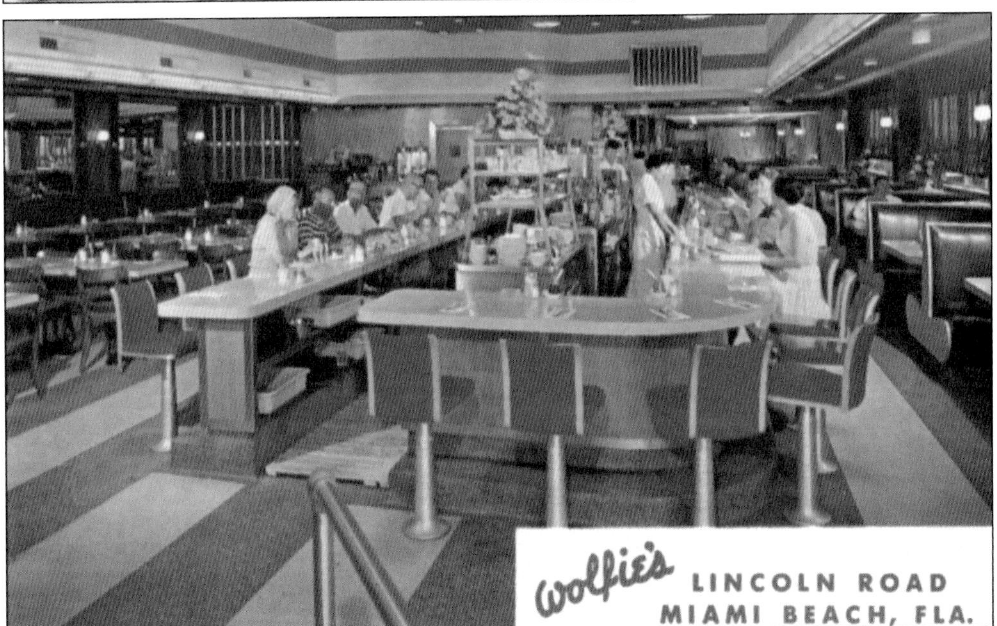

WOLFIE'S RESTAURANT. Wolfie Cohen came to Florida in 1932. In 1947, he opened the original Wolfie's Restaurant at Collins Avenue and Twenty-first Street, the first of seven restaurants in the area. The deli, the last vestige of Miami's Yiddish past, was the site of many political events. Wolfie's had continuous Jewish owners—Cohen, 1947–1953; Edwin Lassman, 1953–1984; and Joseph and David Nevel, 1984–until it closed in 2002.

Miami's Only Jewish Mayor, Abe Aronovitz, 1953–1955. Abe, who came to Miami in 1922, was one of 10 sons of David Aronovitz, who had arrived in Key West in 1889. After serving in World War II, he went into law practice. As mayor, he battled antisemitism, the police department, and slums. Also, he forced Florida Power and Light to cut rates. This was a time when Jews were scarce in the public life.

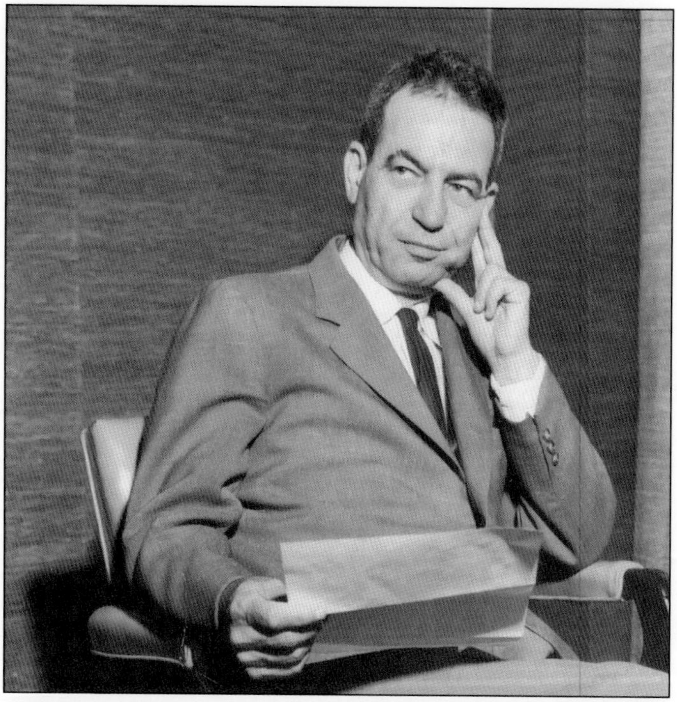

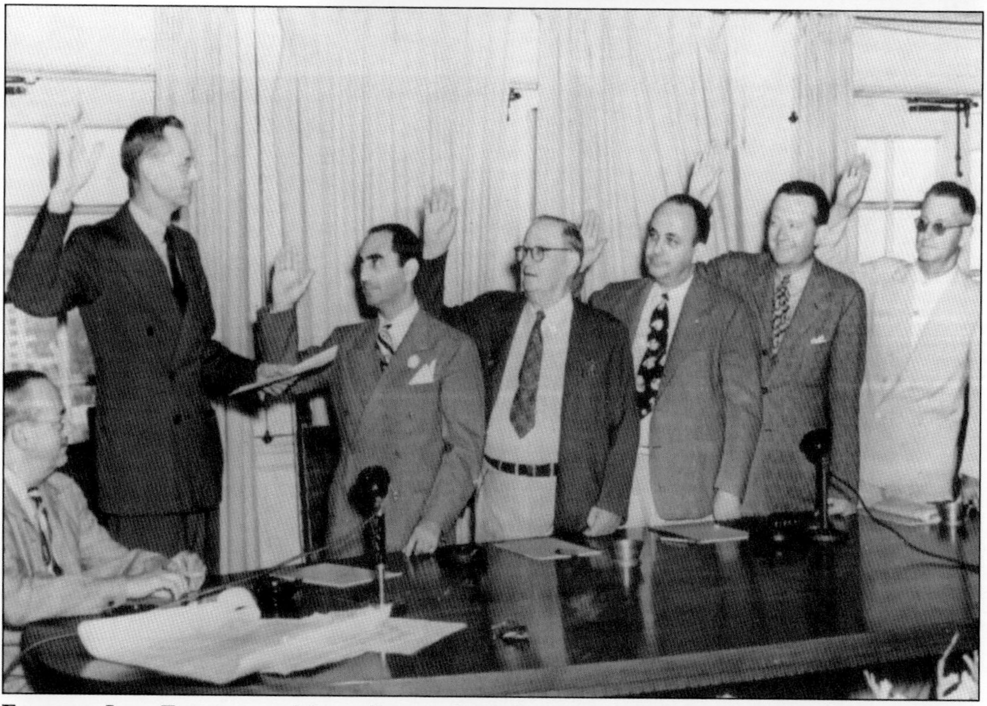

Earliest Jews Elected to Miami Beach City Council, 1939. Baron de Hirsch Meyer (third from left) arrived during the real estate boom and became a successful attorney and banker. In 1934, he was elected to the city council. In 1939, he was reelected and Mitchell Wolfson (second from right) was also elected. Meyer's contribution to the University of Miami funded five buildings and a law library that bears his name.

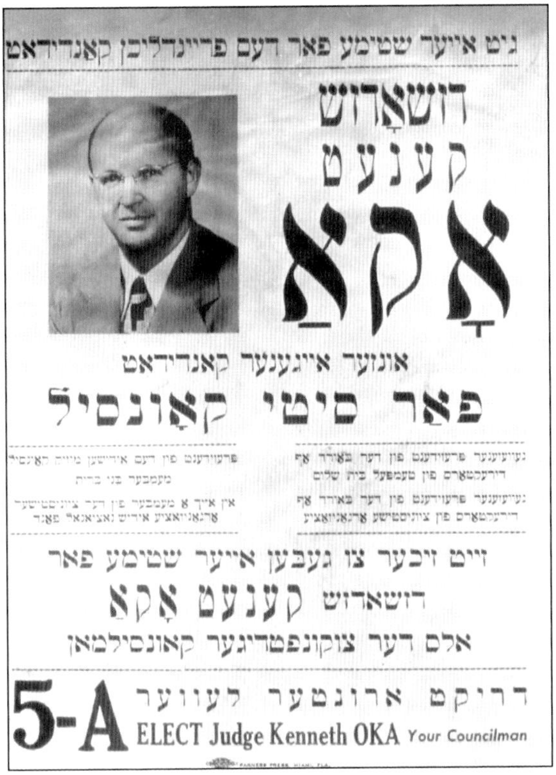

CAMPAIGN POSTER IN YIDDISH. This is a reflection of the heavily Jewish population on the Beach. Kenneth Oka, who served two terms as one of 15 Jewish mayors of Miami Beach (1957–1959, 1961–1963), was a lawyer and judge. His daughter Michele Oka Doner is an internationally acclaimed artist and designer whose prolific career spans four decades. She is best known for her public art commissions, including those at the Miami International Airport.

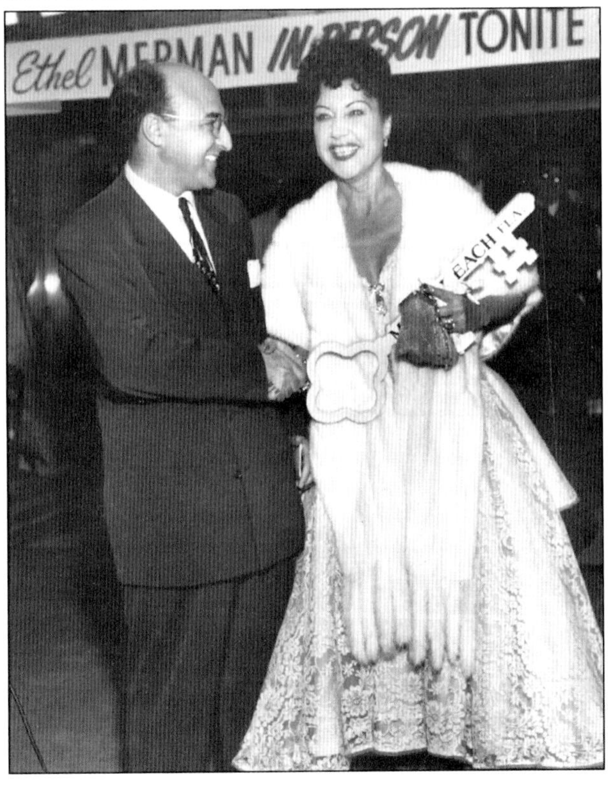

COUNCILMAN BURNETT ROTH PRESENTS KEY TO CITY OF MIAMI BEACH TO ETHEL MERMAN, 1951. This was the year Roth called a meeting of representatives of the taxi, hotel, motion picture, and restaurant industries to convince them that to continue their policy of "whites only" would destroy the convention industry and negatively affect the economy. The restrictions were lifted. Three years later, Roth held a meeting to talk about desegregation of the schools.

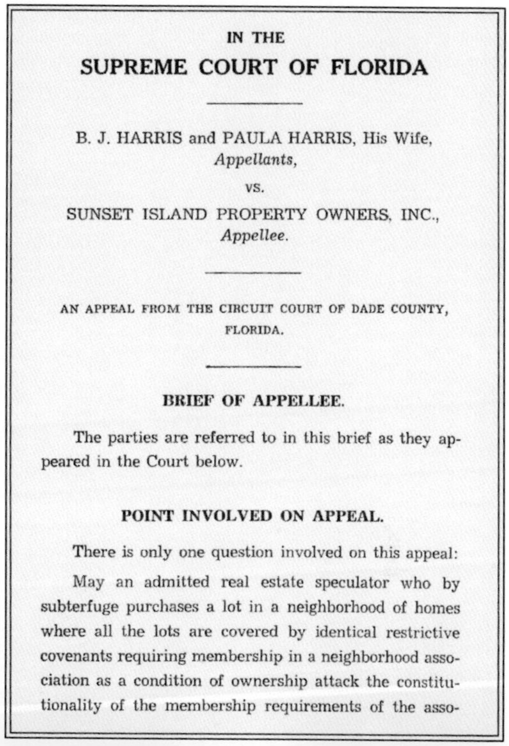

IN THE

SUPREME COURT OF FLORIDA

B. J. HARRIS and PAULA HARRIS, His Wife,
Appellants,

vs.

SUNSET ISLAND PROPERTY OWNERS, INC.,
Appellee.

AN APPEAL FROM THE CIRCUIT COURT OF DADE COUNTY, FLORIDA.

BRIEF OF APPELLEE.

The parties are referred to in this brief as they appeared in the Court below.

POINT INVOLVED ON APPEAL.

There is only one question involved on this appeal:

May an admitted real estate speculator who by subterfuge purchases a lot in a neighborhood of homes where all the lots are covered by identical restrictive covenants requiring membership in a neighborhood association as a condition of ownership attack the constitutionality of the membership requirements of the asso-

SUNSET ISLAND CASE, MIAMI BEACH, 1959. This community had a covenant that no one could buy a lot unless he or she were a member of the association, which excluded Jews. A Jew purchased a lot, was refused membership, and sued. The attorney was David Catsman. The Florida Supreme Court ruled that any attempt to prohibit property ownership because of race or religion was unconstitutional, a decision that changed the practice of illegal restrictions against Jews.

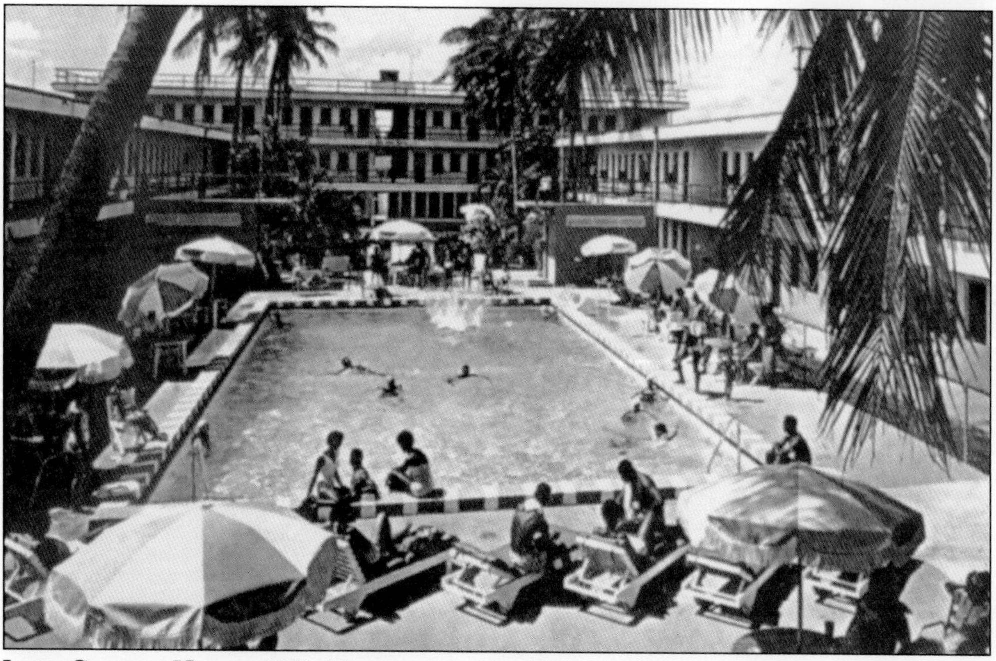

LORD CALVERT HOTEL, 1951. Miami was a segregated city when Ben Danbaum built this hotel for blacks. The best customers were the black entertainers who performed at Miami Beach hotels but were not allowed to sleep there or use the beaches. The hotel's name came from the popular whisky with the same name, as Danbaum owned a liquor distributorship. Ben's son-in-law Sam Rabin ran the hotel until 1962.

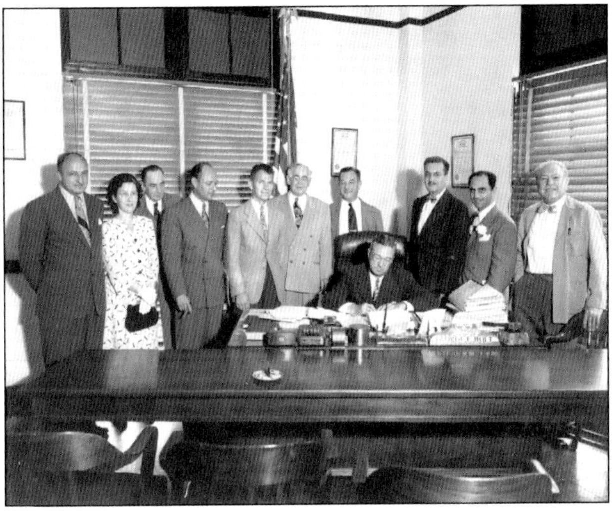

Mount Sinai Hospital, Miami Beach. When Jewish doctors returned from World War II, they were denied staff privileges in Greater Miami hospitals. Jewish leaders created their own hospital and received their charter from the State of Florida in 1946. Judge George E. Holt (seated) is the one signing, and from left to right are William D. Singer, Lois Dobrin, Arthur A. Ungar, Henry D. Williams, Dr. Morris Goodman, Monte Selig, Sam Blank, Max Orovitz, Baron de Hirsch Meyer, and Alex Van Straaten.

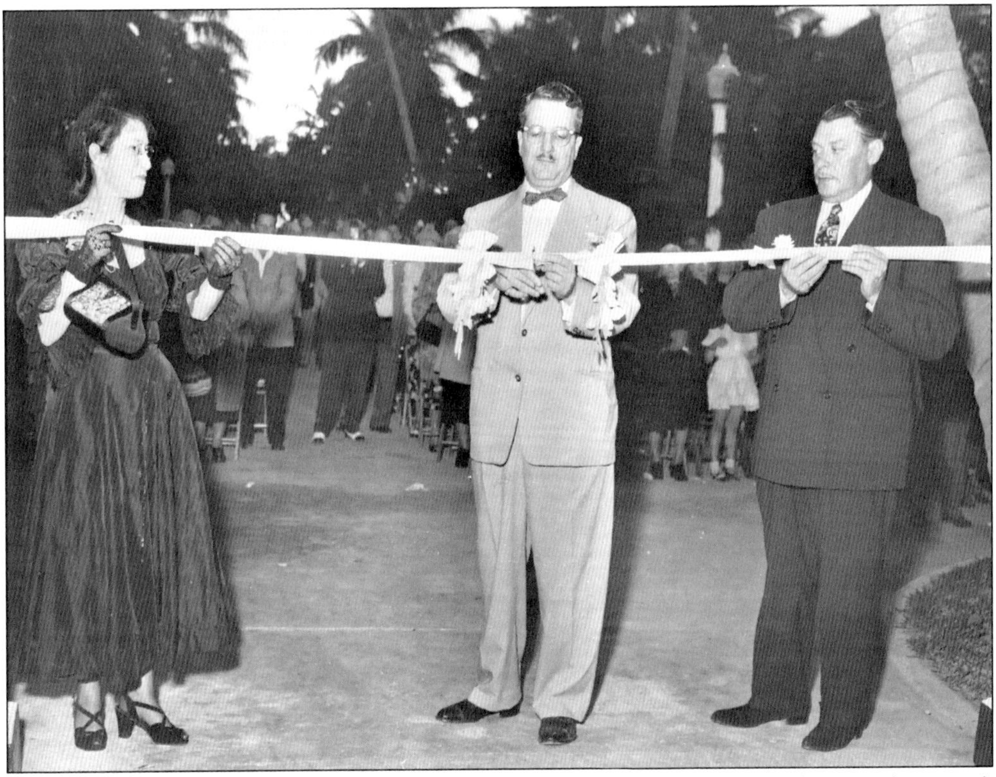

Ribbon Cutting at Mount Sinai Hospital, 1949. The first facility was Alton Road Hospital. Three years later, more space was needed, so the group purchased what once was Carl Fisher's restricted Nautilus Hotel from the City of Miami Beach at a cost of $1 per year for 20 years. The hospital opened with 258 beds. The ceremony was led by president Max Orovitz (center). Dan Ruskin (right), chairman of the building committee, and Lois Dobrin (left), president of the Women's Auxiliary, assist.

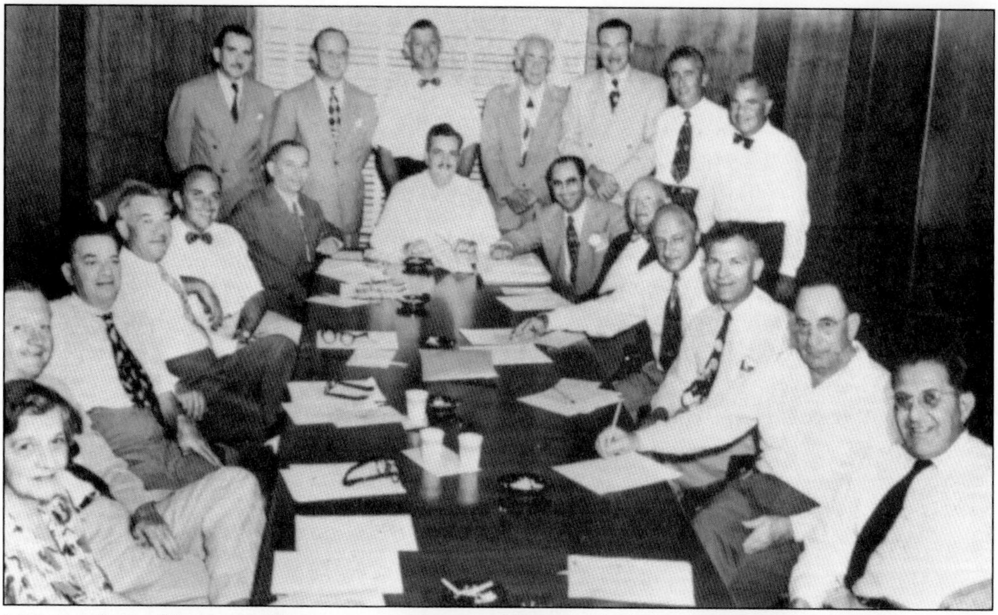

MOUNT SINAI HOSPITAL BOARD OF TRUSTEES MEETING, 1951. Pictured are, from left to right, (seated) Fannie Selig, Mitchell Wolfson, Joseph Stein, Sam Blank, Leonard Wien, Abe Goodman, Max Orovitz, Baron de Hirsch Meyer, Harry Sirkin, William Singer, Dr. Morris Goodman, Arthur Ungar, and Herbert Scher; (standing) Samuel Gertner, Leonard Abess, Carl Weinkle, Monte Selig, Stanley Myers, Sam Friedland, and Jack Ablin.

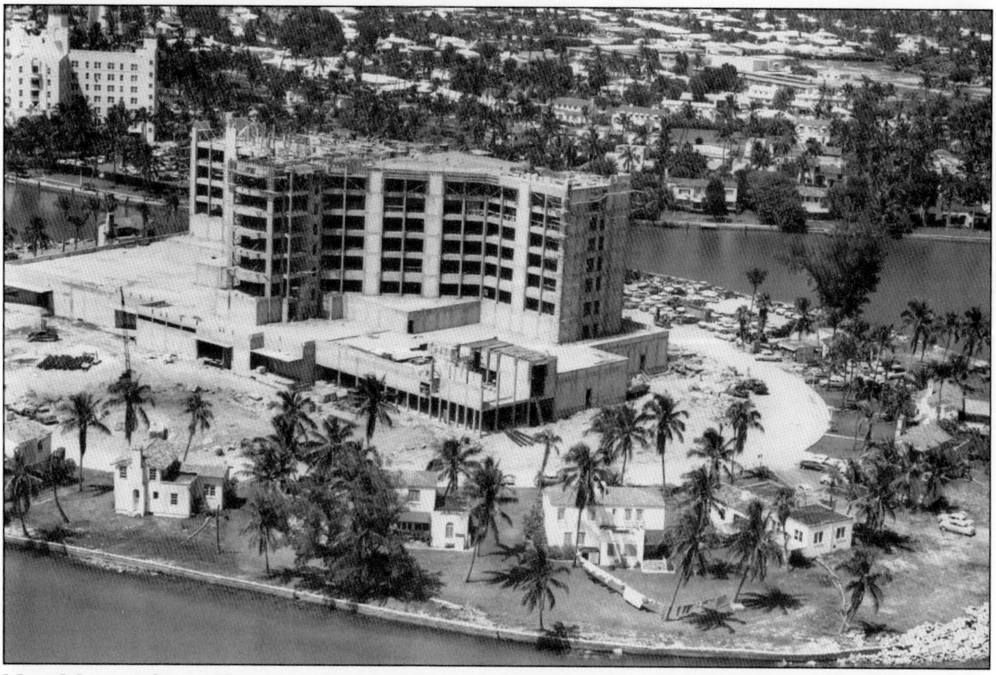

NEW MOUNT SINAI HOSPITAL UNDER CONSTRUCTION, 1959. The former Nautilus Hotel can be seen in the background of this 55-acre campus. Again, more beds were required to meet the needs of the growing population. Today the hospital is a state-of-the-art medical facility and teaching hospital that continues to expand and is the largest employer on Miami Beach.

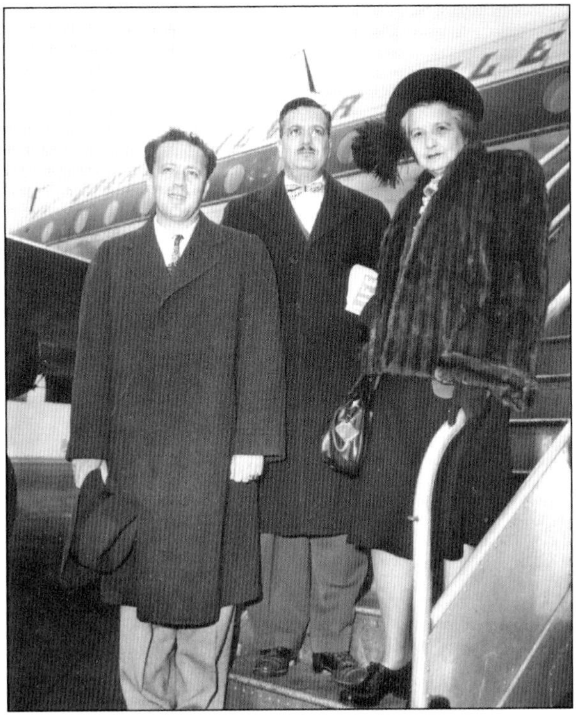

Greater Miami Jewish Federation Delegation to Europe and Palestine, 1947. From left to right are Rabbi Irving Lehrman, president Max Orovitz, and Women's Division chair Fannie Selig. They visited Displaced Persons camps in Europe, then arrived in Palestine on November 29, the day the United Nations voted for partition. Orovitz was approached by Xiel Federmann, from the Haganah, to lend him $5,000. Orovitz agreed but under the condition he see why the money was needed; thus, he witnessed the landing of a boatload of "illegal" immigrants from Europe. The captain had to be handed the $5,000 before he would allow disembarking of his human cargo.

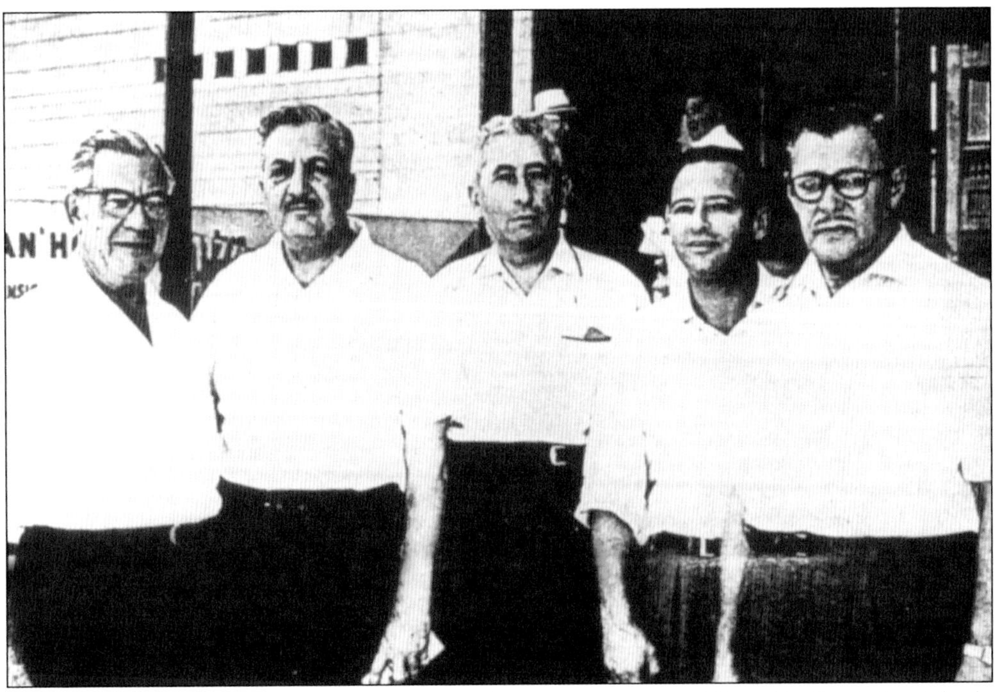

Miami Group. When Max Orovitz returned to Miami, he interested Sam Friedland, Sam Blank, Dan Ruskin, I. L. Mintzer, and Louis Stein in creating a joint venture to boost Israel's economy. They funded the construction of the Dan Hotel in Tel Aviv, which opened in 1953. This was the first of many hotels that were built or operated by the Dan Hotel chain, which became the largest in Israel. From left to right are Blank, Orovitz, Friedland, Federmann, and Ruskin.

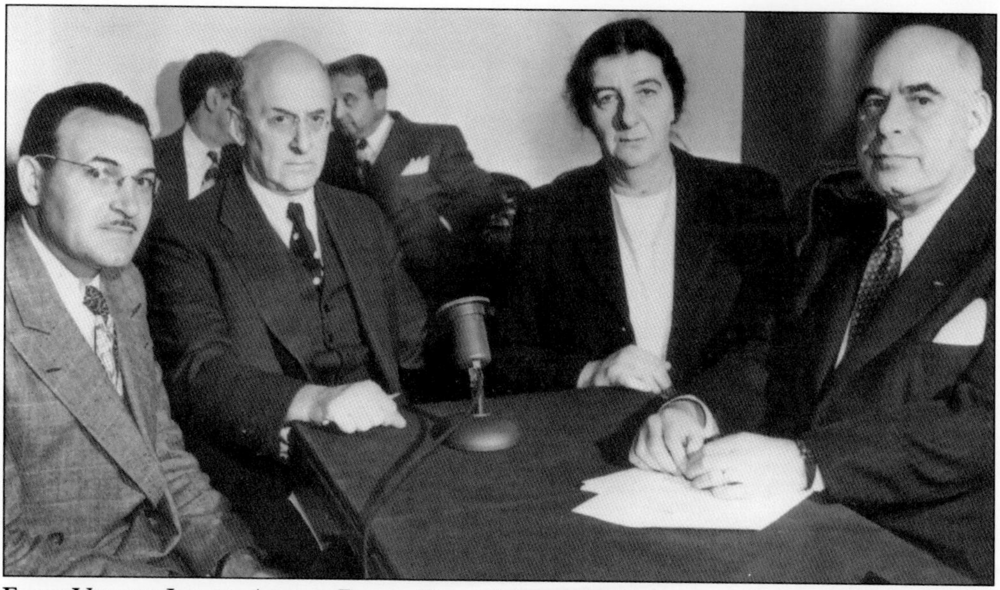

FIRST UNITED JEWISH APPEAL RADIO-THON, MIAMI, 1948. Prior to the United Nations vote for Israeli statehood on May 14, 1948, Golda Meyerson (Meir) appealed to American Jewry for $50 million so that Israel could defend herself against the Arab states. Top leadership appealed for funds. From left to right are Stanley Myers of Miami, president of the Council of Jewish Federations; Henry Morganthau, first national chairman of United Jewish Appeal; Golda Meyerson (Meir); and New York governor Herbert Lehman, first chair of the State of Israel Bonds.

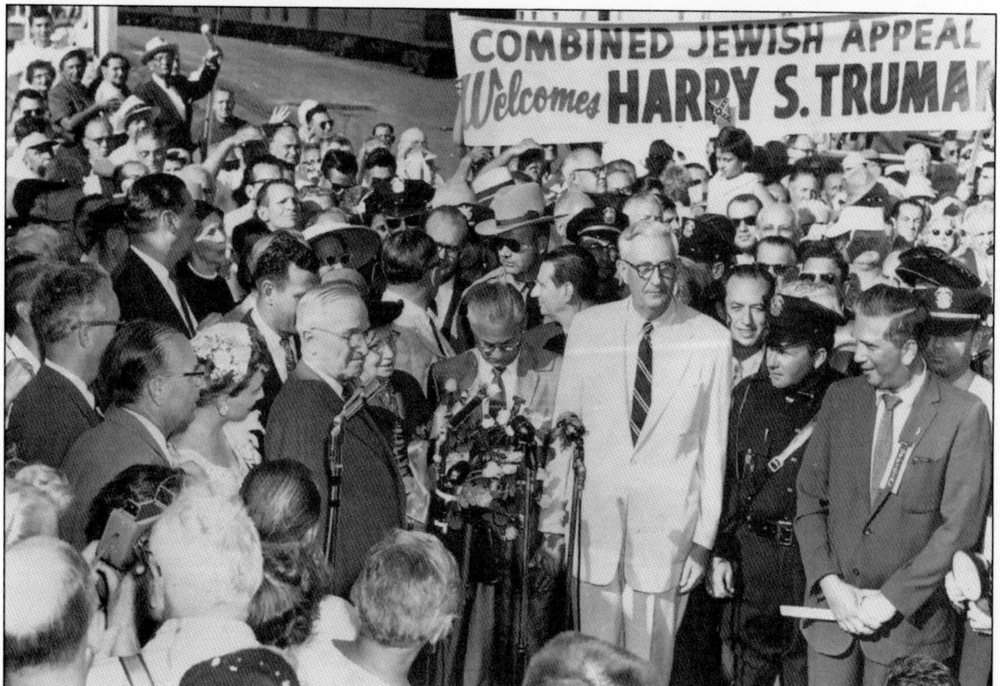

RALLY FOR COMBINED JEWISH APPEAL, MIAMI, 1949. The Miami Jewish community greets U.S. president Harry Truman as they express their appreciation for his recognition of an Israeli statehood.

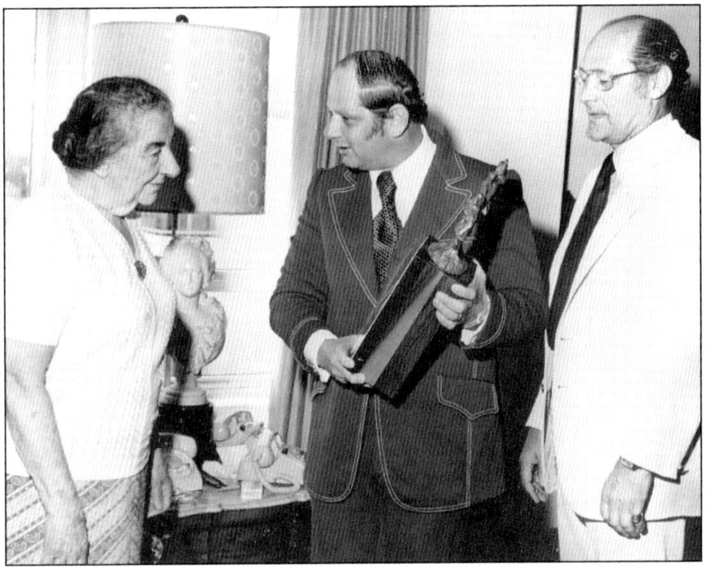

UNITED JEWISH APPEAL (UJA), MIAMI BEACH, 1973. Robert Russell (right) was the first Floridian to serve as a national officer of UJA. Golda Meir (left) played a major role in raising money for Israel. She often traveled to Florida communities where she received support and friendship. The Miami Jewish community responded generously to her appeals, such as this one with Robert Russell and Harry "Hap" Levy (center).

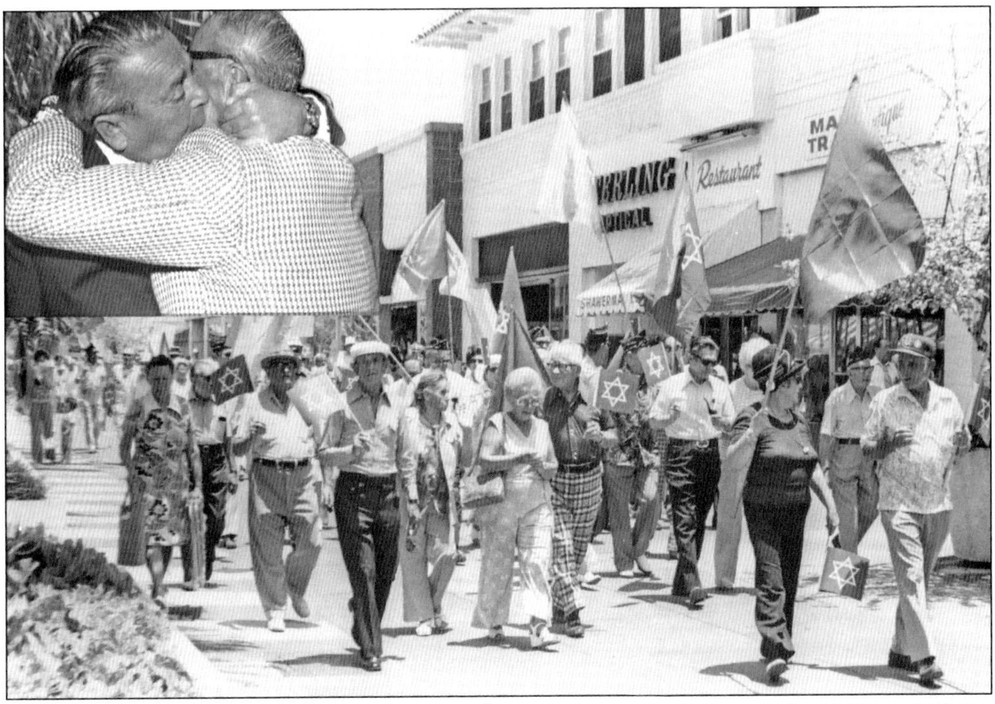

SPEAKING OUT FOR SOVIET JEWRY, LINCOLN ROAD MALL, 1977. During the 1960s and 1970s, Miami Jews protested the Soviet Union's attempts to destroy their Jewish communities, close down synagogues, and deny permissions to emigrate. The Soviets often imprisoned leaders of the Jewish movement. In response, Jewish communities in Florida joined others in staging demonstrations and rallies, lobbying in Washington, and by (shown inset) sponsoring Soviet Jewish families to resettle in U.S. communities.

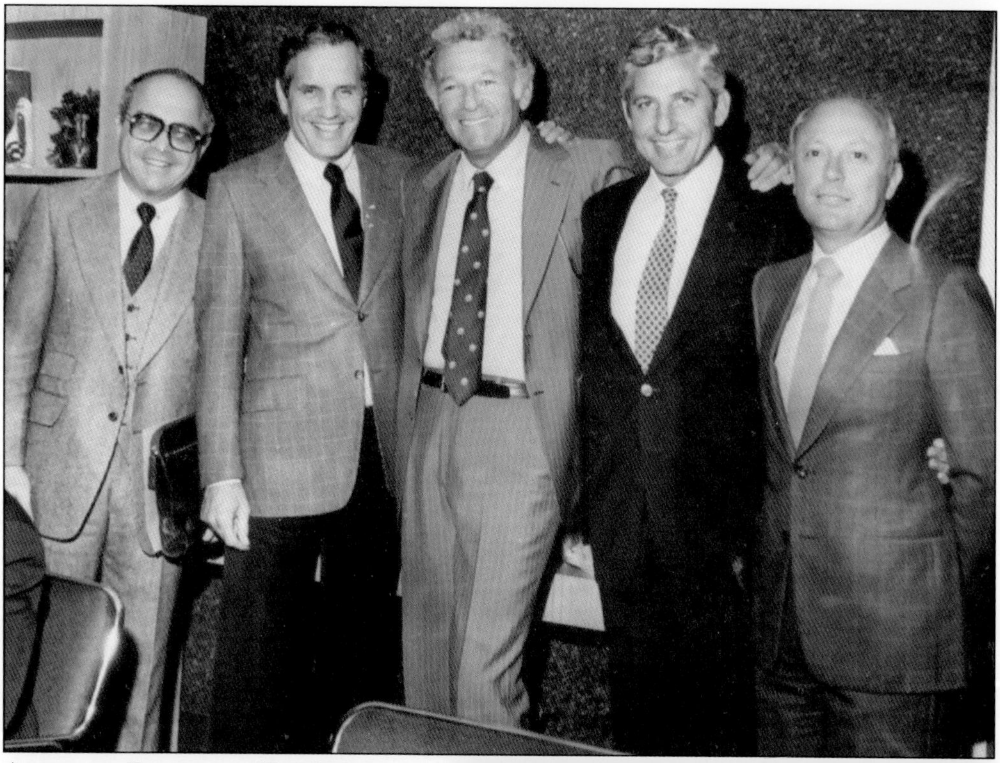

AMERICAN FRIENDS OF TEL AVIV UNIVERSITY RECEPTION, 1981. Miami Jewish leaders host fund-raisers to support all Israeli organizations. From left to right are Haim Wiener, Kenneth Schwartz, Norman Braman, Norman Lipoff, and Bernardo Batievsky. Norman Lipoff, in Miami since 1950 and an attorney with Greenberg Traurig, was national chairman of the UJA (1990–1994). In 1984, he joined the Board of Governors of the Jewish Agency for Israel and served on the executive committee in the 1990s.

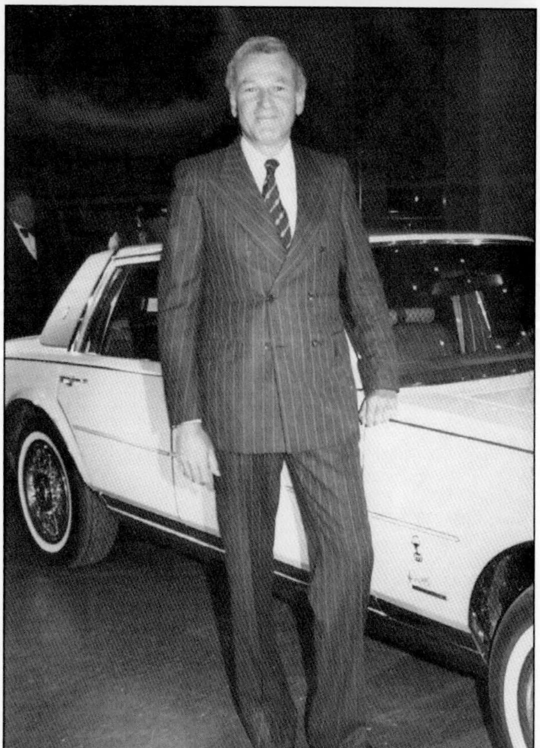

NORMAN BRAMAN. Braman moved to Florida in the early 1970s, bought a Cadillac dealership in Tampa, and then in 1975, he bought another in Miami. Today he is chair of dealerships in four cities. Braman and his wife, Irma, are avid art collectors. Civic activist Norman is one of the founders of the Holocaust Memorial on Miami Beach and served as president of the Greater Miami Jewish Federation.

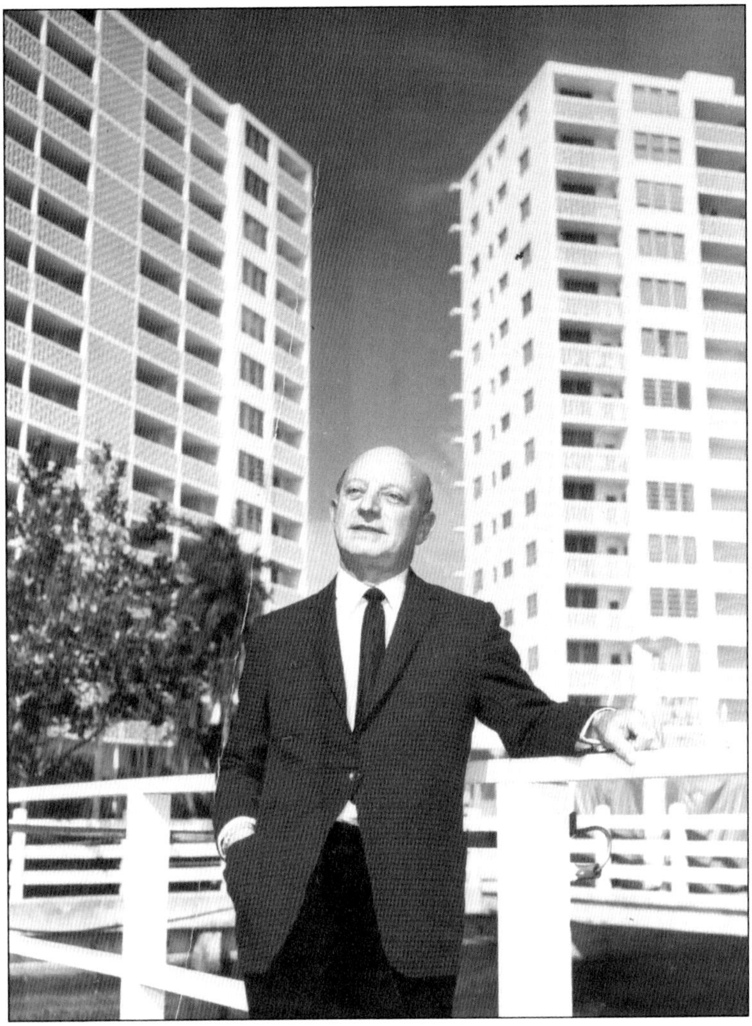

NATHAN GUMENICK. When Nathan Gumenick decided to build high-rise apartments on Miami Beach in 1959, mortgage lenders snickered. They said nobody needed apartments there year-round. Gumenick, known as the "granddaddy of high-rise living in South Florida," died in 1996. He left a legacy of community participation and philanthropy, especially at Mount Sinai Hospital and Temple Israel. A grandson continues the business on the Beach.

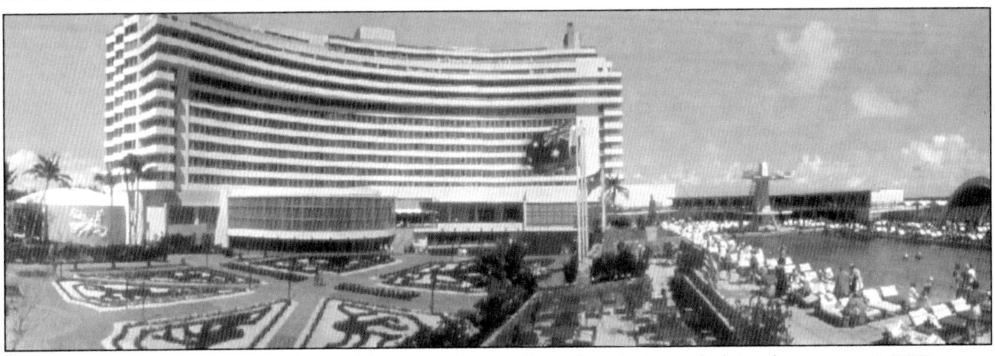

FONTAINEBLEAU HOTEL, MIAMI BEACH. Morris Lapidus designed this glamorous 1,200-room hotel that Ben Novack built in 1954 on the former Firestone estate. Featuring a curved facade, this was perhaps the most famous hotel in the world. Its amenities and live entertainment options lured tourists and attracted the attention of both the movie and television industries. Stephen Muss bought the hotel out of bankruptcy in 1978. In 2005, it was sold again and reopened in 2008 after an extensive renovation.

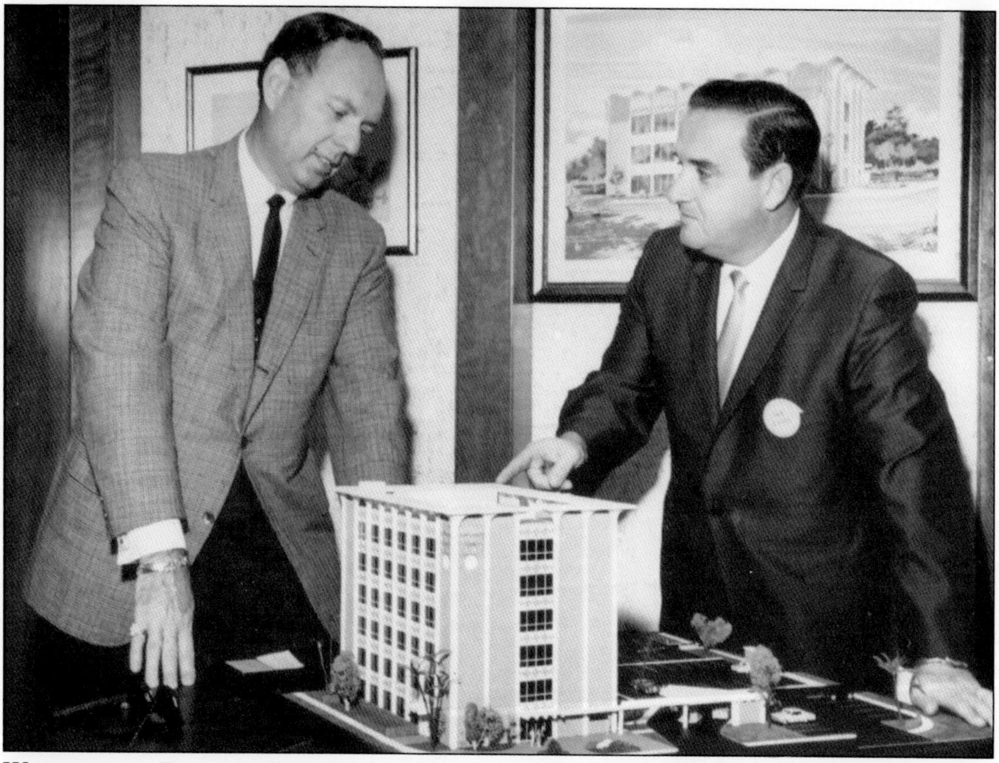

WASHINGTON FEDERAL SAVINGS AND LOAN AND JEFFERSON BANK. Arthur Courshon (left) started Washington Federal in 1951 and Jefferson Bank in 1963 with Jack Courshon, Jack Gordon, Milton Gaynor, and Ben Giller. The public side of Courshon included chairing the Inaugural Ball for Pres. John Kennedy and chairing Miami Beach's Convention Hotel selection committee. Pictured here in 1968, Courshon is reviewing the expansion model of Jefferson Bank with executive vice president Bart Goldberg.

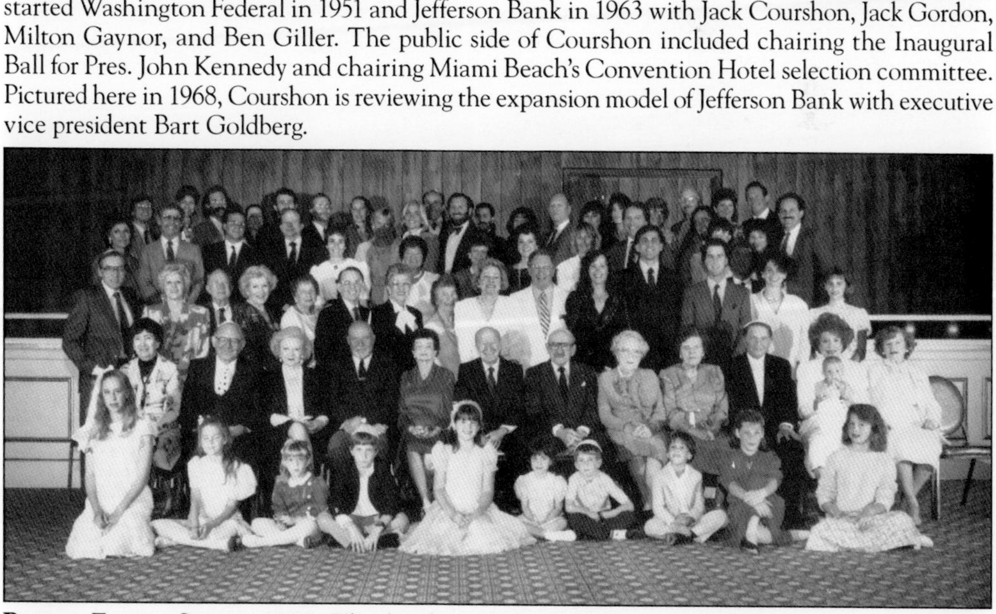

PALLOT FAMILY SEDER, 1986. The family settled in Miami in the 1920s and each branch had its own seders, as no one could accommodate the entire clan. In 1951, E. Albert Pallot initiated a single, unified seder that has been continuous. The first was held in the mansion built by the antisemitic Carl Fisher; it had been converted into Mendelsohn's Kosher Restaurant! Mitchell Horwich has been the religious leader since 1983.

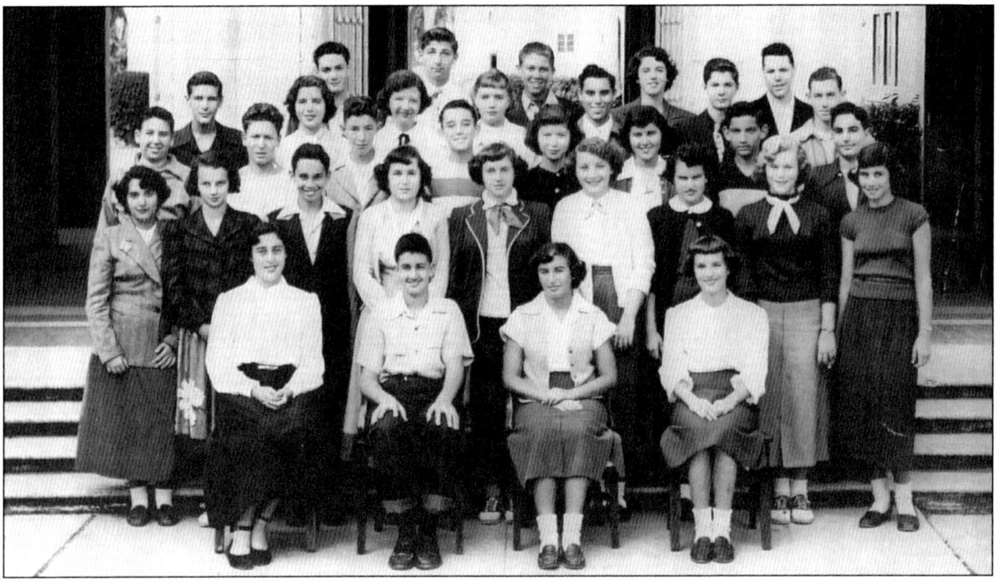

MIAMI BEACH SENIOR HIGH CLASS, 1949–1950. The following from left to right are (first row) Rhoda Berman, Paul Rappaport, Janice Klein, and Sandy Miller; (second row) Marcia Jervis, Pat Grimly, Cliff Fried, Barbara Himmelstein, Eileen Kagen, Arlene Sprafkin, Ester Gerson, Susie Jacobs, and Bunny Zwagenthal; (third row) Joe Ginsberg, Teddy Wallman, Jerome Barach, Leslie Gluckmann, Zeva Quitney, Carole Berman, Lenny Moebel, and Phil Sassoon; (fourth row) Don Sinandres, Louise Lefkowitz, Cynthia Hecter, Beverly Dells, Harry Bailey, Joe ?, and Jerry Schwartz; (fifth row) Buzzy Gold, Warren Tepper, Richard Brickman, Terry Landy, and Stanley Jacobs.

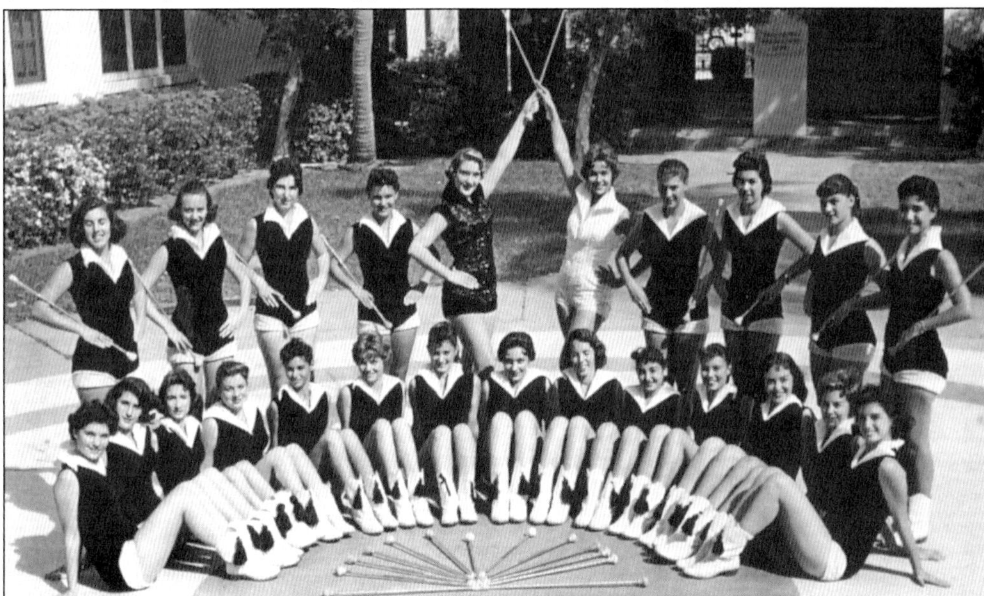

MAJORETTES OF MIAMI BEACH SENIOR HIGH, 1957. In the 1960s, when asked if the school was integrated, the response was, "Yes, there are a few gentiles here!" For many years, it was mostly Jews who attended this school, including Robert Rubin, who served as the U.S. Secretary of the Treasury (1995–1999). Those identified here are Gail Rosen, Bette Paris, Judy Grafias, Madeleine Fisher, Elaine Dernis, Sandra Applebaum, Joan Ruby Rochelle Kradman, and Carole Miller.

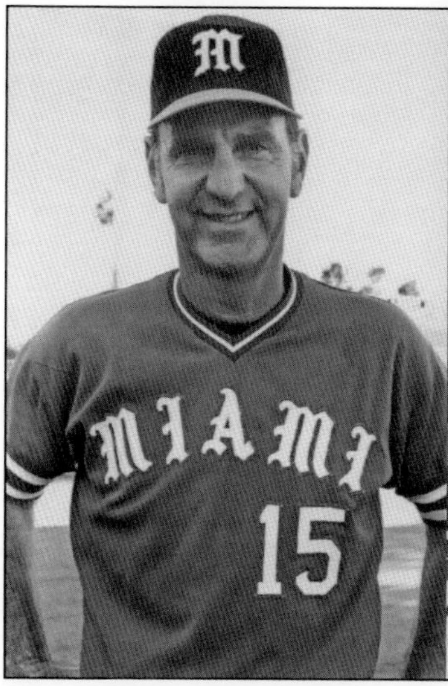

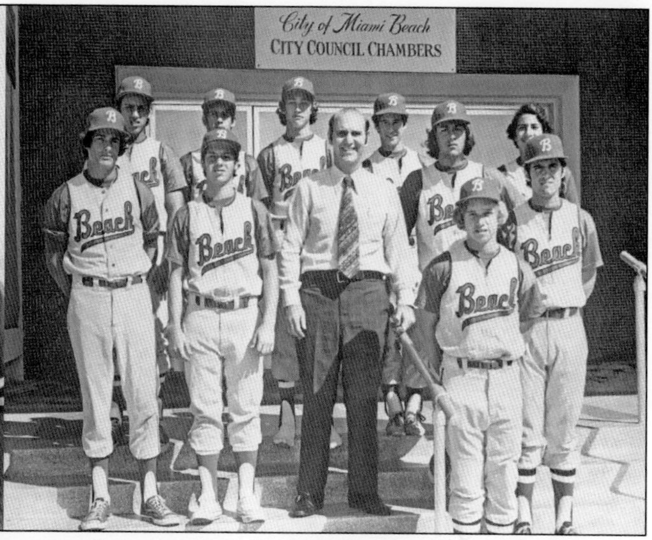

BEACH HIGH ATHLETE SKIP BERTMAN. Bertman played on Miami Beach's first Little League team in 1948. He received a baseball scholarship to the University of Miami (above left). Skip coached at Beach High (above right), leading the team to many championships. After coaching at the University of Miami, Skip coached at Louisiana State University, winning many titles. Receiving the title of National Coach of the Year three times, Skip served as pitching coach for the U.S. Olympic gold medal team in 1988.

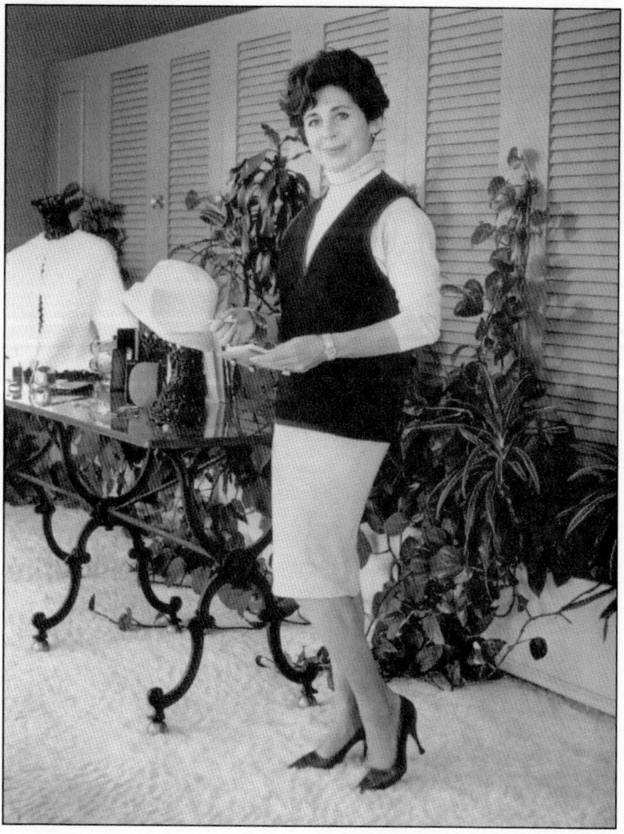

DRESS DESIGNER DEBORAH REGAL FETERSON. Feterson was crocheting gloves at the age of six and, at age 22, was one of New York's youngest dress designers. She moved to Miami Beach in 1939, where she established four Regal Stores. Feterson made 65 crossings to Europe to get the feeling of the fabrics and designs, then created her own designs and had the fabrics made into clothing and accessories for her shops.

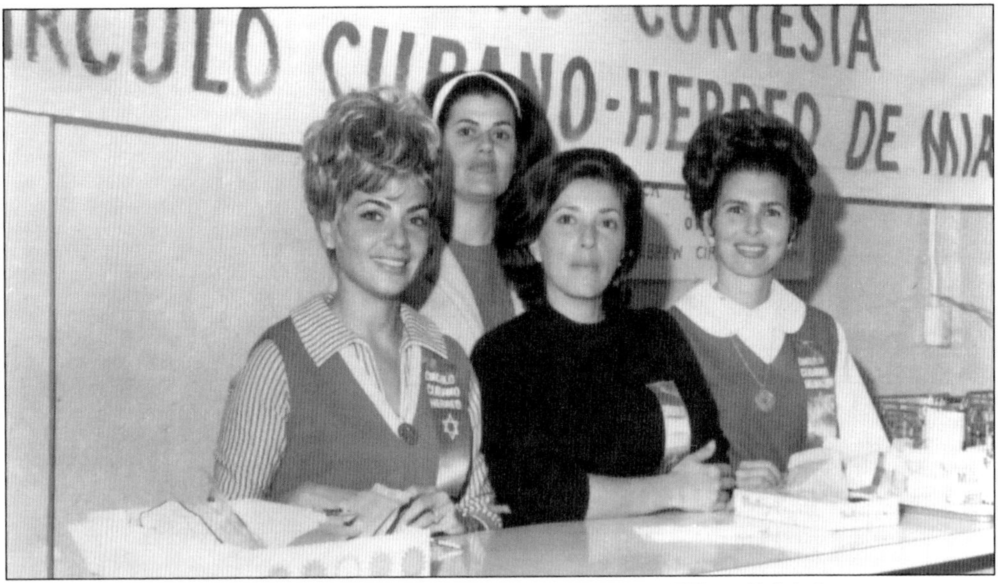

CUBAN-HEBREW CONGREGATION WELCOMES EXILES, 1965. When Fidel Castro came into power in 1959, about 10,000 of the 12,000 Cuban Jews fled to South Florida. It was up to the community to create a home for them. In 1965, "Freedom Flights" brought more Cubans; the flights ended in 1973. From left to right are Estela Egozi, Esther Egozi Garazi, Alegra Barrocas, and Raquel Egozi Silverstein.

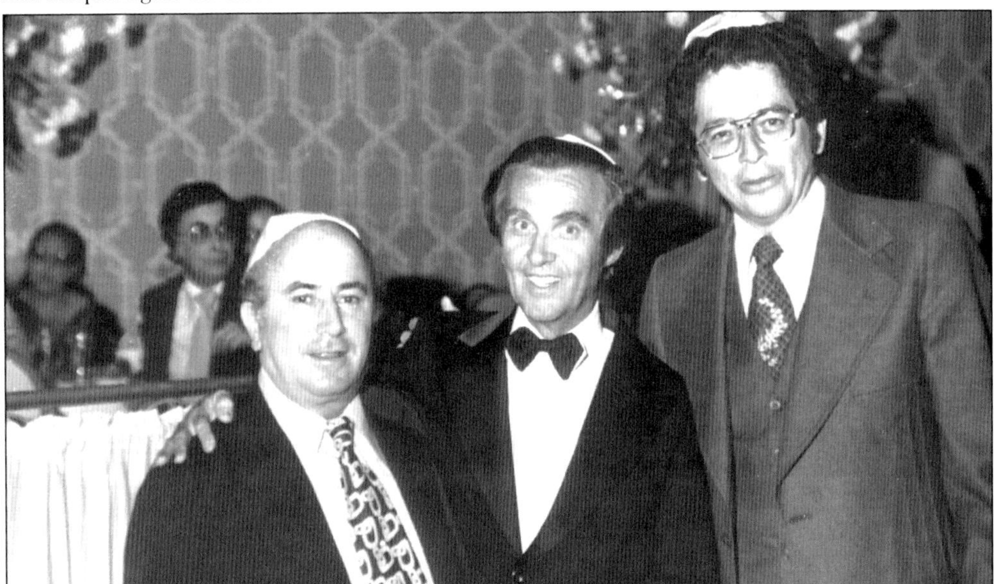

GREATER MIAMI JEWISH FEDERATION CUBAN DIVISION, 1978. From left to right are Jack Chester, Rabbi Mayer Abramowitz, and Rafael Kravec. Upon the arrival of Cuban Jews in Miami, Rabbi Abramowitz opened the doors of Temple Menorah to them. Ordained in 1944, Abramowitz went to Europe in 1945 as a U.S. Army lieutenant and military chaplain. He also helped close Displaced Persons camps and get survivors out of Europe. He moved with his wife, Rachel, who he met in a camp, to Miami Beach in 1951. They continue to live there, where Abramowitz serves as rabbi for the Cuban Hebrew Congregation.

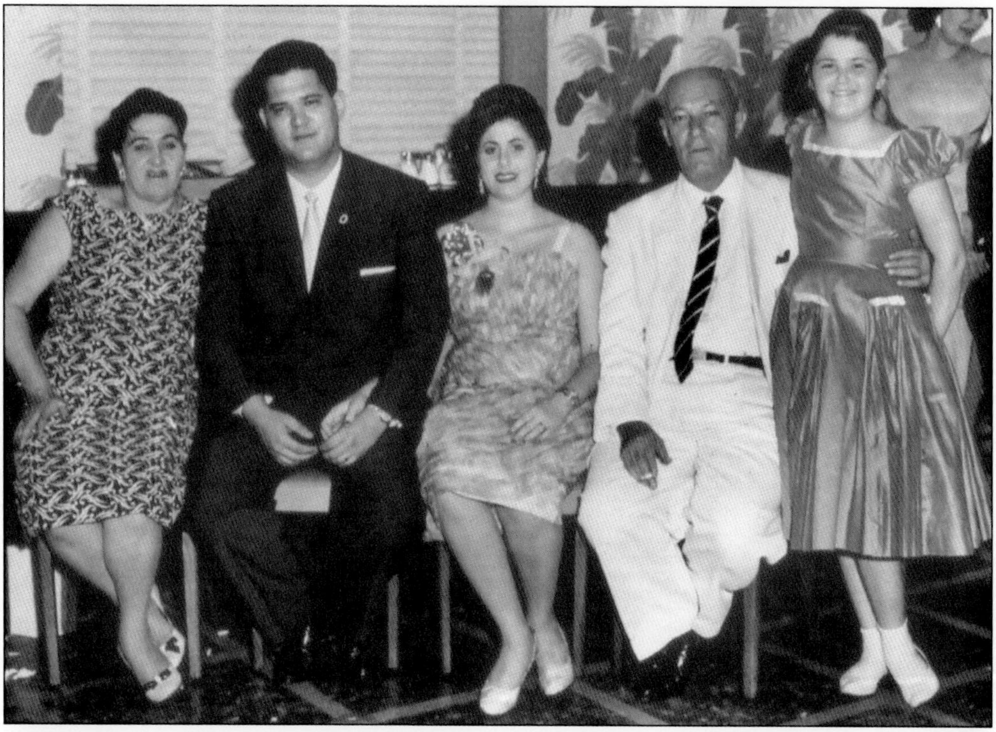

GEORGE FELDENKREIS WITH FAMILY, CUBAN REFUGEES. Cuban Jews began new businesses and professional careers in Miami. Feldenkreis, born in Cuba to parents who had fled Poland, was a Zionist youth leader there. In Miami, he founded Carfel Incorporated in 1961. Having the feeling of insecurity passed down to him by his family's experiences, he diversified into several other businesses and, at the same time, took major leadership roles in the Miami Jewish community.

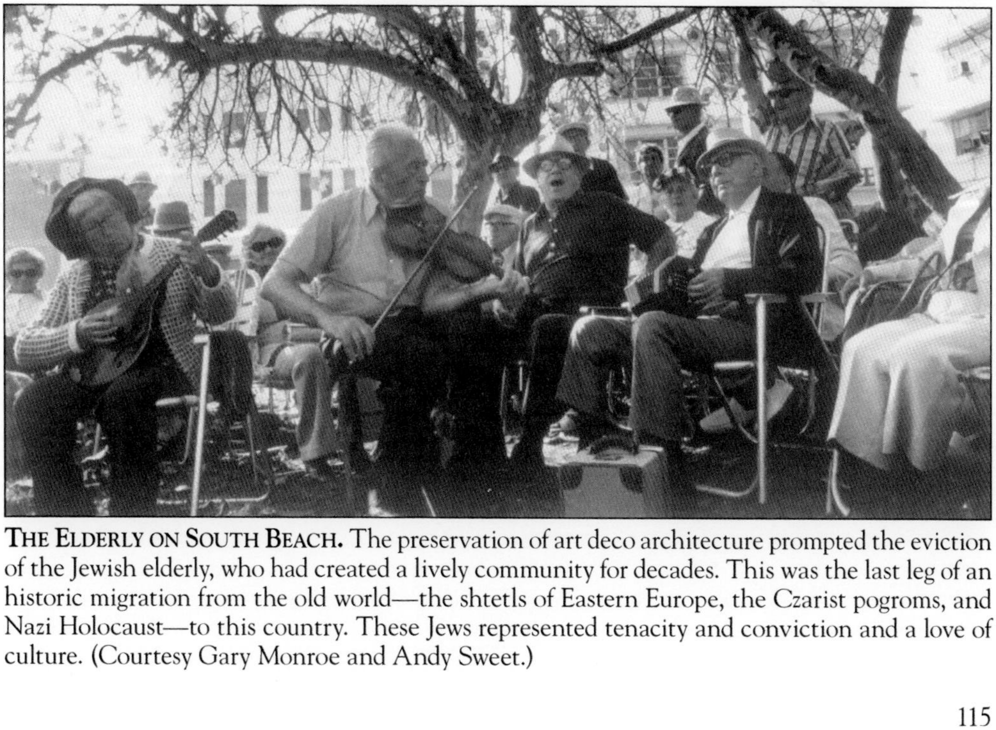

THE ELDERLY ON SOUTH BEACH. The preservation of art deco architecture prompted the eviction of the Jewish elderly, who had created a lively community for decades. This was the last leg of an historic migration from the old world—the shtetls of Eastern Europe, the Czarist pogroms, and Nazi Holocaust—to this country. These Jews represented tenacity and conviction and a love of culture. (Courtesy Gary Monroe and Andy Sweet.)

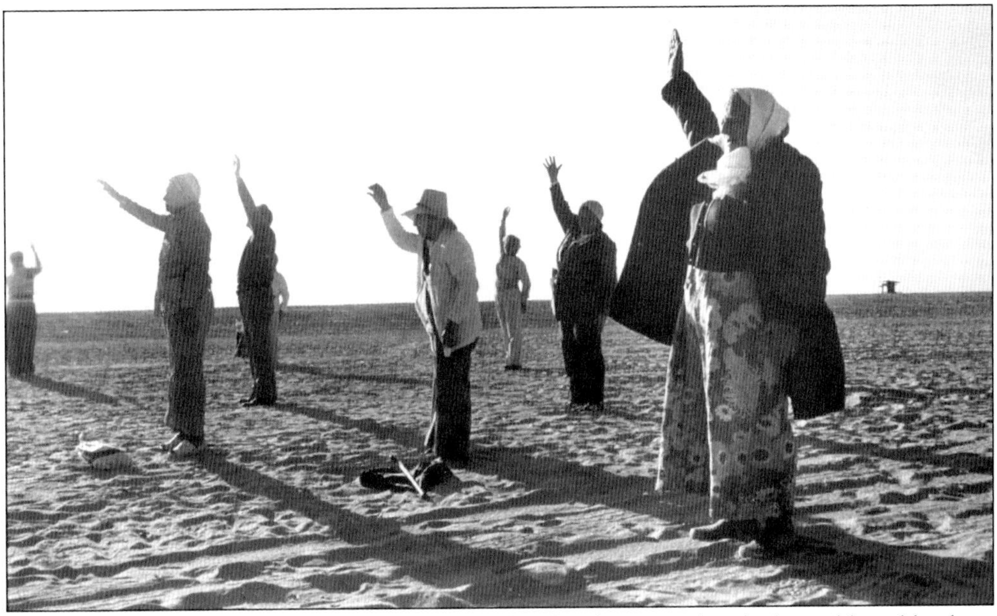

ELDERLY EXERCISING ON THE BEACH, 1970S. They lived in accord with their old-world values. The ocean was therapeutic, the streets were lively, and everything was in walking distance; social agencies and neighbors met their needs, and for *Shabbat*, card rooms became shuls. But the ethnic community was out of touch and out of time. Crime soared with the 1980 Mariel boat lift, and sunrise swims came to an abrupt end. (Courtesy Gary Monroe.)

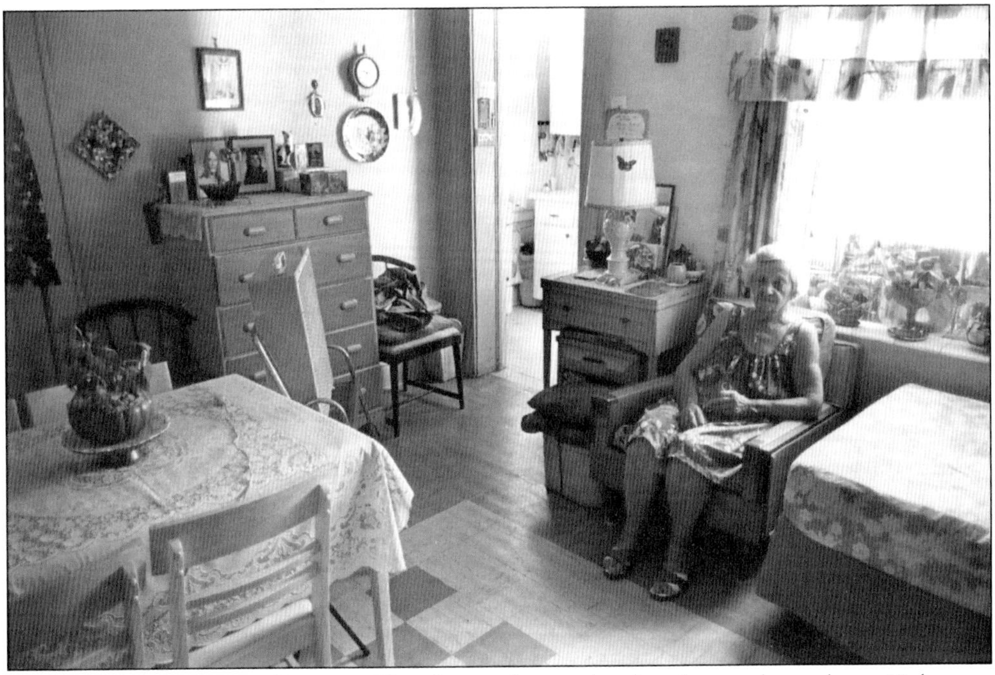

LIFE SUMMARIZED ON A BUREAU TOP. In a rush to redevelop the southern shore, Holocaust survivors were told that they would be "relocated." The precious legacy of the culture they had established in South Beach came to the end of the line. The average age of "trendy" South Beach's population dropped by about 50 years within a decade. (Courtesy Gary Monroe.)

Five

Jews Making a Difference in their Community

Achievements Trump Discrimination

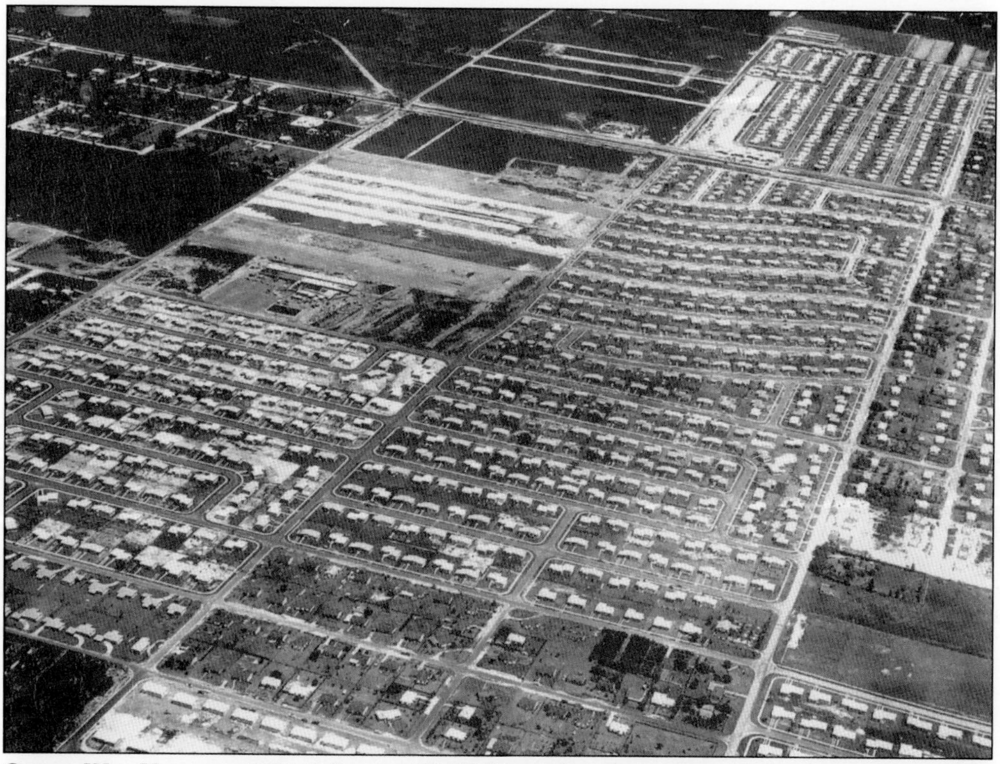

Coral Way Village, 1957. Following World War II, Jewish developers helped meet the demand for housing. Arnold Rosen built these homes, which were designed by Norman M. Giller. Rosen began his building career on a $50 lot. In 1954, he started F&R, which became Lennar Homes (Leonard Miller-Arnold Rosen). The company went public in 1969 and has become one of the nation's largest homebuilders. Rosen retired in 1977 and passed away in 2001. After Leonard Miller's death in 2002, his family donated $100 million to the medical school at the University of Miami. Stuart Miller succeeded his father as CEO of Lennar. (Courtesy Ira Giller.)

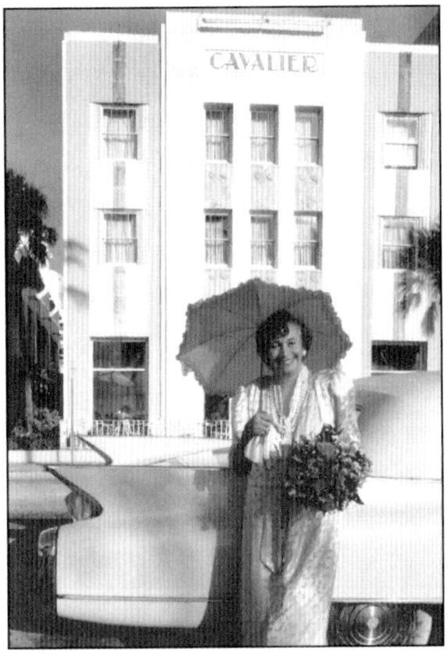

MIAMI BEACH ART DECO DISTRICT. Barbara Baer Capitman founded the square-mile Art Deco District, bounded by Fifth Street to Twenty-third Street, and Lenox Avenue to Ocean Drive. Composed of the largest concentration of 1920s and 1930s resort architecture in the world, this was one of the earliest (1979) U.S. National Register of History listings to recognize the importance of the designs of this period. The vibrantly colored buildings represent an era when Miami was developed as a "tropical playground." (Courtesy Tom Hollyman.)

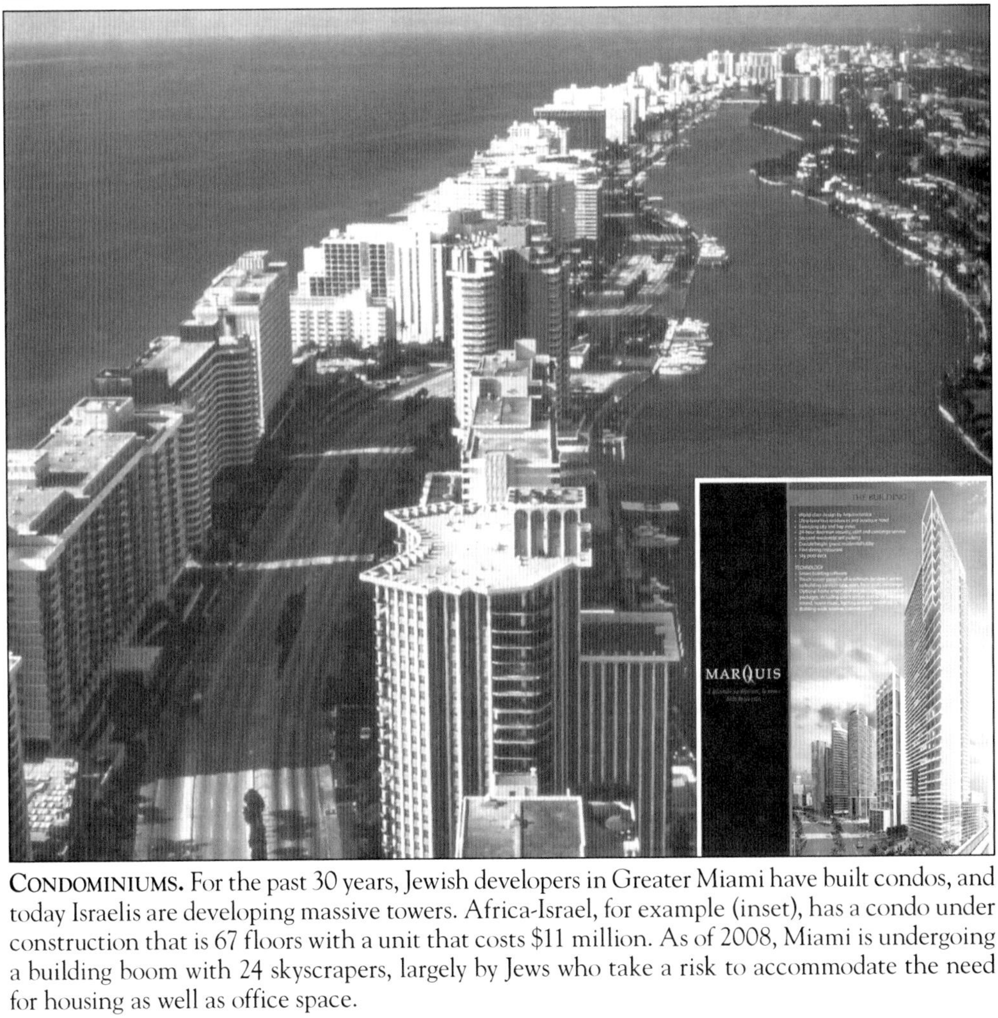

CONDOMINIUMS. For the past 30 years, Jewish developers in Greater Miami have built condos, and today Israelis are developing massive towers. Africa-Israel, for example (inset), has a condo under construction that is 67 floors with a unit that costs $11 million. As of 2008, Miami is undergoing a building boom with 24 skyscrapers, largely by Jews who take a risk to accommodate the need for housing as well as office space.

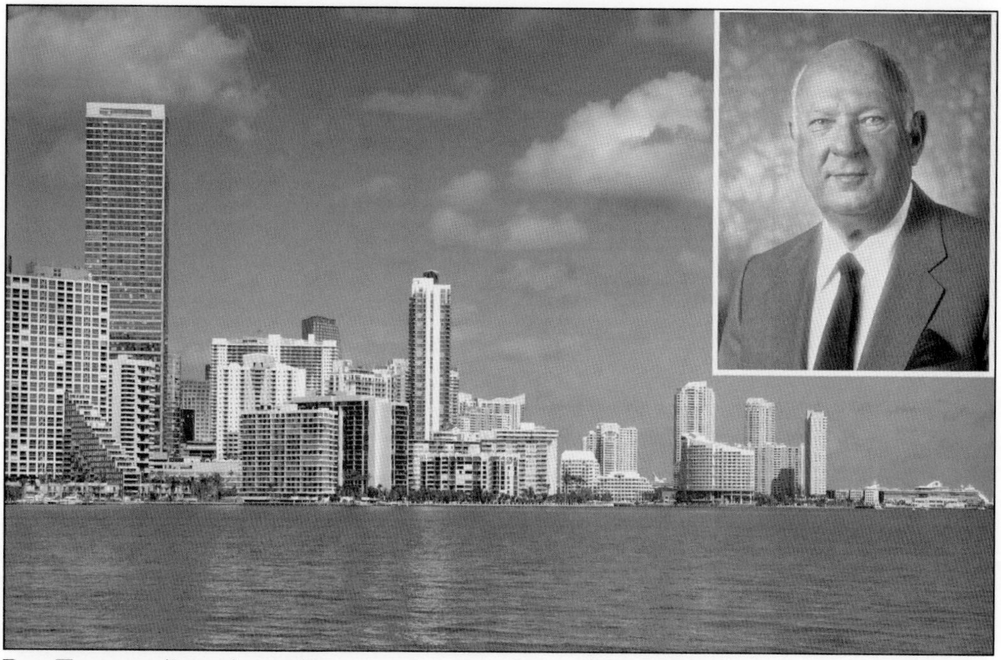

Bob Traurig (Inset) and Brickell Avenue. Most of this development is a result of Traurig's legal skills. As the area's premier zoning attorney for nearly one-half century, this so-called "land lawyer" advised many Jewish developers and builders following World War II. Traurig came to Miami in the 1930s. In 1967, he cofounded Greenberg Traurig, P. A. and has been instrumental in the growth of the law firm and in the community.

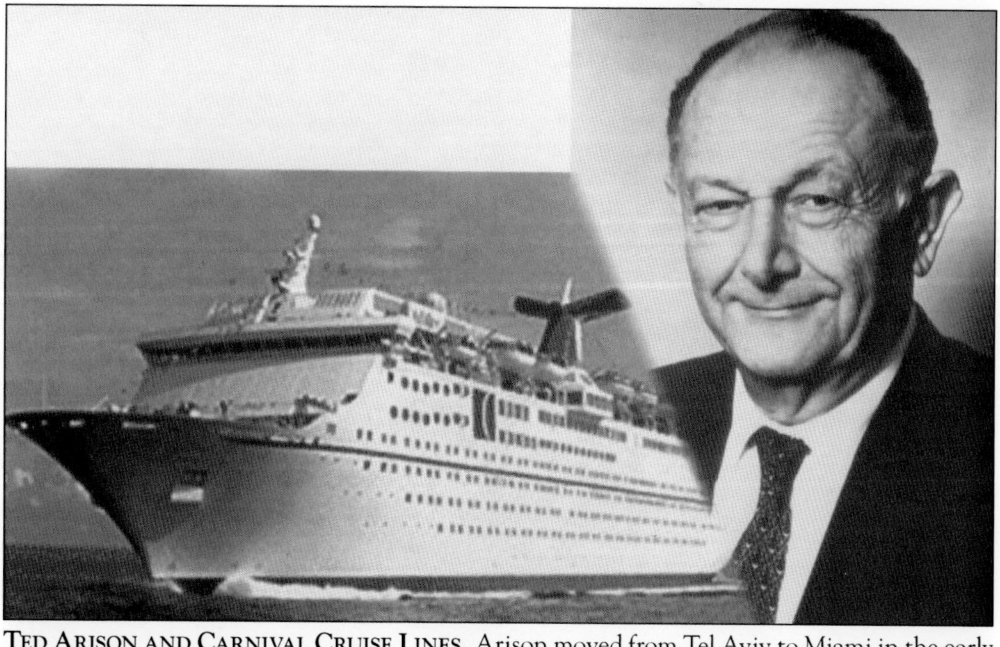

Ted Arison and Carnival Cruise Lines. Arison moved from Tel Aviv to Miami in the early 1950s and created Carnival Cruise Lines in 1972, which is now the world's largest cruise company. He was part of the group that formed the Miami Heat basketball team in 1988. Ted's son Micky now controls the Miami Heat and Carnival Cruise Lines.

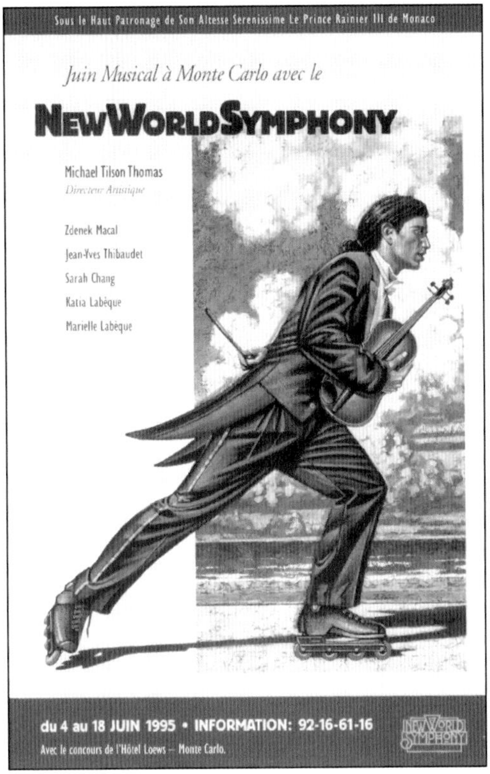

NEW WORLD SYMPHONY. In 1996, Ted Arison contributed $40 million to Miami's youth orchestra. Michael Tilson Thomas founded the group as a place where young musicians could refine their skills. As alumni move on to professional music careers around the world, the goal is realized. Thomas is a grandson of Boris and Bessie Thomashefsky, who were founding members and stars of the Yiddish Theater in America.

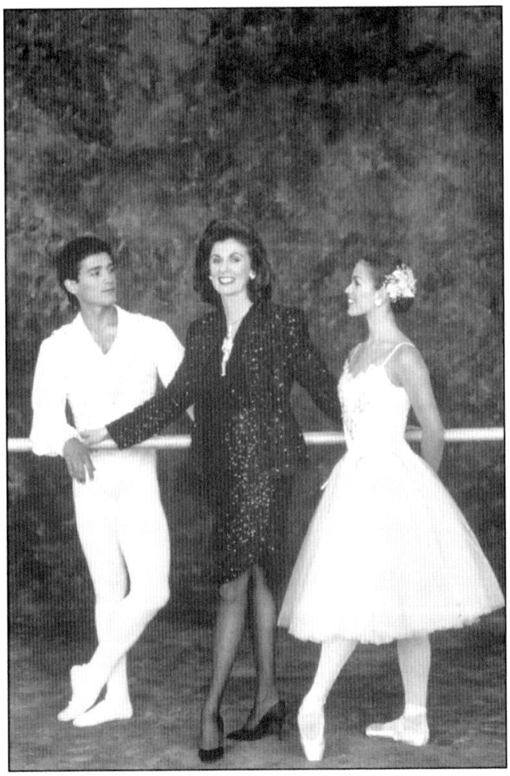

MIAMI CITY BALLET FOUNDER TOBY LERNER ANSIN (CENTER) WITH MIAMI CITY BALLET DANCERS, 1997. In 1985, after a conversation with Edward Villella to hear his 10-year plan and after enticing six friends to join her in each contributing $1,000, Ansin decided this is what South Florida needed to round out its cultural life. Today the Miami City Ballet is one of the nation's major dance companies and performs globally.

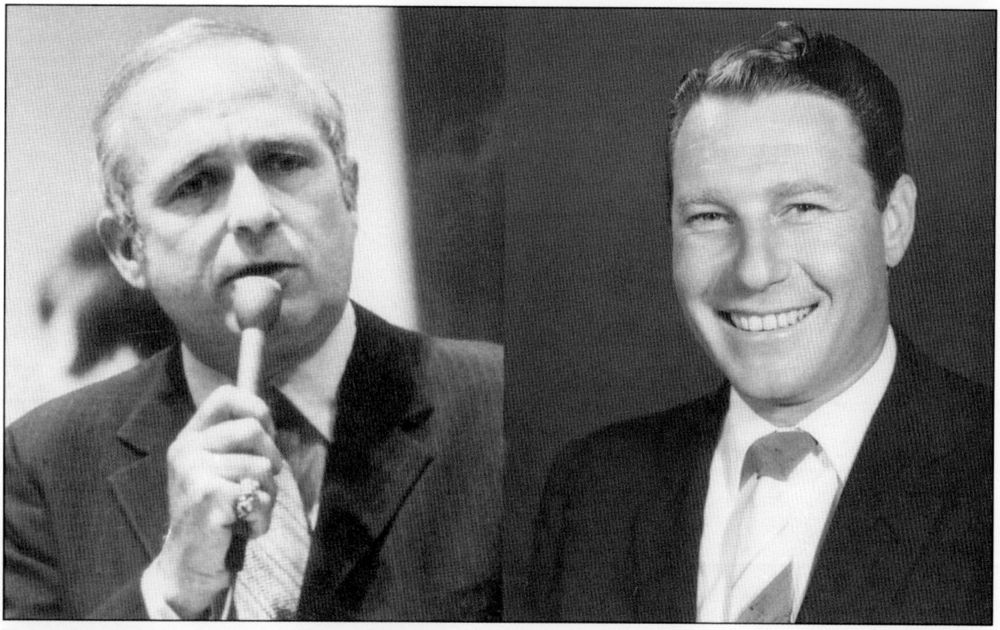

FIRST JEWS ELECTED FROM SOUTH FLORIDA TO STATE LEGISLATURE, 1963. It was very late in Florida history when native Miamians Murray Dubbin (left) and Louis Wolfson II were elected in 1963. They were reelected in 1967 along with two other Jews, Gerald Lewis and Kenneth Myers. Dubbin served 12 years and chaired the Florida State Legislature House Rules Committee.

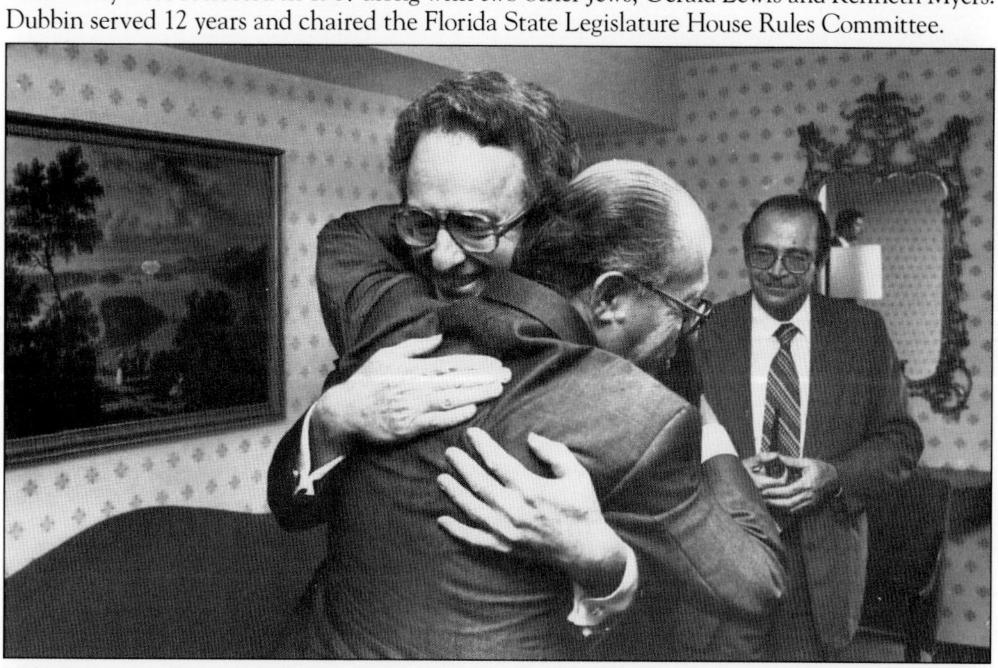

U.S. SENATOR RICHARD STONE WITH ISRAELI PRIME MINISTER MENACHEM BEGIN, 1978. Growing up at the Blackstone Hotel on Miami Beach gave Stone a unique vantage point to prepare him for 40 years of public service. He was an attorney for the City of Miami, served in the Florida Senate, and was the secretary of state in Florida. In 1975, he became Florida's second Jewish U.S. senator. He served as the U.S. ambassador-at-large to Central America and then as the ambassador to Denmark. Israeli U.S. ambassador Simcha Dinitz is in the background.

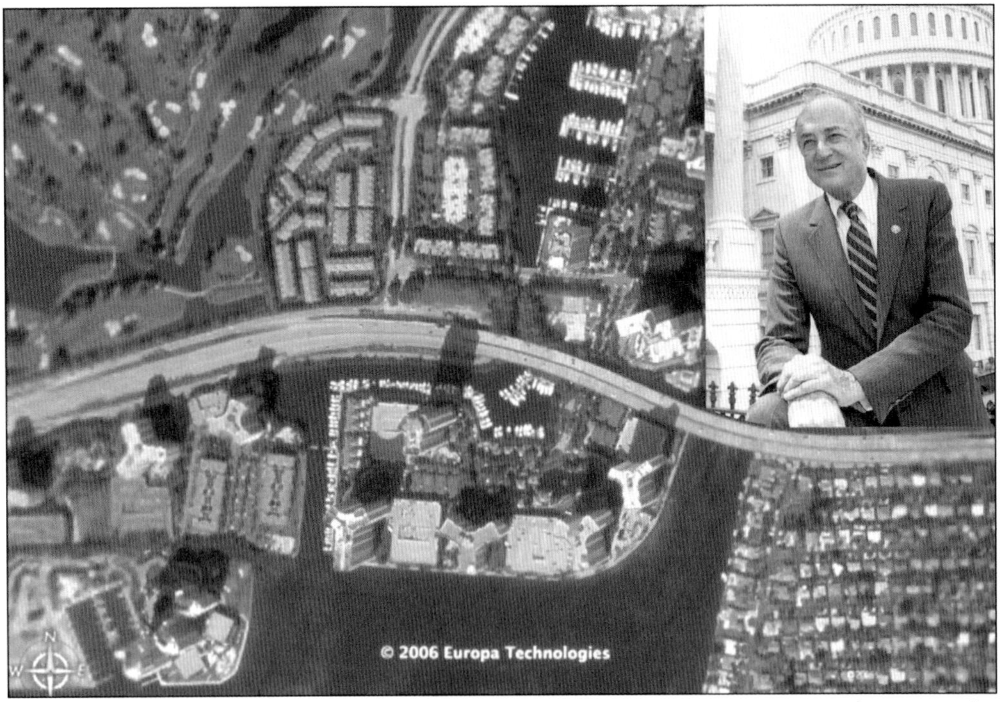

U.S. CONGRESSMAN WILLIAM LEHMAN, 1972–1992 AND LEHMAN CAUSEWAY. Lehman was the first Florida Jew to serve in the U.S. Congress since Florida's David Levy Yulee in 1845. Lehman, who had a car dealership, helped the county of Miami-Dade as chair of the transportation subcommittee and was responsible for getting the Metrorail and Tri-Rail systems into Miami. The Lehman Causeway that connects Aventura to Sunny Isles honors his name. Florida has been served by four other Jews in the U.S. Congress: Larry Smith, Peter Deutsch, Robert Wexler, and Debbie Wasserman Schultz.

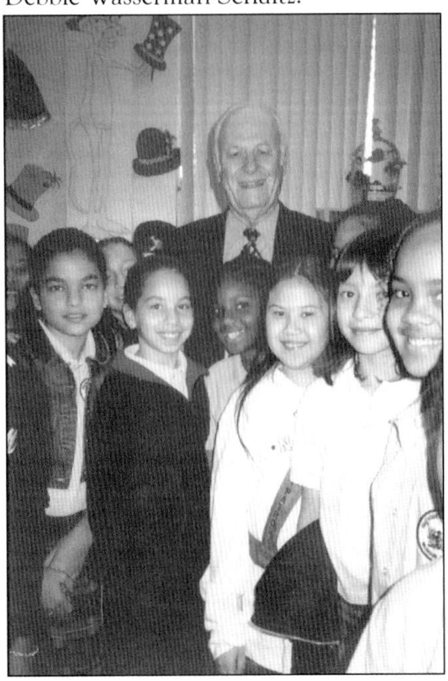

STANLEY TATE PREPAID COLLEGE PROGRAM. Since 1954, Stanley Tate Builders has been constructing apartment houses, private homes, office buildings, and shopping centers. Tate's High Point Delray Builders, in operation since 1969, has developed more than $275 million in condominiums. Tate (center) spends time with civic, Jewish, political, and charitable endeavors and is most proud of starting, in 1987, the Florida Prepaid College Program, which now bears his name.

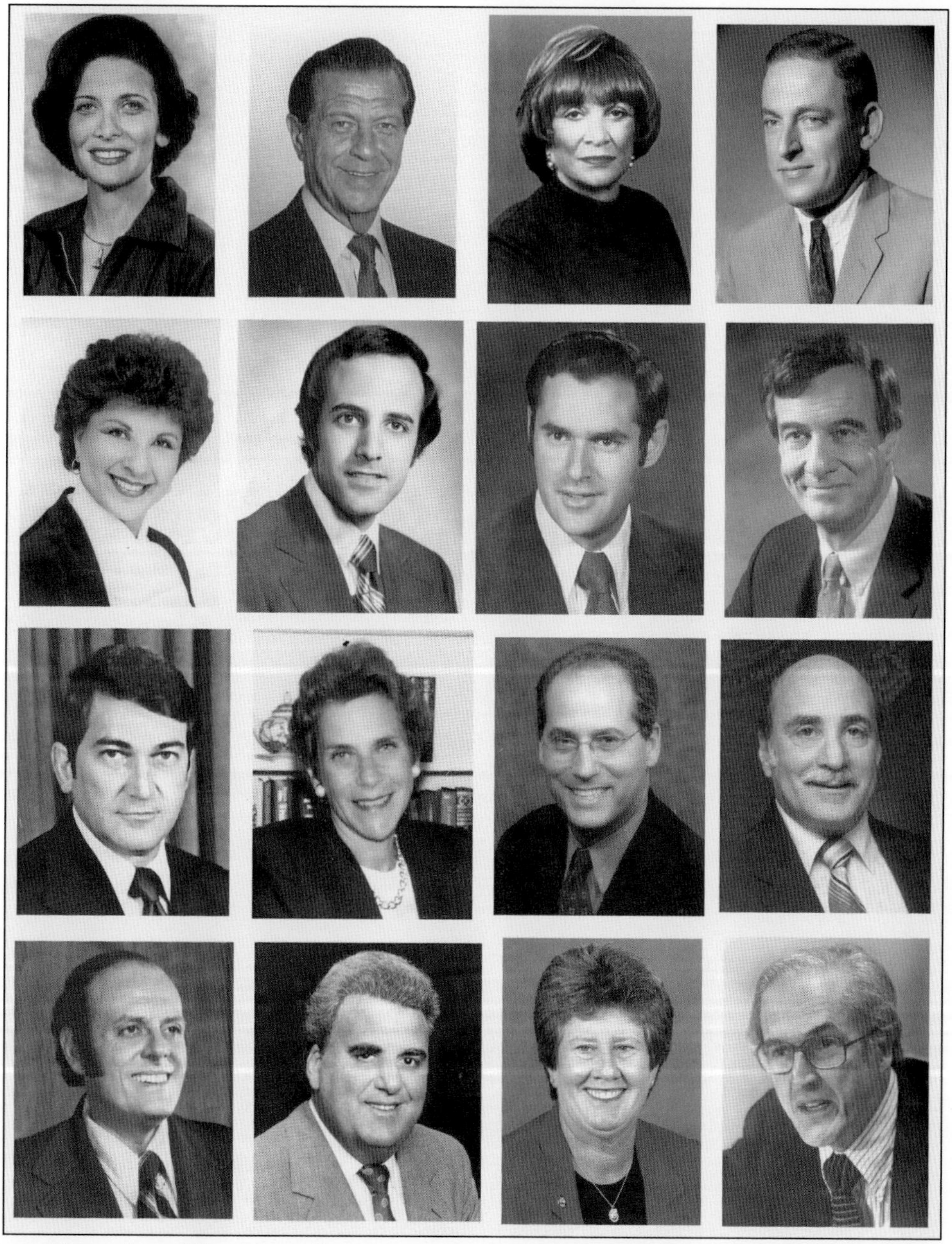

Some Miami Jews Who Have Served in the State Legislature. From the left to right are the following: (first row) Elaine Bloom (1974–1978, 1986–2000); Sherman Winn (1970–1982); Gwen Margolis (1974–1992, 2002–2008), who was the first female Senate president in the nation and also served as chair of the Miami-Dade County Commission (1994–2002); and Marshall Harris (1966–1974); (second row) Elaine Gordon (1972–1994); Alan Becker (1972–1978); Paul Steinberg (1972–1982); and Kenneth Myers (1964–1980); (third row) Gerald Lewis (1966–1972, and as comptroller 1975–1995); Susan Guber (1986–1992); Dan Gelber (2000–present); George Firestone (1966–1978, and as secretary of state 1970–1987); (fourth row) Robert Shevin (1964–1970) and as Florida's attorney general (1971–1979); Ron Silver (1978–2002); Sally Heyman (1994–2000); and Jack Gordon (1972–1992).

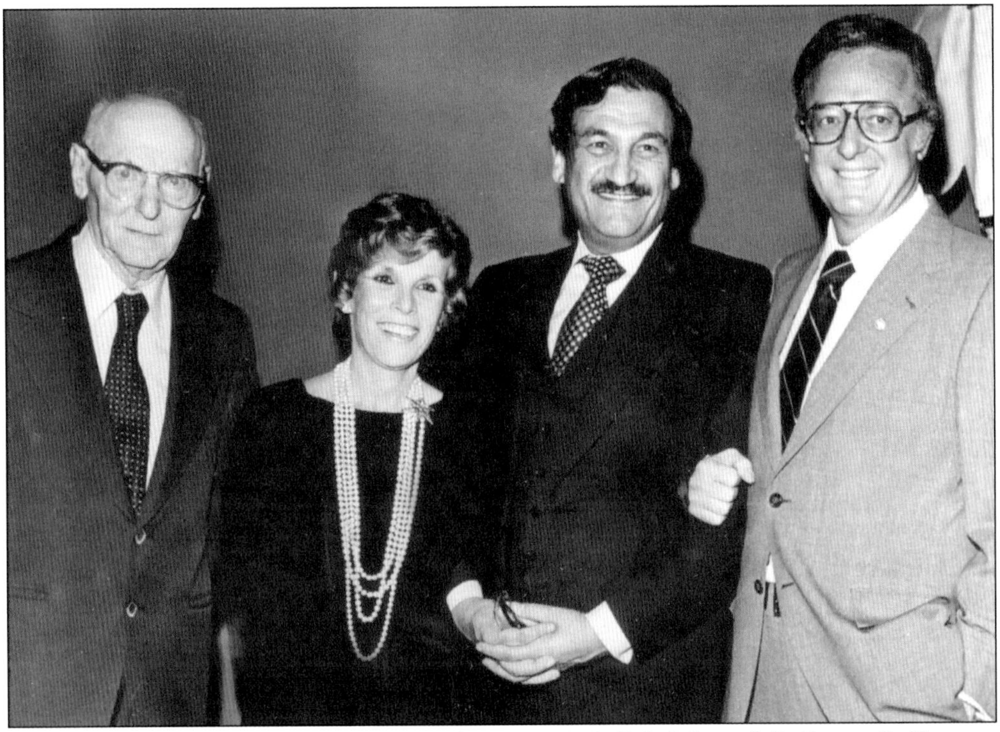

NOBEL PRIZE WINNER, ISAAC BASHEVIS SINGER, 1978. Polish born I. B. Singer (left) wrote in Yiddish and was known for his romantic and legendary stories, some of which had a Florida setting. His works were translated into English and many other languages. A longtime Miami Beach resident, Singer was awarded the 1978 Nobel Prize for Literature; he died in 1991. He is pictured here with Bunny and Sam Adler (center) and U.S. senator Richard Stone (right).

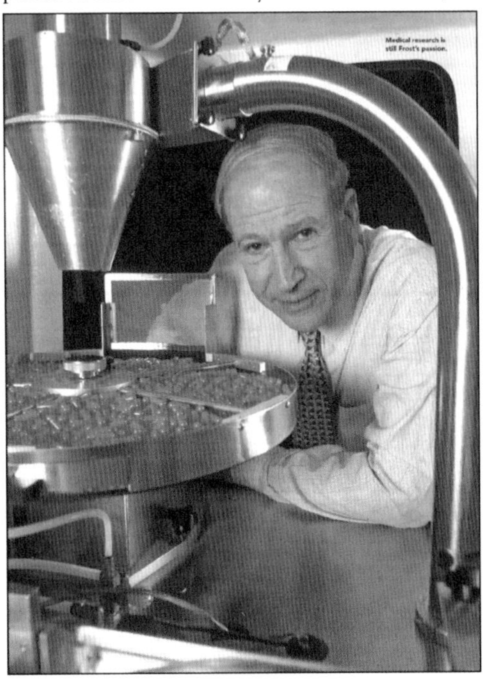

DR. PHILLIP FROST. Frost founded Ivax Corporation, the world's top producer of generic drugs, as a public company in 1987. He was chair of the Department of Dermatology at Mount Sinai Medical Center (1972–1990) and chairman of the board for Key Pharmaceuticals (1972–1986). Ivax was acquired by the Israeli company Teva Pharmaceutical Industries in 2006. The University of Miami music school and the Florida International University art museum bear his and wife Patricia's names. (Courtesy Michael Price.)

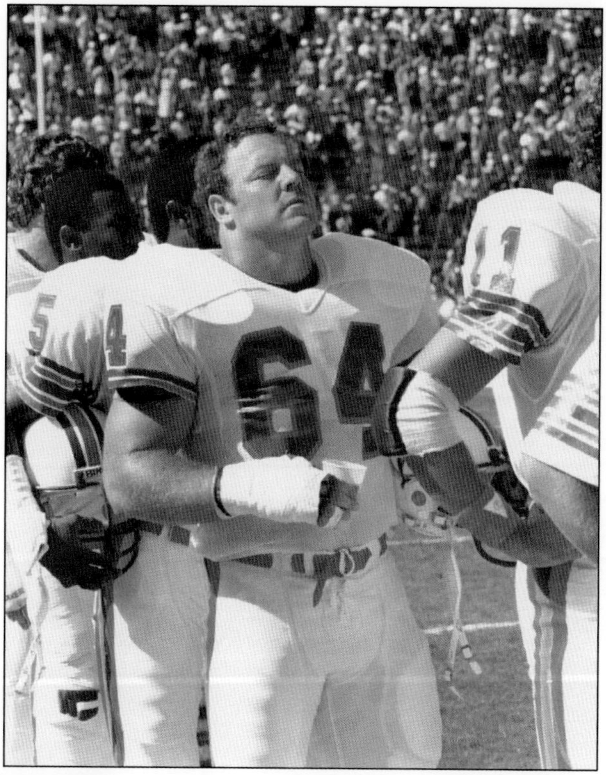

MIAMI DOLPHIN ED NEWMAN, 1984. Newman played for the Miami Dolphins, 1973–1984, and participated in three Super Bowl games. At the end of his football career, he went to the University of Miami law school and currently serves as county court judge in the 11th Judicial Circuit. All of Miami's major professional sports teams have Jewish owners: NFL Dolphins, NBA Heat, MLB Marlins, NHL Panthers, and FC (soccer).

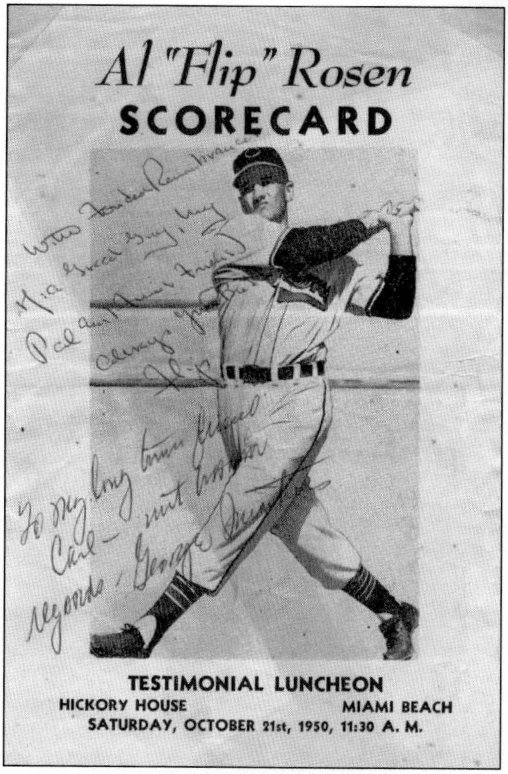

AL "FLIP" ROSEN. Rosen was All-City at Miami High and played for the University of Miami. He won a World Series ring with the Cleveland Indians in 1948. He has been a Major League Baseball executive with the New York Yankees, Houston Astros, and San Francisco Giants. He was one of the best all-time Jewish players with his friends Hank Greenberg and Sandy Koufax, who also refused to play baseball on the Jewish High Holy Days. (Courtesy Frances Gardner.)

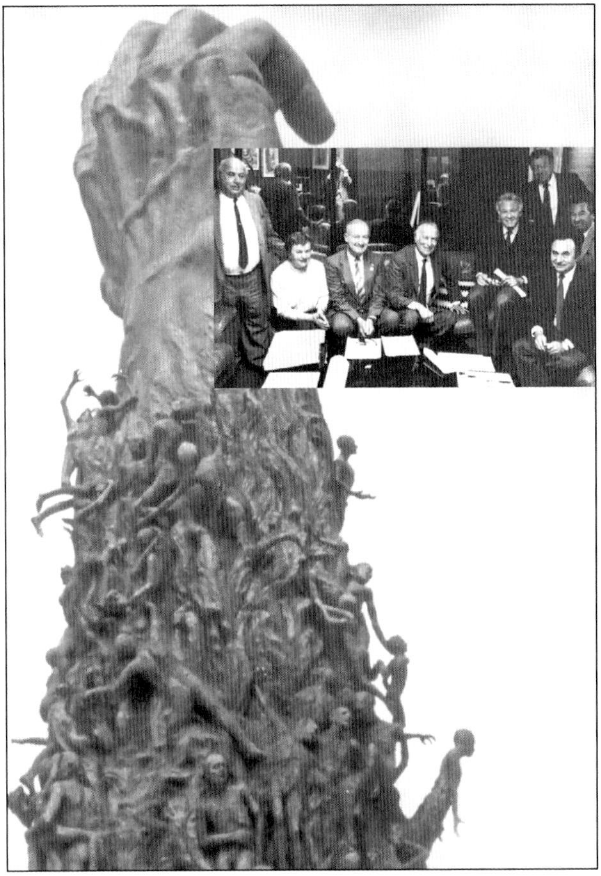

HOLOCAUST MEMORIAL, MIAMI BEACH, 1990. Designed and built by Kenneth Treister, the centerpiece is a 50-foot-high bronze sculpture of a hand with a number, surrounded by 130 bronze figures that cry out in anguish. Treister came to Miami Beach as an infant in 1930. His architecture and sculpture can be seen all over South Florida. The founding group (inset) are, from left to right, Jack Chester, Helen Fagin, Abe Resnick, Kenneth Treister, Norman Braman, Harry Smith, George Goldbloom, and David Schaecter.

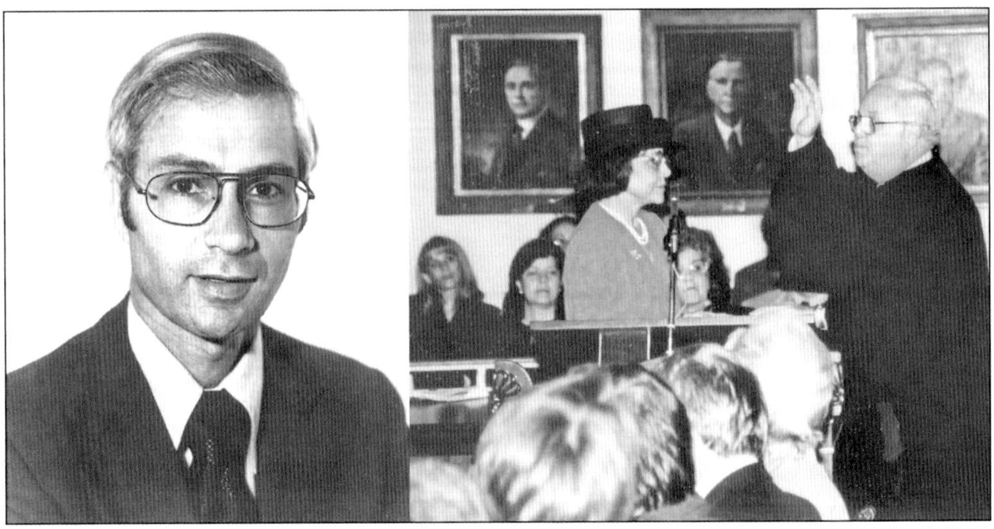

JUSTICES ARTHUR ENGLAND AND GERALD KOGAN, FLORIDA SUPREME COURT. England (left) served the court from 1975 to 1981 and served as chief justice. Kogan (right) was appointed in 1987. On June 3, 1996, Kogan took the oath of office as the chief justice in the first public inaugural ceremony in the court's 150-year history; his wife, Irene, joins him. Kogan moved to Miami Beach in 1947, graduated from Beach High, and attended the University of Miami through law school.

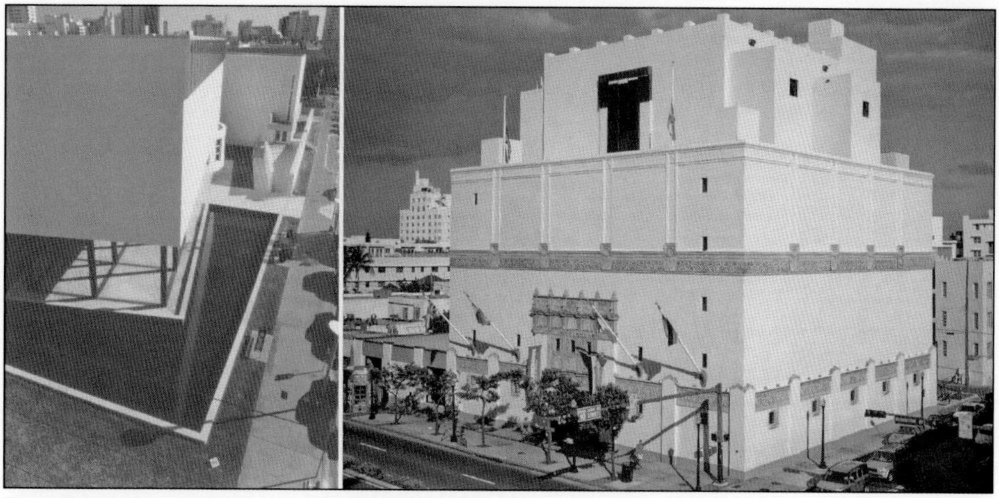

BASS MUSEUM OF ART AND WOLFSONIAN MUSEUM. Jewish collectors John and Johanna Bass founded the Bass (left) to house their 16th- and 17th-century paintings, textiles, and sculptures; the museum belongs to the City of Miami Beach. Mitchell Wolfson Jr. founded this museum (right) to preserve his 70,000 objects, which include furniture, decorative arts, paintings, books, prints, and ephemera. In 1997, Wolfson donated his collection to the State of Florida. (Above left, courtesy Simon Hare.)

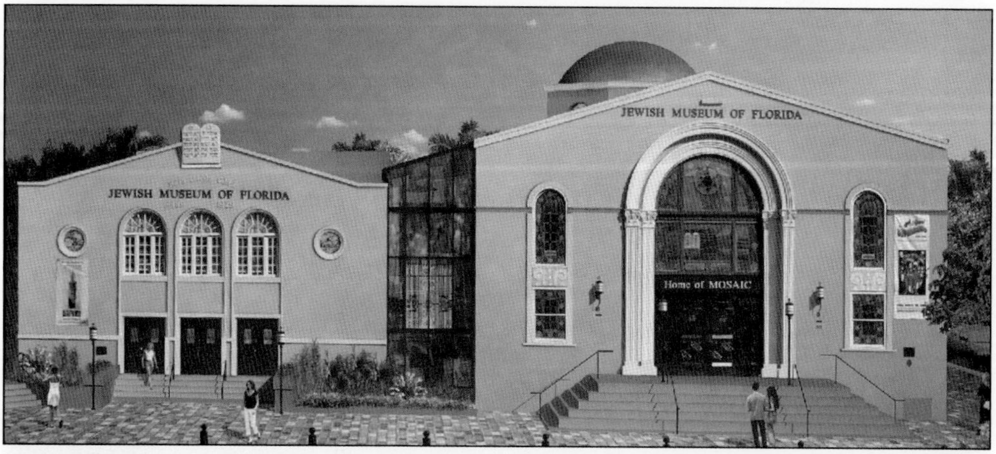

JEWISH MUSEUM OF FLORIDA, HOUSED IN THE FORMER BUILDING OF CONGREGATION BETH JACOB. The museum collects historic memories, tells stories of Jews helping to develop the state, and presents Jewish art and culture. This mission gives pride to strengthen Jewish identity and future generations. For non-Jews, this is education to increase tolerance among diversity. Americans are all immigrants or descendents of immigrants. This story is an example of the ethnic acculturation process of one group—as each has a unique narrative.